Doing Business in the European Community

3rd Edition

Doing Business in the European Community

3rd Edition

John Drew

Whurr Publishers
London

19B Compton Terrace
London N1 2UN
England

This edition first published 1992
Reprinted 1992

British Library Cataloguing in Publication Data
Drew, John
Doing Business in the European Community
- 3rd ed.
I. Title
382.09172

ISBN 1-870332-80-6

Typeset by Sarah Vicary and Mildmay Typesetters
Printed in Great Britain by Athenaeum Press, Newcastle-upon-Tyne

Preface

This book is dedicated to those who have contributed to it, some acknowledged and others not. I should like to thank the Commission of the European Communities for making available material. I am particularly indebted to Sir Leon Brittan, David Elliott, Richard Hay, Denis Kennedy, Robert Pendville, Bill Poeton and Tom Spencer for very useful and interesting insights into their Community functions. Laura Jackson played a major role in helping to produce this edition and without her help, it would have remained unrevised and out of date. Marguerite Brenchley, the Librarian at Jean Monnet House is responsible for most of the useful bibliography. Claire de Longeron did much to update section one. The distilled experience of section two was gleaned from countless managers studying at business schools in the United Kingdom and I am most grateful for their accumulated wisdom and advice. Martyn Bond, Peter Dixon and Peter Sandler made helpful comments on the draft.

While much of the material describes Community policies and actions and is intended to be as up to date and accurate as possible, it does not necessarily represent official Commission or Community thinking. Any errors or omissions are my own.

John Drew
April 1991

Contents

Introduction

The European Community is well on the way to becoming a single market by the end of 1992. Goods, people, services and capital will then move freely between Member States. As a result, new opportunities will arise. Ways of doing business in Europe will change significantly. Companies will need to develop new European strategies and management skills and recruit and train people differently. Do not be deceived into thinking that European business in the nineties will be the same as the eighties. While Europe becomes more a Community, it will also develop into a new civilisation based more on electronics, services and communication than on electrical and manufacturing skills. The rest of the world is fast changing too, but with steady growth forecast to the end of the century, Western Europe will be the largest and one of the richest consumer markets in the world for the foreseeable future. It is for this reason that those doing business in Europe need to ensure that their European operations are carried out by those who understand these trends.

The intention of this book is to help clarify your thoughts about European business and in particular about how the European Community and its policies might affect the strategic development of the company or the industry sector in which you are interested. There is a tendency among those involved in European business to polarise their thinking. Some take the European Community too seriously and exaggerate the impact that it will have on their day to day operations. They put too many resources into tracking draft legislation in Brussels and Strasbourg and forget that business in Europe is much like business anywhere. European legislation and European business culture are just part of the framework within which wealth is created. At the other extreme, business underestimates the growing importance of this European legislative framework. It fails to take into account that all trade negotiations with countries outside the Community are negotiated centrally in Brussels. It is sometimes unaware of the supervisory and policing role accorded to the Commission by Member States and the opportunities and threats presented by a Single Market of some 340 million people.

Europe is finally nearing the completion of what the Treaty of Rome set out to achieve over 30 years ago. The process has been speeded up considerably with the drawing up of the 1985 White Paper by the European Commission. This sets out a comprehensive and integrated package of some 300 proposals aimed at removing completely the various barriers to trade still existing. This programme for completing the Single Market was endorsed by the 12 Member States of the Community who also signed the Single European Act (SEA) which entered into force in 1987. The SEA improves significantly the workings of the Community's institutional system by extending qualified majority voting in the Council of Ministers to some two thirds of the proposals set out in the White Paper.

The White Paper describes the 300 actions (282 to be exact) required to complete the Internal Market. It acts as a programmed checklist of those actions needed to be taken by Community countries to bring about a Single European Market and indicates by what date they need to be achieved.

As Europe moves closer towards economic union, companies across the world, both large and small, are reviewing the European dimension of their activities. For some, the process is well under way; for others it is just starting. It is not just that there will be more exports and imports across Europe, more joint ventures, more investments in other Community countries - yet all these will inevitably follow the easing and eventual abolition of frontier controls. More important will be the fact that European industrial standards, European systems, Europe-wide ways of doing business will become part of the local operating business environment for individual companies throughout the Community.

The removal of barriers means you have a chance in other EC markets previously reserved for local firms. It also means a choice of strategy - export alone or seek a partner or partners in other parts of the Community. Furthermore, an increasing number of companies from other EC countries will enter and compete in your traditional and local markets.

Some large companies have already carried out a '1992 audit' to assess the opportunities and challenges of the changing business environment; many more are considering doing so. Details of such an audit are included in Chapter 7. Significant cost savings will follow the removal of frontier controls on goods, workers and services. Lower cost transport and insurance, harmonization or mutual recognition of standards, the approximation of national company law, increased competition among suppliers of financial services, telecommunications and transport, joint ventures and business cooperation could lead to higher profit and growth opportunities.

The imperative need of firms is to secure access to a larger European home market. This will provide economies of scale through higher sales volume and enable greater research and development expenditure. In this way, Europe's companies will be better prepared to meet the increasing challenge from Japan, the U.S. and the newly industrializing countries.

The first section of the book explains how the Community works and how you can work with the institutions to explain your issues, influence events and help shape your European strategy, taking into account the gradual but relentless drive towards bringing about the freedom of movement of goods and services, people and capital which Europe 1992 entails.

The second section indicates the considerations you will need to take into account in developing a company European strategy. The third and fourth sections describe in outline different EC policies and the ways in which they might affect your business. The boxes throughout the text illustrate the policies and provide check lists for you in developing your thinking. The final section provides up-to-date sources of further information. The book is meant to be dipped into rather than to be read from beginning to end. It will provide a framework for your reflection and a ready source of reference. If you are serious about developing your European business strategy, you will visit Brussels and Strasbourg at least once in your life. Europe is on the move and you will best feel this by moving and seeing it for yourself.

Section I: How the European Community Works and How it Affects Business

1. The Decision-making Process: The Relationship Between the Commission and the Council of Ministers

The key to understanding how the Community works is the relationship between two institutions. The Commission makes proposals for European laws and the Council of Ministers decides whether to accept or reject them. The increasingly important role in the legislative process of the European Parliament is described in Chapter 4.

Box 1: European Legislation

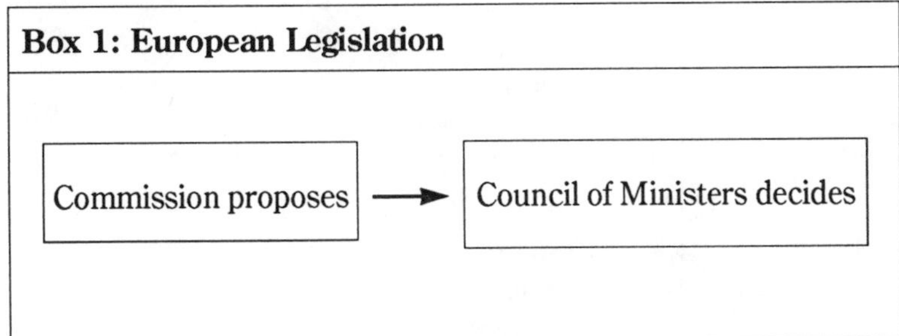

The Commission

Many of the functions of government departments are carried out by the Commission which is also partly responsible for policy formation, acting as a mediator between the governments of the Twelve and executing agreed policies. The Commission staff is headed by seventeen Commissioners. Each Commissioner is nominated by his or her national government and appointed by the Council of Ministers for a renewable four-year term. Senior politicians or other influential personalities are usually appointed.

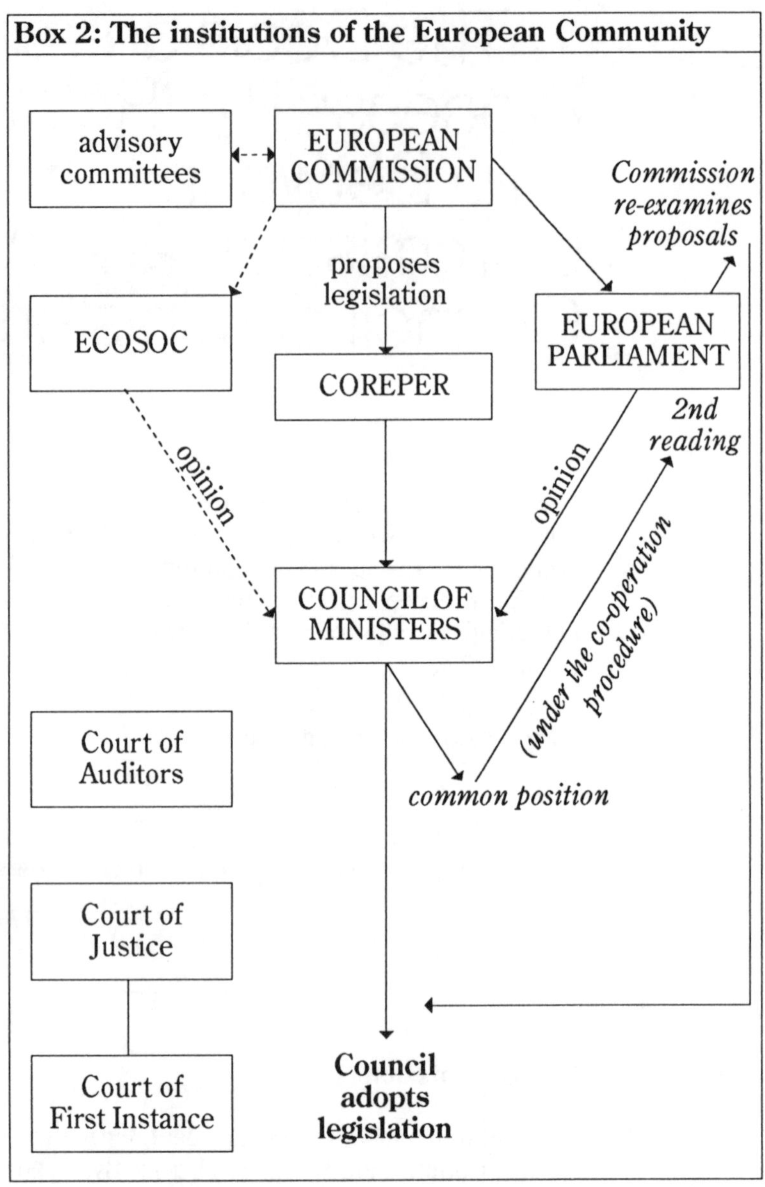
Box 2: The institutions of the European Community
advisory committees
EUROPEAN COMMISSION
Commission re-examines proposals
proposes legislation
ECOSOC
EUROPEAN PARLIAMENT
COREPER
2nd reading
opinion
opinion
COUNCIL OF MINISTERS
(under the co-operation procedure)
Court of Auditors
common position
Court of Justice
Court of First Instance
Council adopts legislation

In practice, two come from each of the larger countries of the Community and one from each of the others. Commissioners are individually responsible for a number of departments known as Directorates-General (see Box 3), but they are collectively responsible for proposals put forward to the Council of Ministers. If they cannot reach agreement unanimously they make decisions by a simple majority vote, in other words at least nine out of the seventeen Commissioners must be in favour. They form a collegiate body and therefore once the Commission takes a decision all the Commissioners are bound to go along with it and support and defend the Commission line to other Community institutions and outside bodies.

Box 3: Special Responsibilities of Commissioners

President:

Jacques Delors -	Secretariat General Legal Services Monetary Affairs Spokesman's Service Joint Interpreting and Conference Service Think Tank Security Office

Vice-Presidents:

Frans Andriessen -	External Relations and Trade Policy Cooperation with other European Countries
Henning Christophersen -	Economic and Financial Affairs Relations with the European Parliament
Manuel Marin -	Cooperation and Development Fisheries
Filippo Maria Pandolfi -	Research and Science

	Telecommunications Information Technology and Innovation Joint Research Centre
Martin Bangemann -	Internal Market and Industrial Affairs Relations with the European Parliament
Sir Leon Brittan -	Competition Policy Financial Institutions

Members of the Commission:

Carlo Ripa Di Meana -	Environment Nuclear Safety Civil Protection
Antonio Cardoso e Cunha -	Personnel and Administration Energy Euratom Supply Agency Policy on Small and Medium Sized Enterprises Tourism Social Economy
Abel Matutes -	Mediterranean Policy Relations with Latin America North-South Relations
Peter Schmidhuber -	Budget Financial Control
Christiane Scrivener -	Taxation Customs Union Questions relating to obligatory levies (fiscal or social levies)
Bruce Millan -	Regional Policy
Jean Dondelinger -	Audio-visual Policy Cultural Affairs

	Information and Communication Policy Citizens' Europe Office for Official Publications
Ray MacSharry -	Agriculture Rural Development
Karel Van Miert -	Transport Credit, Investments and Financial Instruments Consumer Protection
Vasso Papandreou -	Social Affairs and Employment Education and Training Human Resources
January 1991	

The President of the Commission is one of the most powerful jobs in the Community. Jacques Delors who was first appointed in January 1985 is responsible for sharing out portfolios among six Vice-Presidents and the other Commissioners. This is a complicated task as some portfolios are of greater interest than others.

Box 4: Solemn Declaration Made by Newly Appointed Commissioners Before the Court of Justice

I solemnly undertake:

• To perform my duties in complete independence, in the general interest of the Communities;
• In carrying out my duties, neither to seek nor to take instructions from any Government or body;
• To refrain from any action incompatible with my duties.
• I formally note the undertaking of each Member State to respect this principle and not to seek to influence Members of the Commission in the performance of their task.
• I further undertake to respect, both during and after

my term of office, the obligations arising therefrom, and in particular the duty to behave with integrity and discretion as regards the acceptance, after I have ceased to hold office, of certain appointments or benefits.

The Commission buildings are in Brussels, close to, but separate from, the Council of Ministers building (see Figure 1). The Commission is the European conscience of the Community. Officials help make proposals in the interests of the Community as a whole and not in the interest of their own nationality. The two German Commissioners, for example, will have good formal and informal contacts in Germany which they will use extensively, but they do not represent German interests in the Community any more than the French Commissioners represent French interests. Commissioners are sworn in before the Court of Justice (Chapter 5), and promise to act for the Community as a whole (Box 4).

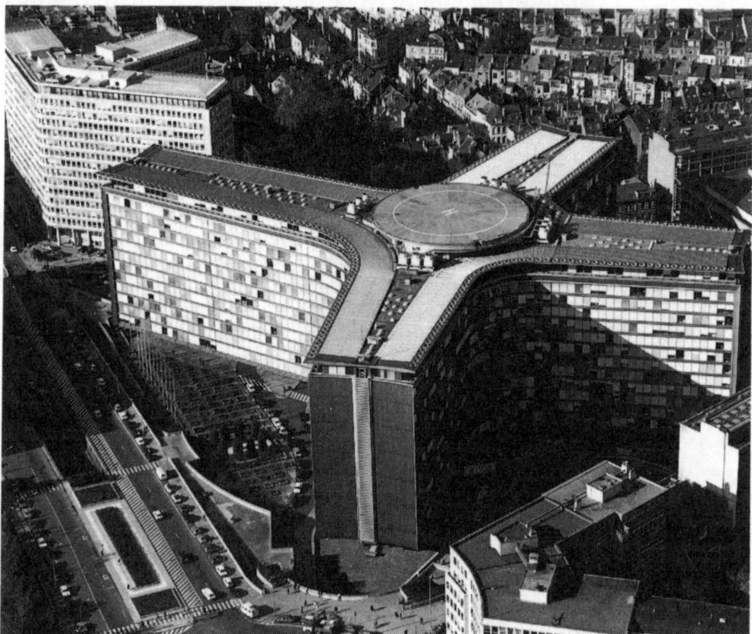

Figure 1 Two main seats of European Community power. The principal Commission building, the Berlaymont, is the X-shaped building on the right. The arrow-shaped Charlemagne building on the left is the Council of Ministers.

Policies are not conceived in a bureaucratic vacuum. The Commission seeks to propose legislation that will help develop the Community along the lines laid down in the founding Treaty of Rome or in subsequent legislation, and which has a reasonable chance of being accepted by the Council of Ministers and the European Parliament. Suggestions for developing policies come from industries, trade associations, pressure groups, member governments and, in particular, from the six-monthly European Council meetings of the Heads of State of the Twelve (Chapter 5). If broad agreement is reached at a European Summit, as these meetings are more popularly called, there is a good chance of detailed legislation on the subject proposed by the Commission being agreed by the Council of Ministers.

As well as specific proposals for legislation, the Commission also sends official communications and guidelines to the Council on a wide range of subjects. The 'Eurocrats' in Brussels, as the popular press calls them, are mostly officials of the Commission.

Box 5: How Many Eurocrats in Brussels?

There are about 9,500 Commission staff in Brussels, with 2,500 in Luxembourg and a further 4,000 elsewhere - these being mainly scientific research staff, and staff in the Commission's 90 or so delegations in overseas countries. The total of about 16,000 is smaller than many a UK local authority.

Moreover, about 2,500 staff are needed because the Community has to work in the different languages of the Member States, and another 2,600 are engaged in the Community's scientific research programmes. So there are only about 11,000 staff of all grades to handle the development of policy and the administration of agreed decisions - a tiny number for a Community of 340 million citizens.

Richard Hay, Director-General
DG IX Personnel and Administration
Commission of the European Communities
December 1990

There are in fact relatively few of them - only about 11,000 - of whom the large majority are interpreters, translators, secretarial and administrative staff (Box 5).

Box 6: The Commission
Makes policy proposals after consulting experts and interested parties; Mediates between governments of the Twelve; Carries out policies once agreed by Council of Ministers. President: (currently Jacques Delors) is one of the 17 commissioners from the Twelve Member States. 800 senior civil servants; 16,000 total staff of which 11,000 involved in policy and administration. The European conscience of the Community; Multinational, multilingual; Career service but top jobs still tend to be government nominees.

The Council of Ministers

If the Commission is the European conscience of the Community, the Council of Ministers is the guardian of the interests of individual member countries. A Commission proposal can only become law when all twelve governments agree unanimously or by simple majority through their representatives at the Council of Ministers.

The Council consists of a minister from each member government. The ministers change according to the subjects on the agenda. If the proposed legislation deals with transport, then the twelve ministers for transport make up the Council; if energy, then the ministers for energy. Ministers represent the interests of their own governments, but try to arrive at agreements which are in the Community interest. When the media suggest, for example, that France or the Netherlands is blocking a certain proposal, this probably means that a French or Netherlands minister is preventing the proposal from being accepted until satisfactory amendments are made to it.

The Treaties provide for three methods of decision-taking depending on the nature of a given proposal and the Treaty Article on which it is based:

- unanimity, which strictly means 'nobody against' as abstention does not prevent unanimity.

- simple majority voting, ie at least seven Member States in favour.

- qualified majority voting under which each Member State has a weighted number of votes depending on its size (Box 7).

The Single European Act (which entered into force in July 1987) has substantially extended the Council's scope for taking majority decisions, particularly as regards the Internal Market, and has subsequently improved the Community's decision-making process.

Box 7: Council of Ministers: Weighting of Member States' Votes

France	10
Germany	10
Italy	10
United Kingdom	10
Spain	8
Belgium	5
Greece	5
Netherlands	5
Portugal	5
Denmark	3
Ireland	3
Luxembourg	2

A qualified majority is 54 out of 76 votes. 23 votes constitute a blocking minority, for example, two larger Member States and one smaller State (except Luxembourg).

Qualified majority voting applies to some two-thirds of the items for action set out in the Commission's White Paper. Only items relating to taxation, the free movement of people and the rights and interests of employees are excluded and will therefore still require unanimity under the Treaty.

This change towards greater use of qualified majority voting has already helped accelerate Council decision-making on Internal Market items and should continue to help speed up agreement on the remaining White Paper proposals to which it applies.

There are, of course, inevitable trade-offs behind the scenes, when one Member State gives way on one proposal in return for agreement on another. This bargaining procedure is not new and occurs at national and local government levels in most countries.

The Council of Ministers meets only for a certain number of days during the year and for the rest of the time the ministers concerned go about their business in the capitals of the Twelve. The ministers, unlike the Commissioners, are not resident in Brussels and only go there for meetings.

Box 8: The Council of Ministers

Guardian of the interests of individual states;
One minister from each Member State;
Effective veto on Commission proposals.

Its President is the Foreign Minister of a Member State on a six-month rotation;
The twelve minister members change depending on subject;
COREPER - ambassadors of the Twelve prepare agenda aided by small permanent secretariat of the Council.

Each country takes a six-month turn to chair Council meetings (Box 9). A national minister of foreign affairs is President of the Council during this period. Commissioners sit in at the Council of Ministers to explain, to defend and if necessary to adjust their proposals. When the Council is not in session, its meetings are prepared by a small permanent secretariat resident in Brussels which is located in the Council of Ministers' building. The main preparatory work and initial negotiations are carried out by the ambassadors of the Twelve accredited to the Community who, with their embassy staffs, are resident in Brussels.

Box 9: The Presidency of the Council of Ministers

1990 Ireland, then Italy

1991 Luxembourg, then the Netherlands

1992 Portugal, then the United Kingdom

The ambassadors, or representatives as they are called, act as a link between the member countries and the Community. They meet in the Committee of Permanent Representatives (called COREPER) to prepare the agendas for the Council of Ministers and to agree, in advance of the Council meetings, many of the non-contentious proposals which have been put forward by the Commission. They draw up points of agreement and difference on subjects so that when the ministers of the Twelve attend Council meetings, much has already been agreed and only matters still in dispute need be negotiated.

Even though most of the draft legislation has been agreed beforehand by the twelve governments, it still has to be placed before the Council of Ministers for legal and constitutional reasons before it becomes law. The first part of the agenda therefore consists of a large number of agreed matters which are taken as so-called 'A' points. Unless any minister wishes to contest them, they are agreed automatically at the beginning of the meeting.

Debate on the rest of the agenda is tense as important national interests are invariably at stake. Non-contentious proposals have already been agreed and accepted as 'A' points. Therefore it is only the policies and draft laws which are close to being agreed which are disussed at the Council (Box 10).

Box 10: A Day in the Life of a COREPER Deputy

1000
Walk across to the Charlemagne building for today's COREPER (Deputies) meeting. Shake hands with immediate neighbours like a good continental.

1030
Meeting opens only 15 minutes after the usual 15-minute delay. We agree the Agenda, noting Other Business points - to be taken after lunch - raised by delegations or the Commission. Move on to the 'i' points (matters purporting to be ready for adoption at a forthcoming Council of Ministers, having been settled at a lower level or a previous COREPER). I place a Parliamentary scrutiny reserve on one of these points since it has not yet cleared the Westminster scrutiny procedure. A colleague asks for a different point to be sent back to the group because he does not agree that it was agreed. The remaining 'i' points are approved and passed on as 'A' points (i.e. not for discussion) to a future council.

1045
Embark on Agenda proper. It is COREPER's job according to Article 151 of the Treaty, to 'be responsible for preparing the work of the Council...'

Today we are preparing Single Market legislation for forthcoming meetings of the Internal Market, Transport and Agriculture Councils. On each item we have before us a report of the working group, the original Commission proposal and any revised texts suggested in the group. The reports tell us what is agreed and what is not and set out any Presidency compromise that has so far emerged. Our task is to take this process to final agreement if possible, and, if not, to the point where the remaining differences are clearly identified for the Council.

I speak in accordance with my instructions, as do my colleagues, each of us trying to draw the others and the

Commission towards our own national objectives, albeit cloaked in Community raiment. If we are at an early stage, the Presidency and the debate are both reasonably open. As we get nearer to the crunch, our Chairman is looking for a decision, which often means a qualified majority. Those on the losing side of the argument seek to adjust their positions in order to find a blocking minority.

1315
Lunch. Sandwiches in the office and catch up with the in-tray.

1515
Despatch Other Business on which, according to our rules, no decisions can be taken.

1530
Work on through the Agenda, our advisers coming and going according to the subject matter. On some points our Chairman has no choice but to send the file back to the group for further work. On others he sees a compromise in the making and urges those on either side of it to come into line. Mostly the Commission's spokesman helps him in this task; sometimes he refuses to contemplate the necessary changes in the Commission proposal. On a few points we reach agreement and send them on to the relevant council.

1900
Meeting ends. There is a Council tomorrow and most Deputies have Ministers arriving this evening.

2000
Briefing dinner for ten chez moi. The UKREP team update the Minister and his officials on the latest documents, Presidency intentions, and the attitudes of other Member States. The Minister makes his objectives for the Council clear; we offer tactical advice.

David Elliott, UK Deputy Permanent Representative (UKREP)

National 'Representations' in Brussels

It is possible to visit the embassy of the Permanent Representative and talk to the staff of the Representation, as it is called. The staff has experts seconded from national government departments and elsewhere, and they represent their countries in day-to-day relations with the Council and the Commission.

A Member State's Representation in Brussels is different from that of an embassy. An embassy has an Ambassador accredited to the Kingdom of Belgium and deals with bilateral affairs between Belgium and his or her country. A Representation is a Member State's day-to-day contact and negotiating arm with the Community institutions. The Representative is a senior diplomat with the rank of Ambassador.

Before the Council meets to discuss a proposal, it will have been thoroughly discussed, not only by the Representation but by the national government departments and working parties of the Council at which Member States are represented. By the time the Council meets there is already a broad measure of agreement. The Council also has the benefit of the opinion of the European Parliament and the Economic and Social Committee before beginning its deliberations on a Commission proposal (see Chapters 4 and 5).

As well as permanent Representatives from each of the Twelve resident with their staffs in Brussels, 144 countries maintain diplomatic relations with the Community and most of them have offices in Brussels. The Commission has 90 delegations in different countries of the world. You may, therefore, contact the Ambassador and staff of your own country's mission to the European Community or one of the delegations of the Commission in your own country. The United States and Japan have well staffed missions in Brussels. Businessmen are well advised to contact their national Representation, as its staff can provide contacts in the Community at every level, depending on the subject to be discussed. The most important contacts will usually be with officials in the Directorates-General of the Commission which is the subject of the next chapter.

2. The Directorates-General of the Commission

The Commission is divided into 23 Directorates-General (DGs) as well as a number of specialized services. The Directorates-General of the Commission are the power house where most can be learned about Community policies affecting business, and where views can be most effectively expressed to officials responsible for initiating, drafting and helping drive through the many proposals likely to be of interest to companies. In developing their relations with Governments, including the Community institutions, managers do not always visit government officials as often as they should. Government involvement in business has been growing for many years, yet many companies still fail to recognize the benefit of personal contacts.

Box 11: The Tasks of a European Commissioner

One thing which distinguishes the European Community from any other international organization is the way in which its institutions have been devised, with the Council of Ministers, the European Parliament and the European Commission interacting together, rather as if they were participating in a formal dance - but hopefully attaining desired objectives, rather than going round in circles.

The European Commission is always at the centre of the dance circle, because we alone are responsible for proposing policies and also for ensuring that they are implemented. The Council of Ministers takes the decisions, but only on the basis of Commission proposals.

This puts my work as one of the 17 members of the Commission into context: developing policy proposals in meetings with my personal staff (the 'cabinet') and with the officials from the policy departments; attending Council meetings to explain proposals and persuade ministers to take decisions; and going to the European Parliament in Strasbourg to convince MEPs of the importance and good sense of our proposals - a very necessary task given the powers which the Parliament now has.

The Commission is a collegiate body, so I also have to convince my own colleagues of the virtues of proposals I would like to put forward - and to examine their proposals as well. This is normally done at our weekly meeting on Wednesdays.

Of course each Commissioner has different portfolios, which is reflected in the nature of the work. As the person responsible for competition policy I have rather special tasks and certain delegated powers which are particularly important in a single European market. Here it is a case not so much of implementing policies agreed by the Council of Ministers but rather of implementing the Treaties themselves.

The Treaties give special responsibilities to the Commission in three main competition areas: anti-trust, state monopolies, and state subsidies, and a large part of my time is spent examining general policy and specific cases in these areas.

At the end of 1989 the Commission's powers were significantly extended when the Council of Ministers adopted a regulation giving the Commission sole responsibility for deciding whether big European mergers do or do not pose a threat to competition, which will of course bring an added work load.

The Commission is a political body. Its role is to act as the motor for the European Community, thinking ahead and using its imagination and foresight to direct the EC in a positive direction. It is a part of the job which I take very seriously. At the same time, we Commissioners have to keep in touch with national feeling in the countries which we know best - in my case the United Kingdom - while in no way taking instructions from governments or anyone else. It is this variety of responsibilities which makes the task so absorbing and stimulating.

Sir Leon Brittan, Vice-President of the Commission

Visiting the Commission

Apart from being the conscience of the Community, the Commission acts as its principal information and public relations agent. A Commission official has at least three good reasons for spending time with visitors: to help them, to learn from them and to promote the Community dimension. Commission officials can be visited to discuss business in the same way as officials in government departments in national administrations. Bureaucrats in Brussels are faceless only to those who never visit them. Those who do, can learn, influence and promote their cause. Not all businessmen can visit the Commission, but there is a good welcome to those who do. When the corridors of the Commission's Berlaymont building become crowded with Community businessmen, the system may have to be changed. This has not yet happened. Few more accessible and open administrations exist anywhere.

Figure 2: The Commission in session

Box 12: Directory of the Commission of the European Communities

The Commission is divided up into 23 Directorates-General and other services, each of which is subdivided into a number of Directorates with responsibility for a specific area of Commission policy.

Directorate-General/ Service	*Commissioner responsible*	*Director-General*
Secretariat General of the Commission	Jacques Delors	David Williamson (Secretary General)
Legal Service	Jacques Delors	Jean Louis Dewost
Spokesman's Service	Jacques Delors	Bruno Dethomas (Deputy Spokesman)
Joint Interpreting and Conference Service	Jacques Delors	Rene van Hoof Hafer-kamp
Statistical Office	Henning Christoph-ersen	Yves Franchet
Translation Service	Antonio Cardoso e Cunha	Eduard Brackeniers
Security Office	Jacques Delors	Pieter de Haan
DG I External Relations	Frans Andriessen	Horst Krenzler
DG II Economic and Financial Affairs	Henning Christoph-ersen	Giovanni Ravasio

Directorate-General/ Service	*Commissioner responsible*	*Director-General*
DG III Internal Market and Industrial Affairs	Martin Bangemann	Riccardo Perissich
DG IV Competition	Sir Leon Brittan	Claus Ehlermann
DG V Employment, Social Affairs and Education	Vasso Papandreou	Jean Degimbe
DG VI Agriculture	Ray MacSharry	Guy Legras
DG VII Transport	Karel van Miert	Robert Coleman
DG VIII Development	Abel Matutes	Dieter Frisch
DG IX Personnel and Administration	Antonio Cardoso e Cunha	Frans de Costa
DG X Information Communication and Culture	Jean Dondelinger	Colette Flesch
DG XI Environment Consumer Protection Nuclear Safety	Carlo Ripa di Meana	Laurens Jan Brink-horst
DG XII Science, Research and Development	Filippo Maria Pandolfi	Paolo Fasella

Directorate-General/ Service	*Commissioner responsible*	*Director-General*
DG XIII Telecommunications Information Industries and Innovation	Filippo Maria Pandolfi	Michel Carpentier
DG XIV Fisheries	Manuel Marin	José de Almeida Serra
DG XV Financial Institutions and Company Law	Sir Leon Brittan	Geoffrey Fitchew
DG XVI Regional Policy	Bruce Millan	Eneko Landaburu Illarramendi
DG XVII Energy Policy	Antonio Cardoso e Cunha	Constantinos Maniatopoulos
DG XVIII Credit and Investments	Karel van Miert	Enrico Cioffi
DG XIX Budgets	Peter Schmidhuber	Jean Paul Mingasson
DG XX Financial Control	Peter Schmidhuber	Lucien de Moor
DG XXI Customs Union and Indirect Taxation	Christiane Scrivener	Henry Chumas
DG XXII Coordination of Structural Instruments	Henning Christoph-ersen	Thomas O'Dwyer

Directorate-General/ Service	*Commissioner responsible*	*Director-General*
DG XXIII Enterprise Policy, Distributive Trades, Tourism and Cooperatives	Antonio Cardoso e Cunha	Heinrich Von Moltke
Consumer Policy Service	Karel van Miert	Kaj Barlebo-Larsen
Task Force for Human Resources, Education, Training and Youth	Vasso Papandreou	Hywel Ceri Jones
Office for Official Publications of the European Communities	Jean Dondelinger	Lucien Emringer
European Foundation for the Improvement of Living and Working Conditions		Clive Purkiss
European Centre for the Development of Vocational Training (CEDEFOP)		Ernst Piehl
Joint Research Centre	Filippo Maria Pandolfi	Jean Pierre Contzen
Euratom Supply Agency	Antonio Cardoso e Cunha	Jean Claude Blanquart

NB Several Commissioners hold multiple portfolios, some of which are not mentioned above as they do not correspond directly to a Directorate-General but to a specific area of policy.

February 1991

Cabinets of Commissioners

In many cases the best contacts are to be found in the Directorates-General of the Commission. But the Commissioners themselves are always ready to receive senior businessmen who have important business to discuss. As they have responsibilities and duties similar to ministers in national governments, their detailed knowledge of specific subjects is necessarily limited. They are also very busy people. Most of their views, and those of the Commission, however, are regularly available in print. Representations on business matters put directly to them, either orally or in writing, will be taken up either by officials of a Directorate-General or by a member of a Commission Cabinet. The Cabinet system does not exist in all Community countries, although the growing use of political advisers by Ministers in the United Kingdom, for example, is perhaps a move in this direction. The system is well known in France and the United States.

Each Commissioner when he is appointed, chooses his Cabinet, a group of people, sometimes but not in every case career officials, who will usually be fellow countrymen/women. Each Cabinet has at least one non-national member.

The 'Chef de Cabinet' holds a powerful position. He is the chief executive assistant of the Commissioner. He will often act on the Commissioner's behalf and stand in for him at meetings. The portfolios of a Commissioner will be shared out among the Cabinet and so, in making an appointment with a member of a Cabinet it is essential to find out who deals with the subject in which you are interested.

Much of the negotiation with the Directorates-General will be carried out by the members of the Cabinet. They write speeches, prepare drafts, accompany the Commissioner on visits, and generally support the work of his sphere of responsibility. They act as a filter to the Commissioner and meet visitors in the same way as any other official of the Commission. It is therefore quite appropriate to call on a member of a Cabinet who is often an effective substitute for the Commissioner himself. Meeting Commissioners, like meeting Cabinet Ministers, will on certain occasions be desirable, but often a meeting with a minister's administrators, or in the case of the Commission, with members of the Directorates-General, can be equally useful for business purposes. In the Directorates-General there are individuals responsible for different areas of policy who will know most of what is likely to interest and affect business in their specialist fields.

How a Directorate-General Works: Example: The Internal Market and Industrial Affairs Directorate-General or DG III

Each Directorate-General (numbered in Roman numerals) of the Commission is divided into Directorates (designated alphabetically) which are divided into Divisions (numbered in arabic numerals).

Each DG is headed by a Director General. A Director-General can be compared to the permanent head of a ministry. The Director-General of DG III is responsible for coordinating the Internal Market and Industrial Affairs. He works closely with the Commissioners and in particular with the Commissioner having special responsibility for industry and may be assisted by one or more Deputy Directors-General.

Box 13: Responsibilities of Directorate-General III: Internal Market and Industrial Affairs

Director-General	Riccardo PERISSICH
Deputy Director-General (with special responsibility for Directorates C and E)	Alexander SCHAUB
Deputy Director-General (with responsiblity for Directorates B and D)	John MOGG
Assistant to Director-General	Mathias REUTE
- Data processing unit	Claude DAVID

Administrative unit	Head
Financial services	Jean SOMERS
Directorate A **Industrial economy, service industries,non-member countries, raw materials**	Robert VERRUE
Adviser	Reginald SPENC
International cooperation in the field of technology Adviser	Peter John LENNON
1. Industrial and technological problems in relation to non-member countries	Fernand THUMES
Deputy Head of Division	Albrecht MULFINGER
2. Completion of the Internal Market	Michel AYRAL
- Special studies	Michael LOY
3. Industrial economy	Jean-François MARCHIPONT
4. Services	Victor POU-SERRADELL
5. Raw materials	José NICOLAI
Directorate B **Internal Market and industrial affairs I**	Ernesto PREVIDI
New approach: standardization and technical harmonization	Ernesto PREVIDI
1. Safeguard measures: removal of non-tariff barriers (Article 30 et seq.)	Alfonso MATTERA RICIGLIANO
2. Foodstuffs	Paul GRAY
Deputy Head of Division	Egon GAERNER
3. Mechanical engineering, electrical engineering and metrology	Luis Sebastian MONTOYA MORON
4. Standardization and certification; relations with standardization bodies; notification procedures	John FARNELL
5. Construction	Karlheinz ZACHMANN

Administrative Unit	Head
6. Pharmaceuticals, veterinary medicines	Fernand SAUER
Directorate C **Internal Market and industrial affairs II**	Daniele VERDIANI
1. Automobiles, aviation and railways	Roger PEETERS
2. Aviation	Jacques SOENENS
3. Textiles and clothing	Paul RUTSAERT
4. Shipbuilding, wood, leather, paper and miscellaneous industries	Abraáo CARVALHO
5. Deputy Head of Division	Louis GRAVIGNY
6. Chemicals, plastics and rubber	György von O'SVATH
Directorate D **Approximation of laws, freedom of establishment and freedom to provide services**	Ivo SCHWARTZ
1. Civil and economic law, criminal law and law of procedure; citizens' rights	Hans Claudius TASCHNER
2. Free movement of self-employed persons and recognition of diplomas	Jean-Jacques BEUVE-MERY
- Management of recognition arrangements	Marcel VAN HOOREBEECK
Deputy Head of Unit	Bertrand CARSIN
3. Industrial property and broadcasting policy	Bertold SCHWAB
- The media	Ulf BRÜHANN
4. Copyright, unfair competition and international aspects of intellectual property	Ludovic BRIET
- New technologies	Bernhard POSNER
Directorate E **Steel**	Pedro Ortun SILVAN
Policy and relations with industry	
Chief Adviser	Hans KUTSCHER

Administrative unit	Head
1. External measures - Management and cooperation in negotiations	Jacobus AARTS
2. Sector analysis, general objectives, structures and administration of controls	Piero SQUARTINI
Deputy Head of Division (with special responsibility for the administration of controls)	Winfried DEUTZMANN
- Production capacity and consultation on Articles 54 and 56, ECSC	
- Raw materials for the steel industry	
3. Forward programmes, market, prices, administration of controls	Vivian EVANS
- Market	Guido VANDERSEYPEN
- Prices	Gerd DREES
- Administration of controls	Georges VOGT
Directorate F **Public procurement**	Robert COLEMAN
1. Public procurement - Policy	David WHITE
2. Public procurement - Application of directives opinions	Giuseppe BONCOMPAGNI
July 1990	

Each Directorate responsible for specific industries is headed by a Director. For example, as can be seen in Box 13, Directorate B of DG III which deals with Internal Market and Industrial Affairs is headed by Ernesto Previdi.

Each division is led by a Head of Division. Below Heads of Divisions there are various grades of administrators and support staff.

In addition to the above job titles, each permanent Commission official holds a personal grade based on seniority and length of service. There are four broad divisions of grades in the Commission namely:
'A' officials (administrators)

'B' officials (junior administrators)
'C' officials (secretaries, typists, etc)
'D' officials (messengers, drivers, etc)
Each of these divisions is split into different grades, for example there are eight 'A' grades numbered from A1 to A8 in descending order of seniority. A commission official who is a Director would normally be an A2 grade official. A1 grades are Directors-General and A2 and A3 grades are senior officials working for them. Most business dealings will be with A2 to A4 grades who are the key administrative officials of the Commission, although some A5 and A6 grades are quite as influential. It may well be that for specialist or technical matters A5 to A8 grades should be your contacts, or certain B grades.

Those who work in a Directorate come from different Community countries. There is in theory no particular advantage in meeting an official of your own nationality, except from the point of view of language and culture, as all officials must take a Community-wide view of their work rather than a national one. In practice an official of a particular nationality is more likely to be knowledgeable about his own country's attitude to a specific subject and there is advantage at this stage in the development of the Commission to making contact, at least initially, with officials from your own country as well as with the officials dealing with a specialist issue irrespective of their nationality. The two working languages of the Community are English and French and officials speak at least one if not both of these. Official documents are translated into the nine languages of the EC, but there are often translation delays.

It can be seen from Box 13 that aircraft (in DG III, Directorate C, 2) are dealt with by Jacques Soenens. In his department there may be two or three other officials, as well as technical and clerical officers. The total numbers are very small, however, in comparison with those working in national governments on different aspects of aerospace. The Commission, therefore, only plays a coordinating and policy-making role. Much of the detailed information on which it bases its policies has to come from national administrations. Commission officials spend a good deal of time briefing and negotiating with national officials. Their task in communicating with national administrations is greatly helped by the Twelve Permanent Representations to the Community described in Chapter 1.

Making Contact with Commission Officials

The Commission produces at intervals a directory of its senior officials. Box 13 is adapted from this directory. It can be obtained from Commission sales agents in about twenty countries including the US, Switzerland and Sweden, as well as direct from the office for official publications in Luxembourg. Details are in Section V.

If your interests are general and strategic then you will probably want to see officials listed in the directory. If your interests are more technical and concerned with the application of, or timetable for, certain legislation for an industry, a lower ranking official may be your contact - not necessarily listed. A telephone call to the key official dealing with your particular interest is as effective a way as any of obtaining meetings with those who can help you. The official will probably arrange a meeting with colleagues involved in drawing up legislation for your industry. From the Commissioner downwards it is unlikely that there are more than a dozen people in the Commission whom a company would find useful to contact on the problems of one industry sector, unless there were many aspects of Community policies affecting that particular business. In practice only one or two might need to be visited.

Box 14: Contact with Directorates-General of the Commission
(1) Obtain up-to-date directory of senior officials of the Commission which is issued periodically. If you are in constant touch with the Commission, obtain an internal telephone directory through a contact. Its circulation is restricted for cost rather than security reasons. (2) Write to or telephone the official dealing with the subject you are interested in, giving as much detail as possible, and set up an appointment. Ask him whether there are any of his colleagues it would be appropriate for you to meet at the same time. (3) Alternatively ask the Commission Representative

Office or a Euro-Info Centre in your country of residence whether they can suggest initial contacts for you. This is perhaps a better way if the nature of your enquiries requires you to meet a wide selection of officials, many of whom you do not know, or if you do not really know whom you ought to meet.

(4) If your enquiries are technical ones, or if the answers to them require preparation, write beforehand setting out what you want to know. The official will be better prepared and may have some documentation available for you which will save time. There are many Commission documents which can be of practical value to businessmen but they are not all for sale because of constraints on time and printing. It is often possible to obtain a copy from the official concerned.

(5) Invite the Commission official to visit you and get him to meet people from your industry. Commission officials are busy, but do need to travel. They cannot accept fees but can sometimes accept travel expenses for conferences etc., which may ease their budgetary constraints.

Offices of the Commission Outside Brussels

It has been suggested that businessmen meet Commission officials concerned with their areas of interest. However, this is only necessary if there is specific business to discuss, or if the intention is to influence Commission thinking or learn what projected, or so called 'pipeline', legislation is being considered.

Box 15: A Working Day in the Life of the Head of One of the Offices of the Commission

08.30
Arrive in office, check overnight fax and telex, go through post with staff.

09.30
Deal with letters which can be answered immediately,

pass others on to information unit. Some set aside for research.

10.00
Reading of newspapers interrupted by call from BBC wanting comment on story in morning papers re cancellation of ERDF grant. Give interim comment, then two phone calls to Brussels for confirmation and further information. Pass on to BBC: want to know if I will say that on camera, for lunch time. Say yes, camera crew coming in half an hour.

10.15
Three phone calls to Brussels for information on EC position on Full Gas Desulphurization, for TV journalist working on documentary.

10.45
BBC TV crew arrive, set up camera, film interview.

11.10
Deal with two awkward phone queries. One man insists European Commission should intervene in his dispute with housing authority over repairs to his dwelling. Irate American lady cannot understand why Commission office does not issue visas for travel to France.

11.30
Fifteen under 11 year olds, plus parents, invade office for prizegiving in Europe week library competition, sponsored by Commission. Distribute prizes, make speech, pose for press photos. Children scoff all the eats.

12.45
Lunch at desk, tuna sandwich and a banana. Over lunch work on contents of next monthly magazine, drafting one article.

2.30
Phone call to Brussels to confirm speaker from Commission for conference being held by major

environmentalist group. No luck so far.

2.45
Leave by car for Portrush to present paper (1992 implications) to private seminar of senior civil servants.

4.00
Deliver paper. Discussion follows.

7.00
Leave Portrush for Coleraine, for public meeting on EC Structural Funds.

7.30
Speak, along with two government officials, at public meeting. Discussion ends 9.30.

10.30
Arrive home. Have missed both lunch and dinner.

Dennis Kennedy, Belfast, January 1990

If your aim is general background briefing on what is happening in the Community relevant to industry and commerce, there are more simple and cost-effective ways. First, there is a team of Commission officials in each of the capitals and other principal cities of the Twelve, Washington, Tokyo and a number of other centres. One of the tasks of each team is to be well briefed on latest Commission thinking. These officials spend much of their time meeting groups and interested individuals. For example, if a businessman wants to learn more about the way competition policy and industrial policy affects his business, there are Commission staff available in London, New York, Tokyo, Paris and Bonn able to help. Similar offices exist in most European capitals and about 90 non-European capitals. The addresses of these Commission offices are in Section V as well as references to other sources, such as Euro-Info Centres specifically set up to assist small and medium-size businesses.

The Offices of the Commission are very useful for keeping in touch with affairs in the Community, not only through meetings with their staff, but through the publications they produce and their comprehensive libraries. All normal bilateral trade and commercial enquiries however, should be directed through national government departments or a national Representation in Brussels. (But see also European Business Information Centres (Box 57) and Section V.)

Briefing in Brussels

Another option is Directorate-General X in Brussels, the Information Directorate-General. It has a staff of officials responsible for disseminating oral, written and audio-visual information about the Community and its activities. A briefing from one of its officials for a businessman and his colleagues on a

Box 16: Briefings in Brussels

The Commission itself organizes briefing sessions for interested parties in Brussels. These sessions, lasting from half a day to a day and a half, are known as 'information visits'.

However, the very great demand for such briefings and the Commission's limited resources to handle them means that the selection criteria have become very strict. In practice, priority is given to group visits (15-60 people) by influential 'multipliers' such as national and regional politicians and high officials, journalists, representative high-level socio-economic and regional associations, etc., from the member countries. Briefings for individuals are no longer possible.

These information visits are in no way to be regarded as 'junket trips'. The travel and accommodation expenses have to be borne by the participants themselves. Furthermore, the programme itself is a heavy series of traditional presentations followed by question-and-answer sessions. More audio-visual methods are likely to be introduced.

Requests for such information visits should in all cases be made first of all to the Commission's offices in the country of origin for initial examination. As regards time scale, three months in advance of the proposed date of visit is a bare minimum, six months is more reasonable and requests nine and twelve months in advance are welcomed.

The great advantage of these information visits is that they allow the participants to talk with the Commission officials responsible for the conception and implementation of Community measures. To be fully taken advantage of, therefore, it is essential that the participants be as well briefed as possible. Asking these officials questions which could be answered from basic written sources is a waste of resources. However, it should be remembered that these are 'information visits', not opportunities for technical consultations and, even less, negotiation sessions.

For schools, universities, cultural associations and the general public, the Commission also organizes shorter information visits consisting of an audio-visual presentation followed by a talk. Again, requests should be made in the first place to the Commission's Office in the country of origin.

The Commission's capacity is limited to four groups a day and groups are accepted on a 'first come, first served' basis. Requests should be made as far in advance as possible, for the programme is generally booked up three months in advance - and even longer in the case of school holidays.

Finally, it should be noted that there are no VIP or general public information visits during the month of August or between Christmas and the New Year.

In view of the Commission's limited capacity to accommodate all the many groups which would like to have an 'information visit', prospective visitors to Brussels should also bear in mind the possibility of visiting instead the European Parliament, the Economic and Social Committee, their country's Permanent Representation to the Community, or one of the many lobbying groups, big and small, in the Belgian capital. It should be noted that more and more regional authorities and major cities now have their own offices in Brussels.

Robert Pendville, Head of Visits, Conferences and Publicity Division, DG X, April 1991

visit to Brussels may be appropriate. This can be arranged by contacting the offices of the Commission prior to the visit. Too many visitors to the Commission are insufficiently briefed. This is wasteful of the time of both the official and the visitor. Managers should obtain pre-visit reading from a wide range of sources including Euro-Info Centres (see Section V for addresses).

3. Community Law: Regulations, Directives and Decisions

Only by understanding the legislative process can companies influence the drafting of laws which will shape their external environment. Community law has precedence over national law if there is a conflict. It stems either from the Treaties themselves, on which the Community is legally based, or on subsequent derived legislation which is known as secondary legislation and appears in the form of regulations, directives or decisions. It is not necessary for a businessman to be familiar with the Community Treaties, although he should be aware in general terms of the powers of the Community to regulate and develop policies which might affect him.

There is sometimes confusion about the difference between regulations, directives, decisions and recommendations. This is not helped by the complication of having not one Treaty for the

Box 17: The Instruments of Community Law; Regulations, Directives and Decisions

Primary legislation of the European Community is embodied in the three Treaties, the EEC, the Euratom and the European Coal and Steel Community Treaties. The Single European Act, now part of the Treaties of the European Communities, is also part of primary legislation.

Secondary legislation is derived from the Treaties through regulations, directives and decisions which are proposed by the Commission and approved by the Council of Ministers. In certain instances the Commission itself is empowered to adopt these acts.

Regulations or Community laws are legally binding on member countries and are applied directly like national laws. In any conflict with national laws, regulations prevail over the national laws of Member States.

Directives are equally binding on Member States as regards the aim to be achieved, but leave national authorities to ensure that they are strictly and fully implemented, where necessary, by national legislation.

Directives concern the business community because harmonization and regulation of trade and industry is achieved largely by means of them.

Decisions are concerned with specific issues and may be addressed to an individual or a company as well as to governments. If addressed to individuals or companies they have direct internal application and are binding in every respect.

Recommendations and opinions do not have binding force but indicate broad lines of current and future policies and therefore need to be monitored if they concern your industry.

European Coal and Steel Community terminology differs somewhat and if you are involved in these industries you need to know what these differences are. Obtain a copy of the ECSC Treaty from HMSO or visit your nearest Commission office.

European Community, but four, nor by the fact that different words are used in two of these Treaties for the same type of legislation! Box 17 defines the different types of secondary legislation.

The Legislative Process

Directives are laws of the Community, but it is up to individual governments to lay down how they are implemented and to enforce them. It is useful to know how a directive becomes law because a company may need to monitor the progress of directives and influence, directly or indirectly, the way in which they are drawn up.

The Role of the Commission

Under the Treaties only the Commission can make proposals for European laws and policies. Where the Council thinks that an action should be taken it may ask the Commission to undertake studies and submit relevant proposals.

Preparatory work on a Directive begins in the appropriate Directorate-General of the Commission. The staff of the Directorate-General will consult with Member States through the Offices of the Permanent Representatives of the Twelve in Brussels. It will also invite officials of the national administrations to committee meetings at the Commission. National and European Trade Associations will be consulted and indeed any groups or individuals interested in the subject or having a contribution to make. Therefore, draft Directives drawn up by Directorates-General and put to the Commission (the seventeen Commissioners as a college) for approval always take into account the views of member governments and the relevant industries and pressure groups in their countries. The intention is to draw up a draft document in legal form as a basis for negotiation by the Member States in the Council of Ministers.

It is important for business to make its voice heard at this early stage when proposals are in draft. Most new proposals for legislation put out by a Directorate-General must be accompanied by a statement assessing the impact of these proposals on business. This impact statement is sent for approval to DG XXIII which deals with enterprise policy. The statements are not confidential and businesses need to be aware of the system and work with the Commission to ensure that they represent adequate assessments of the effect of new proposals on business. National governments too will often distribute explanatory comments on draft directives to encourage full consultation and comment.

If the Commission adopts a draft Directive it is then submitted to the Council of Ministers which must in nearly all cases consult the European Parliament and the Economic and Social Committee.

The Cooperation Procedure

Introduced by the Single European Act, the new legislative process known as the cooperation procedure enables the European Parliament to play an important part in decision-making.

The cooperation procedure involving a first and second reading in the European Parliament is applicable, in principle, to all areas in

Box 18: The Legislative Process: Cooperation Procedure

1. *Commission* proposes legislation

2. *Parliament* adopts an opinion by a simple majority (the 'first reading')

3. *Council* adopts a 'common position' by qualified majority

4. *Parliament*, within three months, approves, amends or rejects the Council's 'common position'. This is known as the Parliament's 'second reading'. Amendment or rejection can only be by absolute majority of those entitled to vote, i.e. by 260 votes - half the number of seats (518) plus one

5. *Commission* may, within one month, revise its proposal 'taking into account' the amendments proposed by the Parliament

6. Where the *Parliament* has proposed an amendment the *Council*, within three months, may do one of four things:
- adopt, by qualified majority, the revised Commission proposal
- adopt, by unanimity, Parliament's amendments not approved by the Commission
- amend and adopt, by unanimity, the Commission's proposal
- fail to act

7. If the *Parliament* rejects the proposal the *Council* can

then only agree it by unanimity

8. The *Commission* may, at any time before the Council has adopted the proposal, amend or withdraw its proposal. Although a final decision still always rests with the *Council*, and the *Commission* still has the power to amend or withdraw its proposal, the *Parliament* now has the ability to send a powerful message to the Commission and Council telling them to think again. If the Commission accepts the Parliament's amendment then together thay can put considerable pressure on the Council since it can only change the revised proposal by unanimity.

which the Council is expressly entitled to take decisions by a qualified majority. Most of the Single Market proposals are covered by this procedure. Box 18 shows the complexity of the process which is not described in detail here.

Within the Council, proposals are considered by the Committee of Permanent Representatives (COREPER). If the proposals are of a technical nature, specialist committees of the Council are set up. They consist of officials from the Member States. Only then will the proposals be referred to COREPER or its deputies. Finally, Ministers themselves, in the relevant specialist Council, will deal with any issues unresolved by officials and take the formal decisions.

Box 19: The Cooperation Procedure - Example of the Influence of the European Parliament

The recent issue of pollution from car exhausts showed just how Parliament can use this procedure effectively. Parliament has for some time been anxious to see high standards of environmental protection and at the first reading of the proposal on small cars' exhausts, voted for US-level controls, while a majority in Council agreed on weaker standards. But at the second reading (April 1989), by threatening to reject the Council's agreement, Parliament obtained the Commission's support and maintained its original position. This meant the Council could only reverse Parliament's opinion through unanimous agreement and as Denmark and the Netherlands also favour the higher standards the Council was under pressure to agree. The alternative of letting the proposal lapse would have left a serious gap in EC legislation and would have opened the way for some governments favouring the stricter standards to introduce national controls.

June 1990

There are several ways in which companies can monitor the progress of legislation likely to affect them and also obtain clear information on which to base their own strategies and make any necessary production or marketing changes. In the UK, the Department of Trade and Industry in the framework of its campaign 'Europe Open For Business' which was launched in 1988, publishes working documents, such as the 'Action Checklist For Business' and '1992 - For You, An Action Guide For Smaller Firms' as well as a comprehensive pack of single market fact sheets regularly updated which can help British business prepare for the Single Market.

In the same way, the CBI Briefing Pack - ('Europe sans Frontieres') covers, in twenty regularly updated briefs, the major Internal Market issues affecting industry. The pack provides reliable information and so enables companies to keep up to date with the latest changes and developments in Brussels, especially at the 'pipeline' stage when there is still time to influence proposed legislation. In many cases, it takes years before proposed legislation finally becomes law. Therefore there is time to make industry's views heard, provided there are good monitoring and lobbying systems in place. However, legislation can sometimes go through quite quickly. An example was the Commission proposal for a Directive for a General System for the Mutual Recognition of Higher Education which applies to all professions not already covered by specific Community legislation. This Directive was drafted in July 1985, received outline approval from the Council of Ministers in June 1988 and final adoption on 21 December 1988.

The Official Journal

When the Commission proposes legislation to the Council of

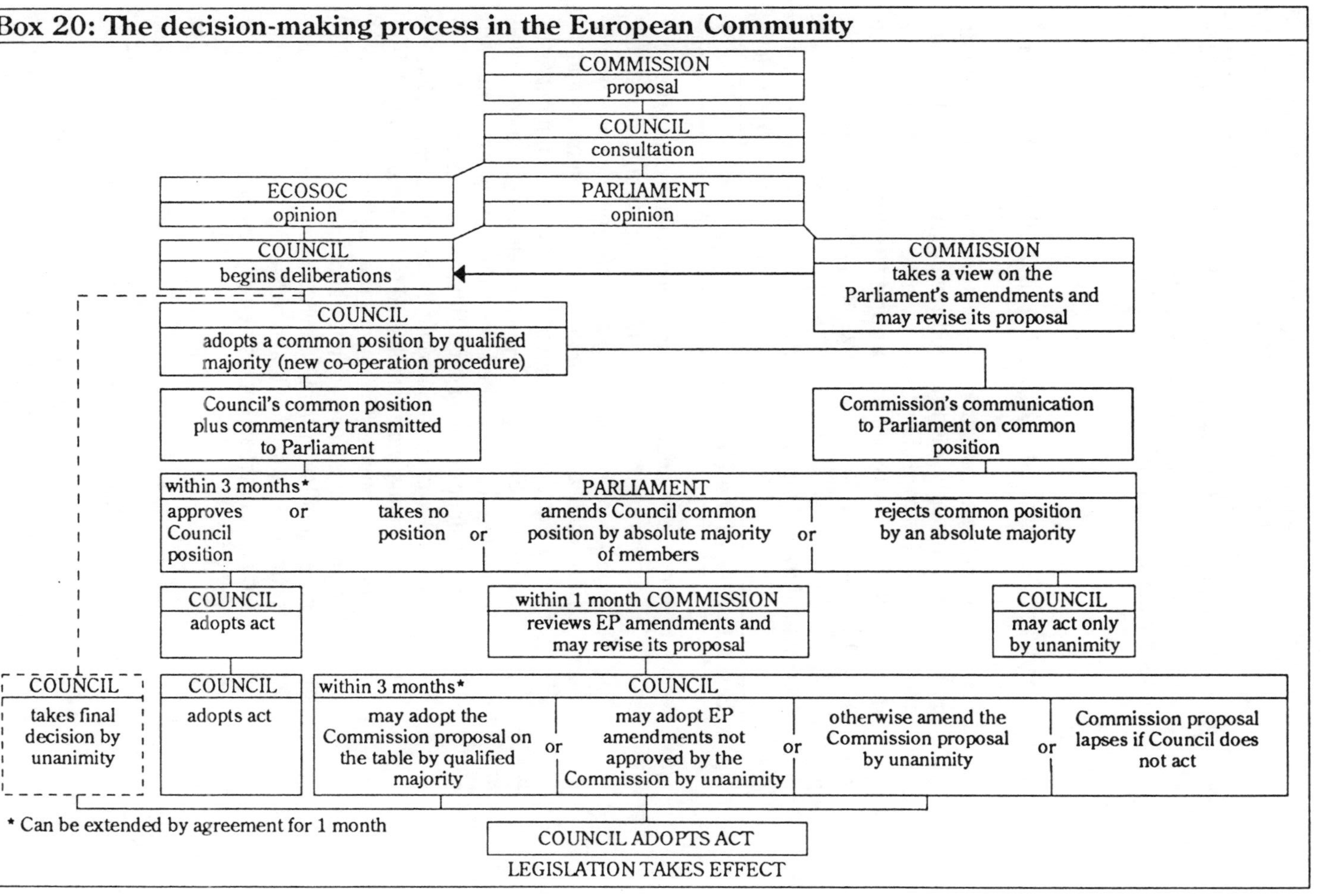
Box 20: The decision-making process in the European Community
COMMISSION
proposal
COUNCIL
consultation
ECOSOC
opinion
PARLIAMENT
opinion
COUNCIL
begins deliberations
COMMISSION
takes a view on the Parliament's amendments and may revise its proposal
COUNCIL
adopts a common position by qualified majority (new co-operation procedure)
Council's common position plus commentary transmitted to Parliament
Commission's communication to Parliament on common position
within 3 months*
PARLIAMENT
approves Council position
or
takes no position
or
amends Council common position by absolute majority of members
or
rejects common position by an absolute majority
COUNCIL
adopts act
within 1 month COMMISSION
reviews EP amendments and may revise its proposal
COUNCIL
may act only by unanimity
COUNCIL
takes final decision by unanimity
COUNCIL
adopts act
within 3 months*
COUNCIL
may adopt the Commission proposal on the table by qualified majority
or
may adopt EP amendments not approved by the Commission by unanimity
or
otherwise amend the Commission proposal by unanimity
or
Commission proposal lapses if Council does not act
* Can be extended by agreement for 1 month
COUNCIL ADOPTS ACT
LEGISLATION TAKES EFFECT

Ministers, it is printed in the 'C' series of the Official Journal of the European Communities. Once the proposals are accepted by the Council of Ministers, the laws or instruments, as they are called, are published in the 'L' series of the Official Journal. This constitutes effective legal notification to the Member States or other parties concerned.

Scrutiny of Community Legislation by National Parliaments

Scrutiny by national parliaments varies from country to country and ranges from fairly sophisticated review systems in Denmark and the UK to less formal methods in some other Member States. In fact the last word on Community legislation, short of abrogation of the Treaties by a national parliament, lies with the Council of Ministers at whose meetings each Member State is represented by a Minister.

Box 21: Role of the UK Parliament

Proposed Community legislation is subject to prior scrutiny by the UK Parliament. Copies of proposals for legislation are sent to the Select Committee on European Legislation in the House of Commons and the Select Committee on the European Communities in the House of Lords. The proposals may then be considered and debated in Committee, or occasionally on the floor of one or both Houses. In January 1991 two new European Standing Committees of the House of Commons were established to work alongside the Select Committee to improve the quality and breadth of scrutiny. The Government will be concerned to take account of Parliament's views, so you may wish to send your views to your MP, and to the Committees at the Houses of Parliament, as well as pursuing them in Brussels.

Source: DTI

The procedure has sometimes been criticized by members of national governments who feel that national legislatures should have the final say. But if all legislation enacted by the Council of Ministers had subsequently to receive the agreement of the twelve parliaments, little would ever be achieved at the European level. The Community, like politics, is the European art of the possible. Progress can only be made pragmatically, by working gradually towards common goals and policies, moving forward where progress seems possible and holding back when it is not. It is generally only possible when the twelve countries and interest groups within them are broadly in favour of the proposed legislation. Very little can be bulldozed through a reluctant Community by a minority of Member States. Although the Parliamentary scrutiny system may not be perfect, the legislation which has emanated from Brussels has been broadly acceptable to the individual countries and has furthered progress towards a genuine Common Market, which remains the common aim of the Twelve Member States. Relations between National Parliaments and the European Parliament and their respective roles in scrutinising EC proposed legislation is one of the key issues of the Inter-Governmental Conference on Political Union which met for the first time in December 1990.

In working out the complex relationship between national and Community legislation there is an increasing number of references to 'subsidiarity'. This is understood to mean that legislation is only enacted at Community level when national (or even local) level proposals would not suffice. It is sometimes further extended by some Member States, particularly when discussing the social action programme, to mean that actions should be taken at the lowest possible level (factory or work place) as close as possible to those likely to be affected by the proposed actions. Keeping legislative activity, wherever possible, close to the grass roots is a concept with considerable popular appeal.

4 The European Parliament

Businessmen interested in European strategy development are taking more interest in the European Parliament (EP) than ever before. This is hardly surprising as its role and competence continues to develop. Lobbying Members of the European Parliament (MEPs) is becoming a normal part of the European parliamentary process for individuals, companies and pressure groups.

Although the Treaty of Rome provided for direct elections, it was not until over a quarter of a century later, that the political will existed to carry out its provisions. The European Parliament, prior to these direct elections, had government-nominated members selected from national parliaments. In 1979, for the first time, voters in the Community were able to elect representatives directly, by universal suffrage, to an organization whose legal powers and influence transcend national frontiers. With direct elections, it became larger and more representative. Its powers are developing by custom and precedent as well as by formal legislation.

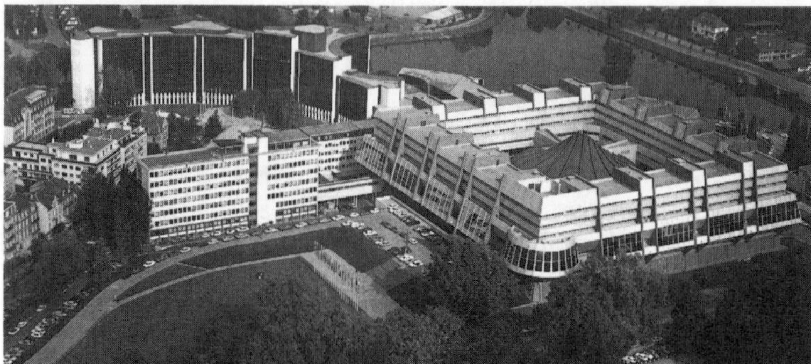

Figure 3: Strasbourg - The European Parliament
The Palais de l'Europe is the square building, standing by the River. The building on the right is where MEPs have their offices. The building immediately in front of the Palais is the European Court of Human Rights. Strasbourg's famous cathedral is visible in the background.
Photo: European Parliament

The Secretariat is based in Luxembourg and Committee meetings are held in Brussels. The future permanent seat is not yet (1991) settled. The decision is delicate and political. There is no doubt the Parliament would like to move to a permanent home. For too long it has shuttled between Strasbourg, Luxembourg and Brussels. This situation costs some £40m per year plus incalculable sums lost through inefficiency and some estimated extra 12% of EP staff, needed because the institution is based in three cities. The Parliament will soon be able to hold 'exceptional' plenary debates in Brussels where a building capable of holding 600 people in one debating chamber is being built.

Figure 4: The Hemicycle of the European Parliament
Photo: European Parliament

How Parliament is Organized

There are 81 members of the European Parliament from each of the four largest countries of the Community out of a total of 518. There are now a further 18 'observers' from what was the GDR. By the next election in 1994 a decision will need to be taken on the new representation for Germany. Although MEPs come principally from the traditional political parties, most of them do not sit in both national and European parliaments. The dual mandate is not legally excluded but political parties are discouraging or forbidding a practice which proved onerous for members of the previously nominated European Parliament.

Box 22: The European Parliament – Distribution of Seats

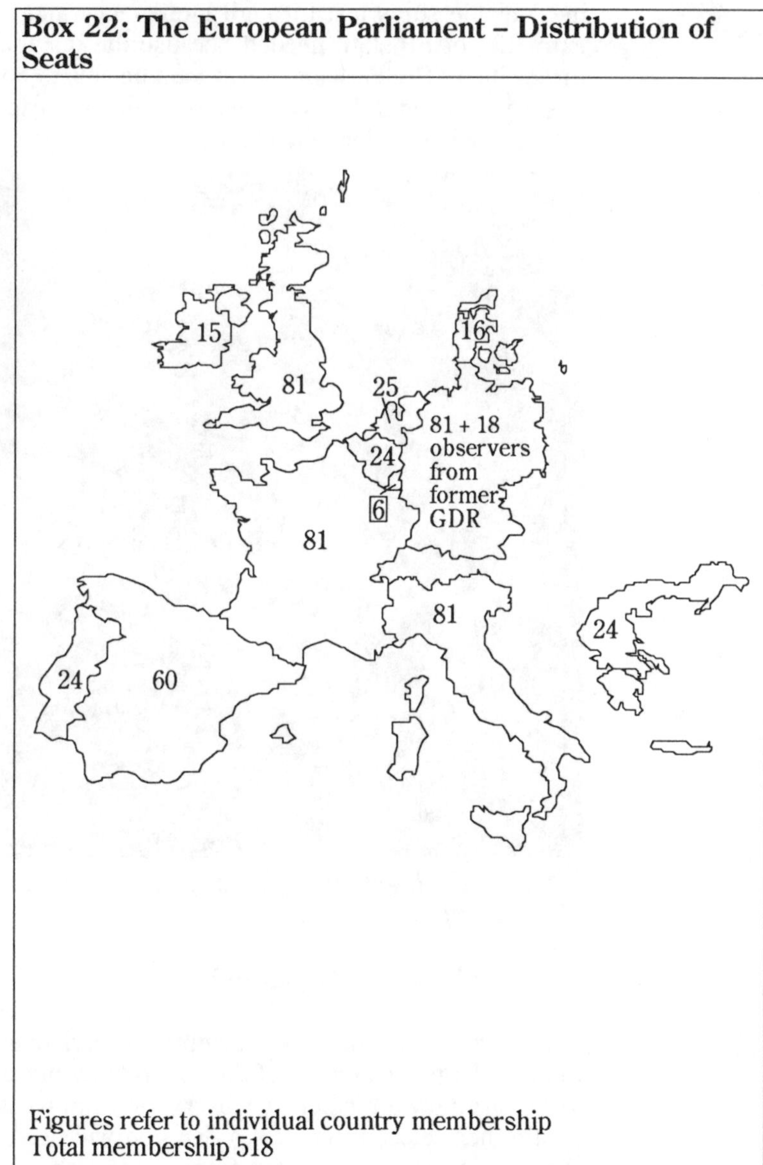

Figures refer to individual country membership
Total membership 518

Members do not sit or vote as national delegations but as European party groups. The manifestos of the European parties are difficult to draw up because of the need to accommodate national differences of policy and the relative inexperience of MEPs in operating a new trans-national parliamentary system.

The President of the EP presides over plenary sessions although the 14 Vice-Presidents can deputize for him. Elected by the Members, he represents the EP both within and outside the Community.

The Bureau which consists of the President, the Vice-Presidents and five quaestors is responsible for organizing parliamentary activity. The enlarged Bureau composed of the members of the Bureau plus the chairman of the political groups carries considerable political influence in deciding the European Parliament's stance on major policy issues.

Box 23: Political Groups in the European Parliament Following the Third Direct Elections in June 1989

	E	Dk	G	Gr	S	F	Irl	I	L	N	P	UK	12
Soc	8	4	31	9	27	22	1	14	2	8	8	46	180
EPP	7	2	32	10	16	6	4	27	3	10	3	1	121
LDR	4	3	4	-	6	13	2	3	1	4	9	-	49
ED	-	2	-	-	-	-	-	-	-	-	-	32	34
Greens	3	-	8	-	1	8	-	7	-	2	1	-	30
EUL	-	1	-	1	4	-	-	22	-	-	-	-	28
EDA	-	-	-	1	-	13	6	-	-	-	-	-	20
ER	1	-	6	-	-	10	-	-	-	-	-	-	17
LU	-	-	-	3	-	7	1	-	-	-	3	-	14
REW	1	4	-	-	2	1	1	3	-	-	-	1	13
Ind	-	-	-	-	4	1	-	5	-	1	-	1	12
Totals	24	16	81	24	60	81	15	81	6	25	24	81	518

The President of the European Parliament is Enrique Baron Crespo (May 1991)

Political Group Leaders

Soc Socialist Group	Jean-Pierre Cot
EPP European People's Party	Egon Klepsch
LDR Liberal, Democratic and Reformist Group	Valéry Giscard d'Estaing
ED European Democratic Group	Sir Christopher Prout
Greens Group of the Greens in the European Parliament co-chairmen	Maria Amélia Mota Santos and Alexander Langer
EUL European United Left	Luigi Colajanni
EDA European Democratic Alliance	Christian de la Malène
ER Technical Group of the European Right	Jean-Marie Le Pen
LU Left Unity	René-Emile Piquet
REW Rainbow Group	Jaak Vandemeulebroucke

Source: 'One Parliament for Twelve: The European Parliament' 11th Edition December 1989 published by The European Parliament

Its Powers

The powers of the European Parliament are developing steadily and depend very much on the political will of the Community and its citizens as well as on its formal rights accorded by the Treaty of Rome.

The Single European Act which came into force in July 1987 considerably extended the European Parliament's powers and influence within the Community, particularly as regards applications for accession to or association with the Community and in respect of legislation concerning the establishment of the Single Market by 1992.

Budgetary Powers

The EP, with the Council of Ministers, is the budgetary authority of the Community. It has the right to reject the budget as a whole, a power it exercised in 1979 and 1984 when it disagreed with the Council of Ministers' spending priorities.

Supervisory Powers

The EP has the power to dismiss the College of all 17 Commissioners by a two-thirds majority, provided over half its members vote. However, it cannot dismiss any one individual Commissioner. It scrutinizes Commission activities through written and oral questions and through its committees.

Box 24: The Cooperation Procedure

The Single European Act, through the institution of the Cooperation Procedure, which applies to a number of Community fields of competence, gives the Parliament an increasingly important part in the decision-making process. The system of two readings led to the fact that from July 1987 to Dec 1988, the Commission adopted, in whole or in part, 60% of Parliament's amendments at first reading, and the Council in its common position, 44%. At the second reading, the corresponding figures were 58% and 23% (see Boxes 18 and 19).

Legislative Powers

As a result of judgements by the Court of Justice, the Parliament's right to be consulted in the framing of Community legislation has been extended. The Council must await Parliament's opinion on all legislative items before being able to adopt laws.

How it Functions

The hemicycle of the Parliament has seats on the floor of the Chamber set aside not only for the Commissioners who regularly attend sessions, but also for ministers and officials from the Council of Ministers. Commissioners answer oral and written questions about the work of the Commission and even take part in the discussions of the eighteen committees (with between 25 and 56 members) through which the burden of the work of the European Parliament is discharged. The eighteen committees (Box 26) scrutinize legislation proposed by the Commission to the

Box 25: A Day in the Life of an MEP

Early Belgian light sidles into the attic room. Last night's dinner was too good. More seriously, it was too late. Why do the Portuguese insist on only coming to the point after midnight? The staircase is steep. The coffee is overly black. The fax machine has not been asleep. The streets in Quartier Leopold are badly paved and tripping up their usual quota of sleepy Euro-folk. The corridors of the International Press Centre are being cleaned - except in the BBC suite. Stale cigarette stubs, yesterday's mugs. It is lonely waiting for the link from the Today Programme to come on line. A swift debate. Two minutes forty seconds of stylized controversy over BSE. A tiny fragment of the 'mad cow industry'. 'Tom Spencer, Member of the European Parliament's Agricultural Committee, joins us from Brussels'..... Back over the paving chaos. Through the building site that lies at the heart of Europe. Rugger skills needed as usual for the over popular lift to the Committee floors of the Belliard Building of the European Parliament. The Agriculture Committee is already in session by 9.03. Interpreters smile wearily from their glass boxes. The coffee arrives courtesy of the fattest man in Belgium. The Spanish Chairman strives to establish agreement on the agenda. Three Irish members speak at length. The Chairman shows signs of needing another cigarette. I speak to my Report on a detail of Sugar policy. A

Commission official slides into his seat just in time to deliver a misleading response to my main point. My Research Assistant hands me a note with further information. Consternation on the Commission bench. A Parliamentary messenger brings news of an urgent telephone call from London. It is 11.00 in Brussels and in London they are just beginning to sketch out the shape of today's Commons script. The PM faces an awkward and technical question. The Deputy Chief Whip of the European Democratic Group (for it is I!) is requested by the Government Whips' Office in London to furnish a suitably barbed riposte sharpish. Forty minutes of voting. The ten political groups find a majority on the future of organic farming and adjourn at 13.00. We will have to meet again during the Plenary Session in Strasbourg next week to finish the agenda.

Back to my office. 144 sq. feet of post-modernism with Belgian Empire overtones. The traffic and a demonstration of Trade Unionists stutter by. In the distance the lift towers of the new Parliamentary Building hold out promise of a Single Centre sanity sometime. The phone rings. My Euro-Agent with news of an extra press interview to be fitted in before tonight's meeting in Guildford. Miraculously the answers to three constituents' questions have been tracked down by the combined efforts of my secretary in Surrey, my wife in London and my Research Assistant, who claims to have infiltrated the elite geography of the 13th floor of the Commission Building. Lunch with a public affairs man who understands that lobbying is about information, not over-eating. He has a brilliant paper on the reform of Europe's corrupt Sugar Regime. I point out a procedural short-cut. Two happy people. The presence of public affairs men is the only truly unbiased measure of Parliament's real significance. There are three times as many such people as there were in 1979. In a different part of the warren, I gather for a meeting with my Leader. Sir Christopher Prout leans forward, puts his long fingers together and uses a law lecturer's skill to show the a-legal nature of the Community's behaviour towards East Germany. A line is agreed. Two telephone calls are placed. It is time for the luggage-ridden dash to Zaventem airport. Sabena to Heathrow. The passport queue of Community Nationals is the usual redundant ritual, but does provide an opportunity to talk to a member of the British Representation in Brussels and a member of the Economic and Social Committee. A deal is struck.

The Volvo waits patiently. The M25 is gracious enough to work. The gym has a reassuring permanence about it. I violently attack a stack of iron. Back to the car. The short cut across the heathland of Surrey works. Somewhere in that scrub lurks an endangered flower on whose behalf I have just written to the Council of Ministers. The village hall is crowded. Surprisingly, I am on time. The questions are precise, well-informed and clearly enunciated. I answer five directly and duck one. More work for the Research Assistant. What is my view on the proposed alterations to the DELTA programme? The journalist settles for twenty minutes at a waterside pub. The car edges through more lanes as the World Tonight outlines a deteriorating situation in Kashmir. Will the European Parliament's South Asian delegation ever make it to Islamabad and New Delhi? The children are sound asleep. The library table has six serious queries from businesses impacted by 1992, fourteen identical letters on overseas aid, several interesting invitations and a letter from a lady who knows that it is the song of dolphins that holds the ozone layer together. Today in Parliament features the PM replying on a point of fact concerning the European Parliament. Thank God for telephones.

Another day; some more small steps for Europe. Lights out. Lights back on again. Post-it note on bedside table - 'Write day in life of MEP'.

Darkness at last.

Tom Spencer, Member of the European Parliament, August 1990

Parliament and the Council. While the Parliamentary plenary sessions are open to the public, the Committee sessions are closed to allow for a free exchange of views between the members who represent different political parties.

When a proposal goes to a committee, a 'rapporteur' or spokesman is appointed to prepare draft amendments and ultimately to draw up a final report which is debated, amended and finally adopted at a plenary session as the Parliament's opinion to be passed back to the Council via the Commission. The debate on the formal report to Parliament may lead to further amendments and the Commissioner responsible for the subject is usually asked to reply to the debate. The Council of Ministers is often represented and its representative also may speak. The procedure therefore provides considerable opportunity for formal and informal contacts between the members of the European Parliament, the Commission and the Council. The informal contacts can be very influential and play a significant part in developing the legislation which finally emerges from the Council of Ministers. The relationship of the European Parliament to the other institutions can be seen in Box 20 in Chapter 3 and Box 2 in Chapter 1.

The effect of this process is that any legislation proposed by the Commission is scrutinized by a Parliamentary committee. They play a key role in the Parliament and the workings of those dealing with subjects of importance to your company need to be followed closely. You should get to know key members such as the Chairman and the 'Rapporteur' - the person who will present a Committee report to the Plenary session of the Parliament.

Committees sometimes produce own-initiative reports for the Parliament. They are debated in the same way as Parliament debates draft legislation, but they have no legal force. They enable the EP to be the prime mover in potential legislation and provide a stimulus to the Commission as well as to the Council. They call on the Commission to take action. An increasing number of these own-initiative reports eventually lead to draft legislation or other actions.

Box 26: The European Parliament: The 18 Committees including number of members & Chairmen/women

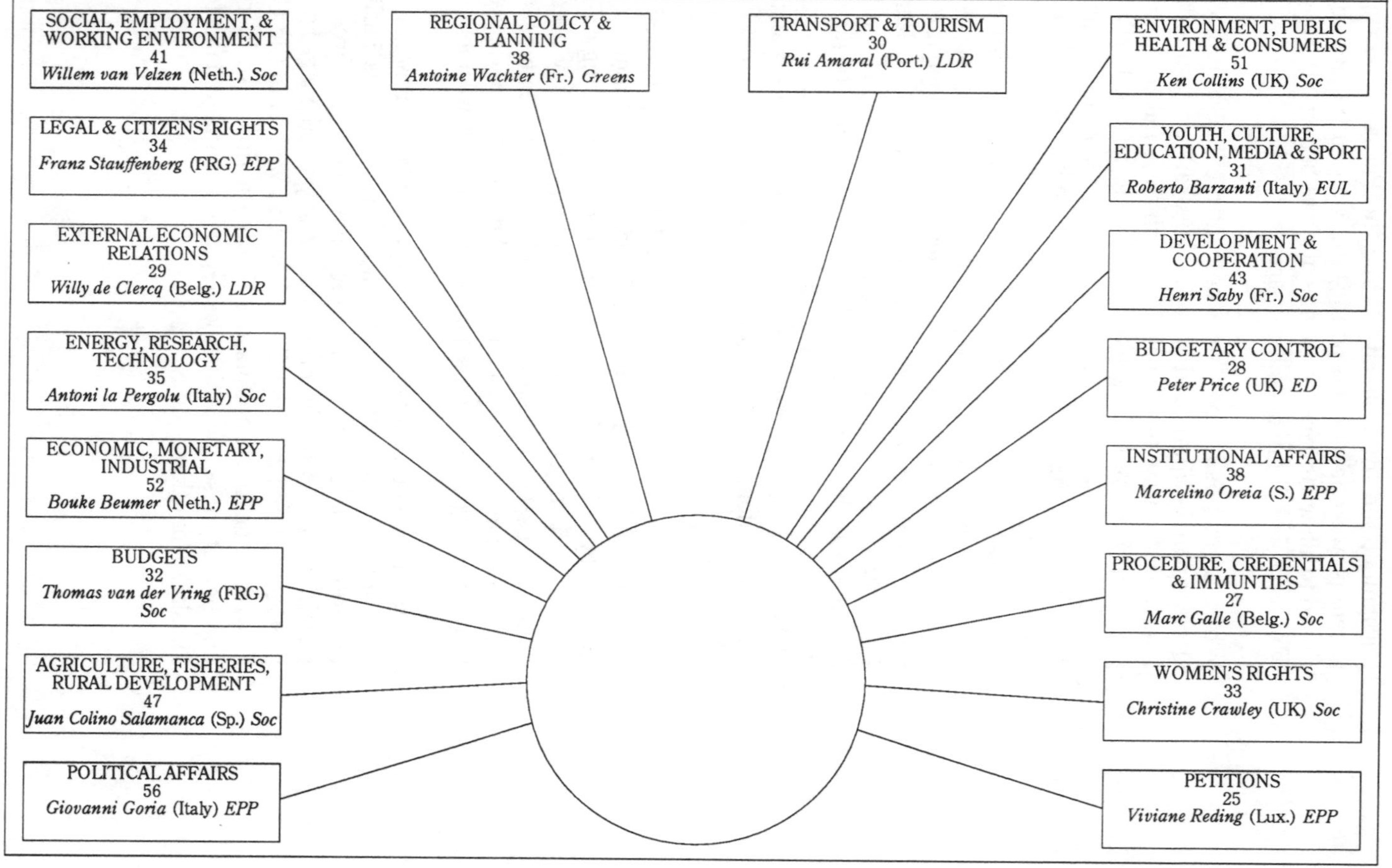

SOCIAL, EMPLOYMENT, & WORKING ENVIRONMENT
41
Willem van Velzen (Neth.) *Soc*

LEGAL & CITIZENS' RIGHTS
34
Franz Stauffenberg (FRG) *EPP*

EXTERNAL ECONOMIC RELATIONS
29
Willy de Clercq (Belg.) *LDR*

ENERGY, RESEARCH, TECHNOLOGY
35
Antoni la Pergolu (Italy) *Soc*

ECONOMIC, MONETARY, INDUSTRIAL
52
Bouke Beumer (Neth.) *EPP*

BUDGETS
32
Thomas van der Vring (FRG) *Soc*

AGRICULTURE, FISHERIES, RURAL DEVELOPMENT
47
Juan Colino Salamanca (Sp.) *Soc*

POLITICAL AFFAIRS
56
Giovanni Goria (Italy) *EPP*

REGIONAL POLICY & PLANNING
38
Antoine Wachter (Fr.) *Greens*

TRANSPORT & TOURISM
30
Rui Amaral (Port.) *LDR*

ENVIRONMENT, PUBLIC HEALTH & CONSUMERS
51
Ken Collins (UK) *Soc*

YOUTH, CULTURE, EDUCATION, MEDIA & SPORT
31
Roberto Barzanti (Italy) *EUL*

DEVELOPMENT & COOPERATION
43
Henri Saby (Fr.) *Soc*

BUDGETARY CONTROL
28
Peter Price (UK) *ED*

INSTITUTIONAL AFFAIRS
38
Marcelino Oreia (S.) *EPP*

PROCEDURE, CREDENTIALS & IMMUNTIES
27
Marc Galle (Belg.) *Soc*

WOMEN'S RIGHTS
33
Christine Crawley (UK) *Soc*

PETITIONS
25
Viviane Reding (Lux.) *EPP*

Parliament and the Commission in Formal and Informal Contacts

Members of Parliament working on Parliamentary committees spend a good deal of time with Commission officials. Most of the committee meetings take place in Brussels. The committees are therefore well informed about 'pipeline' activities of the Commission, and often see informal preliminary drafts and hear about proposed new legislation and policies at a very early stage. Access to 'pipeline' information is important for the further development of the decision-making process between the two institutions and it is of interest to anyone wishing to influence the way in which the EC operates. It may be too late if action is not taken until legislation is debated by the Council of Ministers or even until it is proposed formally by the Commission. If representations are to be effective they need to be made at the earliest possible stage.

The Commission, of course, consults regularly with all interested parties before proposing legislation. But although only the Commission can propose legislation, other institutions can suggest to the Commission that such legislation is formally proposed; for instance, the Parliament, through its 'own-initiative' reports calling on the Commission to take action (see above). The informal links between the Commission and the Parliament are perhaps as important as those legally established by the Treaty of Rome and the SEA. Both the Commission and the Council of Ministers have encouraged the growth of the indirect influence of the European Parliament. This is another example of how, given the political will of the twelve countries, significant progress can be made in developing the role of Parliament whatever the legal constraints of the founding Treaty.

When President Delors took office in 1985, one of his first tasks after taking the oath of allegiance before the European Court of Justice (Box 4) was to present to the European Parliament the Commission's plans. His initial speech and the subsequent detailed report which he presented were debated in Parliament. Had Parliament so wished it could have censured the speech and hence indirectly the President and his fellow Commissioners.

In fact Parliament has often threatened, but never actually used its power to dismiss the Commission. The reason for this is that members of the Community institutions see that their long-term objective is to make an imperfect mechanism work better. This aim can best be achieved by a gradual process, by avoiding confrontation rather than by promoting it. 'Europe will be made by little steps' is the philosophy behind this pragmatic, rather than dramatic, approach to organizational development.

Current Problems

The formal and informal powers of the Parliament make knowledge of its operations and contacts with its members valuable to companies wishing to influence and monitor the progress of European integration and its effect on their activities. Individuals and companies wishing to increase their knowledge and further their interests in the European Parliament can do this directly through their local member of the EP (Box 28). Other

Box 27: The European Parliament

1 Has 518 directly elected members.

2 Has 18 important committees which scrutinize Commission proposals and write reports.

3 Debates proposed European legislation and proposes amendments.

4 Can reject the whole budget.

5 Has the ultimate sanction of dismissing the Commission by a two-thirds majority.

6 Through the Cooperation Procedure, established by the SEA, it plays an important role in the decision-making process.

7 Has a joint decision-making power with regard to relations between third countries and the Commission and association agreements.

8 Given the political will, it could one day become the most important Community institution.

possibilities are through the secretariat of a political group, through the chairman of an appropriate committee or by direct petitioning of the Parliament. Any individual or group can submit a petition to Parliament - even those from outside the Community if the matter is one over which the Community has jurisdiction.

A member of the European Parliament has to spend time in his very large constituency, at Parliamentary sessions in Strasbourg, sitting on committees of the Parliament and making contacts with the Commission in Brussels and at the same time keeping in touch with his national Parliament and Party in the home country. The need also to travel throughout the Community, and have a private life, makes the job very demanding. But MEPs are elected representatives and are ready to help you if you ask. Box 28 suggests how to improve your contacts with them.

Box 28: The Best Approach to Lobbying MEPs

1 Find out which MEP you need to meet from the European Parliament information office, your trade federation or your local MEP's representative in your constituency (called a Euro-agent). Refer to Section V for telephone numbers.

2 Write and/or telephone for an appointment stating your problem.

3 Remember you can see UK MEPs in their constituencies, in London, in Brussels or in Strasbourg.

4 Invite them to visit you. They need to understand your problems to represent you better.

5 Invite them to speak to your managers or workforce. They will explain what they do and how they can help.

6 Bear in mind that many MEPs have considerable experience of industry and commerce and are as dedicated as you are to making a success of European business. They will welcome your interest and be able actively to help you.

To enable politicians from all countries of the European Community to conduct their European Parliament tasks effectively, the working languages introduced from the beginning were those of the founding states. Today, the EP has nine working languages including the official languages of all the Member States of the Community (except Luxembourgish and Gaelic). Thirty-three per cent of European Parliament staff are employed in jobs connected with the large number of languages.

Language is the greatest non-tariff barrier in the Community. There would be considerable opposition if individuals were prevented from speaking and writing in their own languages. Much of the detailed legislation needs to be monitored and applied at quite junior levels within the administration of individual countries. It is therefore not possible to ask administrators, companies or traders to apply laws written in a foreign language. Many of the Community working drafts are available only in English or French. Some committees agree informally only to use French and/or English. European managers will have to speak at least English and French to communicate effectively. As far as the written word goes, there is some hope through computer translation. The EUROTRA project is a research field in which the Community is leading the world. The language question will need to be resolved if the Community is enlarged as there would be an impossible task of interpretation if there were, for example, fifteen official languages.

Parliament will have more influence in the future, both as a result of growing public and media interest in the institution and of its new powers conferred by the Single European Act in the Community decision-making process. Those who aim to influence decisions will have to pay more attention to the EP and not just concentrate their efforts on the Commission and officials in Member States.

In his opening address to the EP in 1989, the President, Enrique Baron Crespo, stressed that its priority should be to develop its role in EC affairs through the SEA without trying to exceed its competence. But it was equally important to increase the EP's supervisory role over the Community's institutions. At the same time, he said, national parliaments should be more involved in Community business. For business, the European Parliament has come of age and this is apparent in the increasing number of business and trade associations which spend time in Strasbourg and Brussels and which work formally and informally with MEPs.

5. Other Community Institutions and Organs: the Court of Justice, the Court of Auditors, the Economic and Social Committee, the European Council

So far we have considered the Commission, the Council of Ministers, and the European Parliament and seen how it is possible for companies to have both direct and indirect contact with officials, elected representatives or ministers who contribute to the functioning of these institutions. We will look more specifically at ways of making these contacts in Chapter 10. This chapter looks at the Court of Justice, the Court of Auditors, the Economic and Social Committee and the European Council. Each plays an important part in the machinery of the European Community but companies will have fewer direct dealings with them.

The Court of Justice

The principal function of the Court of Justice is to ensure that European law is observed and interpreted uniformly throughout the Community. It is the ultimate interpreter of the Paris and Rome Treaties on which the Community is based and the final arbiter of disputes concerning secondary legislation whenever there is a query or disagreement about the meaning of a particular regulation, directive or decision.

(1) **Proceedings against States**. If a Member State does not fulfil its legal obligations, the Court has jurisdiction over the

proceedings brought against that State by another Member State, or more usually by the Commission. The Court, however, does not have powers to impose penalties on a Member State. Like an international court, it can establish whether there is a breach of an obligation and if there is, request the State concerned to remedy it. As Community law is binding on Member States,

Figure 5 The European Court of Justice. The Court sits at Luxembourg.

they almost always comply with its requests although the process can be a very lengthy one when national considerations are politically or economically delicate. The Court of Justice, which sits in Luxembourg, should not be confused with the International Court of Justice at the Hague. The latter is a Court of International Law to which cases are voluntarily referred by countries that wish to resolve their legal differences. The former is the Court specifically set up by the Treaty of Rome to interpret the Community Treaties and the secondary legislation derived from them. Neither should be confused with the Council of Europe's Court of Human Rights at Strasbourg.

(2) **Review of the legality of Community acts**. The Council of Ministers or the Commission can go to the Court if either of these institutions, or a Member State, consider that legislation has been passed which is contrary to the letter or the spirit of the Treaties. In this way the Court is able to ensure that none of the institutions exceed their legal powers.

(3) **Settling disputes**. The Court is empowered to settle a dispute within the Community, where the dispute is covered by Community law. It rules on disputes between individuals, companies or states in disagreement with rulings of the Community institutions. In most instances these disputes are settled between the individual or organization concerned and the Community institution, but if they cannot be resolved then the Court acts as final arbiter.

In matters of competition policy, for example, fines imposed by the Commission can be contested and the case referred to the Court of Justice. The Court's decision on the Commission's ruling is final.

Box 29: The relationships of the Court of Justice to the other Community institutions

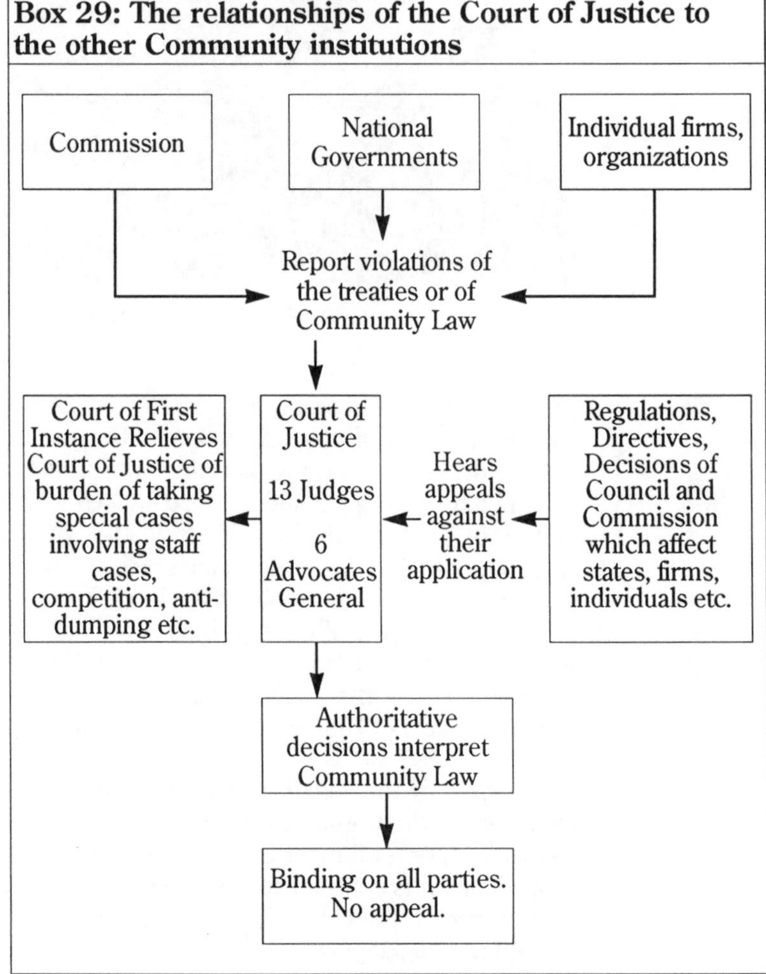

(4) **Preliminary rulings**. The Court will also give, on request from national courts, a legal opinion on points of Community law. It is compulsory to request this opinion when the national court, called upon to decide an issue of Community law, is the court of final appeal on that issue.

(5) **The organization of the Court**. It consists of thirteen judges, appointed for six years by agreement among the governments, and six advocates-general. There is no official requirement for one judge to come from each of the twelve countries, but over time both they and the advocates-general will tend to come from different Member States to give a balance of nationalities.

The Court of First Instance

The workload of the European Court has increased by over 50% during the last decade and the backlog of pending cases has doubled. This led to the establishment of a Court of First Instance in 1988 which deals with at least 25% of cases. Staff issues, competition and anti-dumping cases, coal and steel will initially be transferred, but actions for damages and state aids are other possible future areas which will fall within its competence.

The Court of Auditors

The Court of Auditors of the European Communities, which sits in Luxembourg, became operational in 1977.

It audits the accounts of the Community, examines whether revenue and expenditure have been properly and lawfully received and incurred, checks that financial management has been sound and reports back to the Community institutions.

The EP, which strongly supported the establishment of a Court of Auditors, makes full use of the opportunities offered by the Court's investigatory powers, opinions and annual report to reinforce its own control over Community expenditure and give full weight to its annual decision granting a discharge in respect of implementation of the Community budget.

The Economic and Social Committee

Before a Commission proposal can be adopted by the Council, the opinion of the European Parliament and in most cases of the Economic and Social Committee (ESC) must be obtained. This is a consultative body composed of 189 members, 24 from the UK, divided into three groups: Group I (employers), Group II (trade unions) and Group III (other interests such as consumers and farmers). Members have four-year terms. As a two way communications link, the ESC serves a helpful role which is capable of further development. Officials in Brussels see it as a useful gauge of public opinion and an aid in gaining public acceptance of Community policies. Companies may see it as a means of communication with the Community institutions and a possible way of influencing directly and, more importantly, indirectly, the course of Community legislation. Box 31 gives an indication of the activities of one of its members. They are well informed on Community affairs and invariably helpful as they contribute to the more active role of the ESC. Contact addresses are listed in Section V.

Procedure

Decisions are reached by the ESC in open debate in full sessions. Much of its work is carried out by different sections of the Committee, each one dealing with a number of specialized fields rather like the committees of the European Parliament. Plenary sessions, of which there are nine each year, are open to the public. At the sessions a section of the ESC may present a draft report or opinion which is debated and amended. Much of the detailed work is carried out by small study groups which can be a time-consuming task for some members. There is therefore a necessary trade-off between the jobs that members of the ESC have in their home countries and the amount of time they are able to spend on Committee affairs.

The European Council

Twice a year the Heads of State and/or Government of the Twelve, together with their Foreign Ministers and the President

Box 30: ESC: Genesis of Opinions

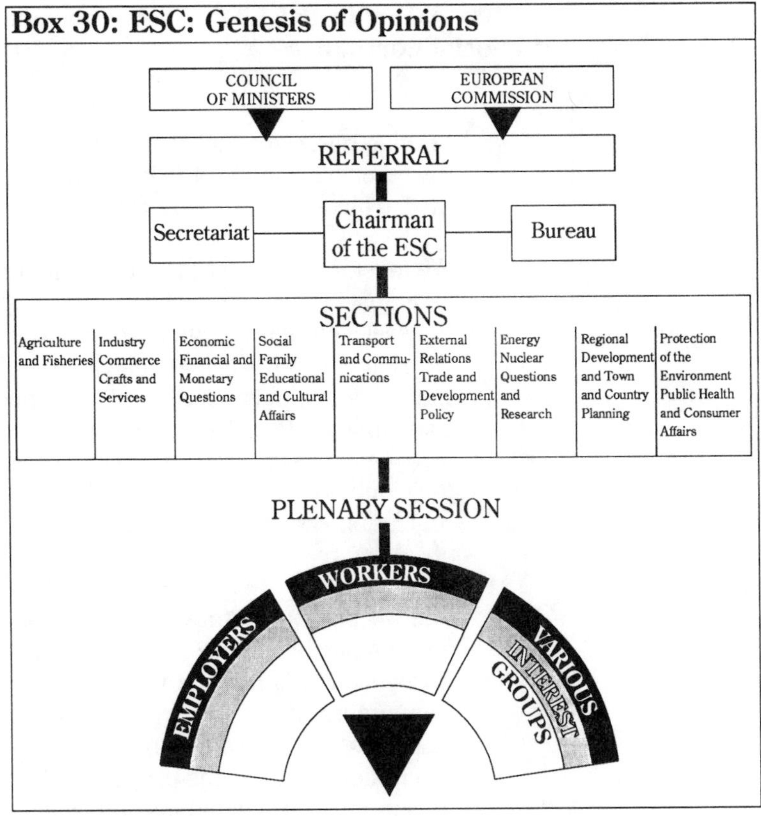

and one of the Vice-Presidents of the Commission, meet at a 'European Council'. This is a key and newsworthy event in the workings of the Community and takes place in the Member State which holds the six-monthly presidency of the Council of Ministers. In recent years there has been a tendency to hold three or four a year because of the backlog of work

Over the last few years the influence of the European Council in the workings of the Community has increased. The personal involvement of the Heads of State and Governments in Community affairs has provided political impetus. The Council lays down guidelines in areas of prime importance (such as direct elections to the EP, the European Monetary System, reform of agricultural policy and the accession of new members).

Box 31: A Day in the Life of a Member of the Economic and Social Committee

Leaving home at 5.30 I can be in my Brussels office by 9.30 even allowing for the hour difference, thanks to the 7 o'clock Sabena flight to Brussels.

We meet in plenary session each month at our headquarters by the Central Station in downtown Brussels, but it is the small study groups where we do our real job brainstorming on Commission proposals. Individual members of the ESC whether employers, trade union officials, consumer organization representatives or trade experts take apart line by line the Commission's draft proposals for directives or regulations prior to their consideration by the Council of Ministers.

The work in these study groups and specialist sections goes on day in and day out in parallel with those in the European Parliament. No laws can become Community laws until Parliament and in most instances, the Economic and Social Committee, have given their views on the proposals. Views are given through the form of publication of an informal 'opinion' drafted by an elected 'rapporteur' - a cross between a secretary and chairman of a select committee.

Today I am appointed rapporteur on HDTV - High Definition Television - the subject involving one of the most important advances in TV technology since the introduction of colour in 1977. At the 10 am meeting there are ten members of ESC present plus three Commission staff, one of whom is the author of the Commission's draft proposal on HDTV. There are a complex series of issues around HDTV to do with mass consumer markets, competition with Japan and Commission and Member State support programmes.

The views of the Economic and Social Committee are useful as they represent a cross section of the various economic and social interest groups. The previous

President of the European Parliament, Lord Plumb, likened the activities of ESC to those of the House of Lords, effective in analysis and scrutiny whatever their legal and formal responsibilities. During the year, practically every senior ESC office holder will have addressed the Committee receiving a 'non-political' grilling by its members.

Today my job is to listen carefully to the DG XIII representative - the Telecommunications Directorate. Mr E Lalor outlines the Commission's proposals with meticulous skill and is then cross-examined by other members until lunch. This is taken in the excellent self-service on the fifth floor of the ESC building and during it I have an opportunity to talk with Rudolph Leiner, a senior official in the ESC responsible to me for drafts and coordination of our opinions and all the other necessary bureaucratic arrangements of keeping to deadlines, arranging dates, translations etc.

I just manage to catch a late flight back to Heathrow which is not always the case. Sometimes I have to stay overnight for several days when there are a number of meetings in succession.

It is a busy, painstaking and complex job but slowly and surely we are winning.

My own company, the CBI and other organizations such as the Union of Independent Companies value the opportunity the Community affords to be on the inside track of the European Community legislative process and to contribute to it.

W G Poeton
Vice-President of the Economic and Social Committee
President of the Union of Independent Companies
President of the Poeton Group of Electro-plating Companies

August 1990

The existence of the European Council has had an effect on the position of the Council of Ministers itself by opening up the possibility of appeal to a higher authority and on the Commission - and in particular its President - which has been given increased political status through its participation in European Councils.

The nature of the meetings (free of any institutional formalities) and the fact that they combine discussions on Community matters with discussion of political cooperation have emphasized the intergovernmental aspects of the European Community. The significance attached to the position of the Presidency of the European Council has strengthened public interest in the Council discussions. At the end of each European Council a communiqué is issued giving the broad outlines of what has been agreed (see Box 32 for an example).

The Committee System

Legislative power, in general, rests with the Council of Ministers. However, the Council has extended the Commission's management and administration function in the EC context by giving it additional responsibility for the implementation of secondary legislation. Such powers are generally exercised by the Commission with the assistance and advice of committees composed of representatives of the Member States and all chaired by a non-voting representative of the Commission.

The Single European Act also envisaged an overhaul of the committee system. This has been achieved by:

Advisory committees: their use is recommended by the Single European Act for measures relating to the completion of the Internal Market. However, the Commission is not bound by the committees' opinions.

Management committees: established since 1962 particularly in the sphere of agriculture to ensure that the implementing legislation is in line with Council guidelines. They are widely used and work extremely well.

The Commission is not bound by a committee's opinion. However, if the Commission decides to go against an opinion, the

Box 32: Presidency Conclusions, European Council, Paris 18-19 November 1989

Emergency Summit to discuss changes in Eastern Europe

A special EC summit to discuss the rapidly developing situation in Eastern Europe was convened on 18 November 1989 in Paris by the French President François Mitterand. The meeting of all Heads of State and Government was called at the request of Chancellor Helmut Kohl of the FRG by President Mitterand in his capacity as President of the Council of Ministers. The 12 leaders of the European Community and Commission President Jacques Delors wholeheartedly endorsed political reform in Eastern Europe and promised substantial economic aid to those Eastern European countries which embrace democracy. 'Solidarity and Unity' were the two watchwords at the meeting. The Community leaders called on the International Monetary Fund to reach agreement with Poland and Hungary on terms for standby credits and German restructuring by the end of the year.

matter is referred to the Council which may reverse the Commission's decision within one month. If on the other hand the Commission's decision is in line with the committee's opinion, or if no opinion has been forthcoming the decision is final and there is no appeal to the Council.

Regulatory committees: apply the management committee formula to other fields.

Special procedure: this is for commercial policy measures or action under the safeguard clause. It enables the Commission to take directly applicable decisions once it has received the advisory committee's opinion. However, these decisions must be approved by the Council within a period of three months, failing which they become null and void.

Through the committee system cooperation and mutual confidence can be developed between the Commission's departments and the national departments which subsequently enforce the Commission's decisions.

The Role of Business in Community Committees

The role of business in many of the committees of the Community has not been thought through either by the institutions or by business. In the US, for example, business plays a much greater advisory role in issues such as the GATT negotiations. Careful consideration should be given to whether it is useful for senior management to be represented on Brussels committees. To what extent is it for reasons of protocol or ritual? A company must decide at what level it should be represented, if at all. Also it must ask whether involvement in committees does much for the individual and little for the company and whether it helps the industry rather than the company. There is also the question of how much senior executive time should be devoted to industry-wide as opposed to specific company business. There is a growing demand for industry input into the Community decision-making process and representation on the wide variety of advisory committees is one way in which industry can meet this demand.

Whatever the specific company approach to these issues, both employers and employees will need to understand and attempt to influence the Community decision-making process.

Section II: Developing Your Business in the European Community

6. Developing an Active Company Approach to the European Market

Introduction: The Community as a Single Market

For over a decade, the senior management of companies doing business in Europe has been asked to consider the EC as a single market but, for quite proper business reasons, they have consistently refused to do so. It has been more useful to look at markets, operating units and fiscal matters at a national level. Even if goods have been produced for more than one market, there have often been adjustments necessary for different technical requirements and standards. Now that the Single Market is well on its way to being achieved, there will come a time when the EC and possibly the rest of the Western world will benefit by a more regional approach. That time is not far off. Standards are fast becoming harmonized, public procurement is open to tender across the EC and increasingly national contracts will not be reserved for national champions. The Statute for a European Company and the European Economic Interest Grouping will be forerunners of other new ways of creating legal entities across Europe (see Chapter 12).

For a company assessing or reassessing its European strategy, the timing of many of these changes is crucial as they will vary from country to country and from industrial sector to industrial sector. The pace of application and enforcement of Community law will vary, as will the ability of the EC to enforce its application through the administrative and legal channels open to it. It is for this reason, in an uncertain but positively and often fast changing business and economic climate, that the managers involved in the strategic aspects of their companies doing business in Europe need to remain on their toes. They must be ready to assess the changes affecting companies while at the same time keeping their lines of communication within the company constantly open as complex decisions may have to be made - often at short notice - to take advantage of the opportunities on offer.

The completion of the Single Market provides an occasion for companies to develop or review their European strategy. Careful preparation will pay off and increase the chances of success. Commitment to the concept of 1992 should be inspired from the top of the company, and will then filter down through the organization.

But commitment stems from conviction. How do you convince your senior managers that Europe 1992 is not a piece of rhetoric, but a fast growing movement, which is gaining momentum by the month? One way might be to run a seminar or briefing session for senior managers to reveal the extent of their knowledge or lack of it. After this you can decide whether it is worth building a European strategy review or company 1992 audit around the suggestions in the next chapter. If you do hold such a seminar, questions you may wish to put to your management are in Box 33.

You will need for this seminar to assemble some facts and views about the 1992 process to illustrate why Europe 1992 - the free movement of goods, services, people and capital - is fundamental to companies doing business in Europe. Material is readily available and references to it can be found in Section V.

Box 33: Possible Questions to be Addressed at a Senior Management Seminar

1. Will Europe 1992 happen on time and even if it does will it affect our company? What happens if we do nothing?

2. What new competition/threats/opportunities will we have? When?

3. What new ways of doing business need to be considered? Joint ventures, licensing, export/import agencies, raising capital in different EC countries, buying in services from other countries, hiring managers with cultural and language skills, effect of labour relations, taking over or buying an interest in a European company?

Will we grow new skills or buy them in?

4. What are the savings for the company of the completion of the internal market?

5. What are the implementation costs of the new strategy in terms of employee communications, consultancy, in-company management, additional resources for company search activities etc?

6. Is Europe 1992 marginal or fundamental to our business?

After such a seminar or discussion, if your company wants to continue developing its European strategy around 1992, there are a number of options:

1. Obtain material from sources in Section V and distribute it regularly to key managers. Use a consultant to ensure the material is readable and company targeted.

2. Arrange a meeting of functional managers - planning, export marketing, personnel, manufacturing, finance - to discuss further actions or monitoring required.

3. Decide whether you need to lobby in pursuit of your firm's priorities. It may be that local contacts and local or national pressure points will have to be supplemented by lobbying at Community level. How can this be done? Through a specialist consultant, a trade association, or by extending the responsibilities of an existing member of the firm?

4. Appoint a board member, and give him or her the specific task of assessing the White Paper and its implications for company strategy.

5. Based on his or her recommendations, decide whether to carry out a Europe 1992 audit - the subject of the next chapter.

7. Designing and Developing a 1992 Company Audit

A 1992 audit need not be difficult once you have obtained senior management commitment. As you follow these guidelines, based on the experience of some companies which have already launched 1992 activities, your work will gain a momentum of its own. The significance of 1992 must be got across to key managers, and they must take responsibility for implementing the necessary changes.

Box 34: Senior Management Review of 1992 - a General Approach

1. Hold a short seminar (about two hours) for senior manager/board level. (See Box 33 for issues which might be discussed.) Smaller companies may wish to hold discussions with two or three senior functional managers. You may wish to use an outside consultant or speaker to animate the discussion.

2. If Europe 1992 is considered of sufficient importance, appoint a senior manager to be responsible for the general action plan and its integration into existing European strategy or activities.

3. After developing the company action plan and proposals, re-convene the seminar to agree a 1992 approach as part of the company European strategy and/or as part of an employee communications or awareness plan.

4. Consider developing a 1992 audit/new European strategy, as part of the company management process.

Then key managers must be encouraged and be well and regularly briefed. 1992 is a complex issue and it is very easy to turn managers off by involving them in too much irrelevant detail. Sweeping generalities about the future of Europe are equally self defeating. The relevance of specific parts of the White Paper to each management function needs to be underlined. For example, that a company can now hold funds and invest them in different European currencies will be of interest to the finance function. The single Administrative Document, which replaced over 150 different documents for moving goods round Europe from 1 January 1988, should be of interest to the marketing and transport departments as it involves long-term savings and short-term costs. So will the eventual abolition of internal Community documentation altogether.

The creation of common standards will affect production and marketing departments. The likelihood that EC competition policy will have to be modified to facilitate new forms of cross-frontier cooperation between firms will concern general management and legal departments. The opening up of national markets for services will in many cases give service companies the choice of providing or 'exporting' the services from their home base instead of being present in the client's national market through a subsidiary, agent or representative. Some questions senior managers might ask are in Box 35.

Box 35: Possible questions from Senior Management about the Development of an In-company 1992 Audit

How will 1992 affect:

* computing and telecommunications systems?
* the raising of contract and finance insurance?
* siting and responsibilities of head office?
* how and where accounts are centralized?
* the way in which the company monitors and inputs

into standards development?
* research and development location?
* production, transport and storage?
* marketing operations?
* staff recruitment and training?

The first steps towards developing a 1992 company audit are listed in Box 36.

Box 36: First Steps in a 1992 Company Audit

1. Obtain the Commission 1985 White Paper and supporting documents, such as progress reports and sectoral analyses. Also a summary of the CECCHINI report on benefits (see index).

2 Take out from the 282 proposals those which seem relevant to your company. Three major European companies recently identified between 140 and 190 which directly affected them - the number will be much smaller for small and medium-sized enterprises (SMEs). While some will have obvious costs or benefits in bottom line terms, others will be more difficult to price. They might, however, be even more important as signposts to further essential preparatory activity, for example training, recruitment, currency management, and adapting to new manufacturing standards.

3. List company departments, or areas of activity, and apportion the proposals among them.

4. Write a short four or five line description of each proposal and an initial assessment of how it might affect the department.

5. Set up a meeting with the heads of department and other staff to discuss materials to send to them. These are key meetings as you need to convince each manager of the importance and relevance of

1992 to his or her function.

6. Refine the proposals and take up detailed points with trade associations, chambers of commerce, consultants, relevant government departments or offices/Directorates of the Commission.

7. Refer back to company departments. Assess costs, benefits, implications and necessary actions of each proposal. Track how far each proposal has got in the European legislative process and its likely date of implementation.

8. Update senior management on progress so far and agree next steps.
   Options are:
   (i) Abandon activity as having achieved its first objective of sensitizing senior management to 1992 implications.
   (ii) Draw up a company 'bible' or audit to be used as a base document to track 1992 progress. It should explain the following:
   - the decision-making process of the EC
   - the key proposals and implications for specific departments
   - implications for the company as a whole
   - suggestions how the 1992 audit can be integrated into company European strategy development.
   (iii) Set up a system for regular update and review of material.

One of the key follow-up decisions is how to sensitize company personnel to the relevance of 1992. Articles in the house journal might be supplemented by a video or in-company seminars. There is a wide variety of commercial seminars and television programmes which can be used.

Some companies are beginning to write about 1992 in their annual reports. This is useful not only for employees but for a wider section of opinion formers interested in the company's activities.

Senior management should also refer frequently to 1992 in their in-company briefings and when talking on public platforms.

Moreover, in order to perform these activities, those concerned need to be well briefed. They need to know the parts of the 1992 programme which particularly affect their company and its activities and where the opportunities and threats lie so that they can demonstrate how it can profit from the former and head off the latter.

The 1992 review process should be continued during the next few years - it is a long-term exercise and cannot be completed and then forgotten.

This is merely an outline of how 1992 might be got across in your company. You will need to adapt it to particular operating conditions. No two audits will be the same, but the key points, judging from other companies' experience, are:

1. Explain exactly what 1992 is and why it is important in a company, national and European context. Because the subject may be seen as irrelevant, unimportant or tedious, even more care is required to get it across in an imaginative way and to underline that it is serious and significant for company success.

2. Show that 1992 provides opportunities, but also threats to those who do not respond actively. The downside risk also needs to come across. There will be increased competition in your traditional markets from other European countries.

3. Designate a senior person in the company, at or near board level, to be responsible for 1992. He or she can delegate the work to managers in public affairs, export marketing or planning, but the approach should be seen as new and company wide and crossing traditional boundaries. If it is seen to be the preserve of the public affairs or planning department, for example, it will not have the same innovatory impact. 1992 will have a major influence on European businesses and this needs to come across to all your managers and employees.

4. Move quickly once you have agreed the approach. It is essential to keep up the momentum and to maintain initial enthusiasm for the idea. A draft letter to heads of departments is in Box 37.

5. Set up meetings with heads of departments as close together as possible - fortnightly intervals - so the impetus is maintained. Your manager responsible will end up with a bulky document which will act as a company reference point and check list for a 1992 audit.

6. Ensure the board or executive committee endorses the approach after the company audit or 'bible' has been completed. This will show in a tangible way that it fully supports the activity.

As a small or medium size firm you will not be able to spare the management resources to develop a comprehensive approach to 1992. Use of the information given in Section V will be even more important and it may be worth buying in some consultancy to support your effort, working though your trade association or attending one of the many seminars on 1992.

Box 37: Sample Letter to be sent to Heads of Department Explaining Company Approach to 1992

'Europe 1992 and your department'

The European Community is on the way to becoming an integrated single market by the end of 1992. Goods and services, capital and people will then move freely between Member States. As a result new business opportunities will arise for all firms including our own. Ways of doing business in Europe will change significantly as you will see from the attached document. (Attach your notes from this chapter.)

All departments of our company are likely to be affected by at least some of the 282 proposals in the Commission's White Paper. The proposals we believe relevant to your department are attached. Would you please read them carefully, assess their importance to you and, if possible, consider with colleagues the possible costs, benefits and changes in operating procedures which may be necessary as a result of their implementation.

> Mr X, who reports directly to me for this exercise, will arrange an appointment with you during the next two weeks. I would be grateful if, after discussing the issues further with him, you could agree a revised draft. After these drafts have been assembled, they will be reviewed by my group and we shall hold a heads of departments' meeting to discuss the report which will be presented to the Chief Executive in two months time.
>
> Please let me know if you have any queries or require further documentation.

The next two chapters suggest more detailed ways of reviewing company European export and investment strategies in the light of the Single Market. They will provide material and checklists but should be seen principally as a source of ideas. It may be that parts of them can be adapted and built into a company's specific discussion paper. There are no new ideas in them, but they do bring together a fairly comprehensive list of points to consider. They are intended to stimulate your thinking and encourage you to act.

8. Export Strategies and the European Community

It is often the simple questions which do not get answered because they do not get asked.

Introduction

Most companies begin their activities outside their home country by exporting or importing, through, for instance, an import enquiry or a request to provide an agency. This may lead to some one-off export orders. Before long there may be a considerable amount of business involved, much of it developed by accident and with no clear strategy behind it. It is at this stage in a small company that an analysis of export strategies might by undertaken. Exporting can be expensive if it is random, and the scatter gun approach rarely makes money. Larger companies may wish to use the material in this chapter to review their existing export programme.

Entering Strategy

Having decided to develop or review a European strategy, a company needs to determine the best method of entering the Community market. The options are:

(1) An aggressive sales policy from a home-based manufacturing and sales facility. In this case it is necessary to determine the scale of effort and tactics. Should licensing or service agreements be drawn up with other Community firms?

(2) Entry from a home-based manufacturing facility by agreement

with existing Community agents, distributors or retailing networks.

(3) Entry from a home-based manufacturing facility but with acquisition of an existing distribution system or the establishment of a new one in the target country or countries.

(4) Merger with a local manufacturer who has a distribution network or access to such a network. This could be a joint venture with equal partnership or a minority holding.

(5) Acquisition of a majority holding in an existing manufacturing and distribution facility. A joint venture with financial control of the enterprise.

(6) New investment: acquisition of a factory for basic manufacture or a plant for assembling from components. A wholly owned foreign subsidiary.

The first three options are progressively more costly. As the list of options continues, what begins as an export sales activity gradually becomes a full-scale foreign investment. One of the early decisions a company needs to take is the target scale of its operations. Although circumstances will change as an export marketing operation develops, it is useful to decide on the size of the operation the company is prepared to consider and the time scale for the operation. What begins as selling surplus production abroad can end as an operation on a sufficiently large scale to affect significantly the profitability of a small company or a division of a larger company.

A major problem for the company which has not yet made a serious marketing effort in the European Community, is that entering a sophisticated market is complicated, time-consuming and costly. Although the Community is in itself a market, it is probably more useful to consider Western Europe as a whole when looking for business opportunities. Provided that the differences, in terms of actual and potential tariffs and other barriers to trade, are appreciated, it may be more sensible to look, for example, at Finland, Norway, Sweden and Denmark as a single market. This is particularly relevant if the objective is to export rather than invest. Since 1977 tariffs in Europe on industrial goods have been reduced to zero between Community and European Free Trade Association (EFTA) countries. (EFTA relations are described in Chapter 23.) It is therefore of relatively little importance to businesses operating within Western Europe whether their markets are in Sweden or Denmark. But if the market opportunity is about equal between these two countries, it must still be in the company's best interests to market within the Community because of the impact of the Single Market and other future legislative changes. For companies outside the Community the situation is somewhat different as the European Community has a common external tariff (see Chapter 14) while the EFTA countries are free to raise or lower their tariffs individually.

Marketing Questions

The following are some of the marketing questions which a company might ask in order to establish a short list of market areas on which to focus attention:

(1) What is the total European market for the products both in the European Community and in EFTA?

(2) At what rate is the market for the products growing?

(3) What is the product market structure by country, and, if possible, by region?

(4) What are the factors which have influenced market growth and structure?

(5) Are these factors changing, and if so for what reasons?

(6) What is the price structure?

(7) How have prices moved over the past five years and what has influenced these price movements?

(8) Who are the competitors and what is their size?

(9) How are products distributed, by country and region?

(10) Where is the competition likely to be weakest?

Much of this research can be carried out from the home base. By using official sources of national information, this work can be done inexpensively. (Useful addresses and contacts are given in Section V.) Most business executives involved in exporting do not use official government services efficiently, and yet they are the cheapest and often the best way of carrying out basic desk research. Official services are underrated because businessmen and businesswomen too often base their assessment of them on past performance or prejudice. Companies often pay for costly advice and consultancy from organizations which themselves use the official government services on behalf of their clients. A more advantageous time for buying in advice is when basic research has been carried out, and when help is needed in the target country to find agents, set up a distribution system or acquire a site.

Market Research

Marketing operations rarely begin at the beginning. There are usually existing products. Questions need to be asked such as: is there a demand for the product? Does it need to be modified? What specific marketing possibilities exist for it? In which area or countries should a start be made? These are the questions on which a company operating in the Community may need advice. Official sources will help to some extent. How many companies are aware, for example, that some Commercial Sections of Embassies have bilingual product officers throughout Community countries working for national business interests?

Market research is usually done in two stages:

(1) An investigation of the market in general.
(2) Identification of specific business opportunities

The first can be approached on a Europe-wide basis as regards sources. As questions become more specific it will be necessary to look for sources of information under national headings. (The main sources of this information are listed in Section V.) Checklists may seem a rather obvious way of ensuring that the groundwork is done, but simple devices can help a company to think through its marketing strategy.

A simple checklist which has been compiled and refined by a number of managers involved in European operations is given in Box 44. The first two parts of the checklist on entering strategy and marketing have been given above. Questions on distribution, business policy, legal aspects and investment aspects follow in Box 38.

Box 38: The European Market - Some Considerations for Potential Exporters

Entering strategy - see text

Marketing questions - see text

Distribution questions

(1) What are the shipping facilities and costs? Port of entry - on-off services and container services?
(2) What are the supportive road/rail facilities and costs?
(3) What are the port and rail clearing charges?
(4) Who are possible clearing agents?
(5) What is the distributive/forwarding agency set-up?

The objective of this research is to determine ability to enter the market.

Business policy questions

(1) Current and future growth factors in the markets under consideration. GNP. Net disposable income.
(2) Current and forward exchange rates and likely strengths of currencies.
(3) Tax structure (including withholding taxes).
(4) Can profits and dividends be freely remitted?
(5) Current and likely future trends in wages and salaries in the markets under consideration.
(6) Are there any price controls?
(7) Labour relations and union structure.
(8) Relative productivity factors of different business

sectors.
(9) Employees' rights - social security payments, pensions, compensation and other benefits.
(10) Engineering and building costs.

The objective is to establish from these questions a second short-list of markets.

Legal questions

(1) Existing and proposed competition and anti-trust regulations.
(2) Existing and proposed company law.
(3) What are the legal rights of minority shareholders?
(4) What is in the pipeline in the way of legislation?

The objective is to establish the pitfalls of different methods of achieving entry and to review EC and national legislation.

Investment questions

(1) Investment incentives. (Regional policies and capital grants.)
(2) Government attitude to mergers and acquisitions.
(3) Banking facilities. Bank charges - working capital, loans, company expansion facilities.
(4) Attitudes to foreign investors.

Sections to add to the checklist might include those on competitors, availability of personnel, sources of finance, required rates of return on investment. The list is by no means exhaustive but time spent on establishing such a list is not wasted. References at the end of the book suggest sources of information and advice on: export marketing decisions; export practice and documentation; marketing in the European Community; markets in the Community; background information on the business climates in the countries of the Community.

A company needs to look at conditions in specific countries in which it seeks a market and also at aspects of Community export marketing. As regards the Community, the points to bear in mind are:

(1) The Community, because it is a customs union and has an external commercial policy, is a market in itself; but, as regards specific products, there may be dozens of markets segmented in different ways.

(2) The policies it develops and the laws it draws up regulating business need to be monitored as well as the national laws of individual countries.

Box 39: Timing plan — a bar chart approach

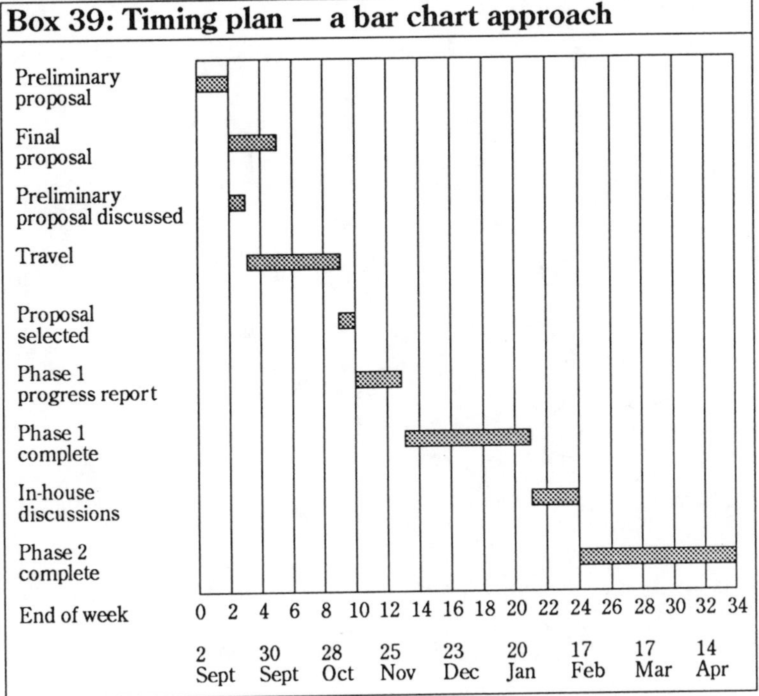

(3) Increasingly it will be legislation and policies emanating from Brussels which will concern those operating within the Community, whether from an external base or from one of the countries of the Twelve.

(4) Apart from the above, marketing in the Community is no different from marketing elsewhere in the world, and the same considerations apply.

In a marketing decision, just as in an investment decision, time is one of the most valuable commodities and, just as it pays to make checklists, it pays also to work to a strict timetable. Dates for meetings at different levels in the organization should be arranged at the beginning of an export marketing operation. They can always be cancelled but are much more difficult to arrange at short notice. A simple bar chart approach is illustrated in Box 39. The considerations which might affect a decision to export to a market in one country rather than another are also relevant to investing in one country or another. It is to the investment decision which we now turn in the next chapter.

9. Investment Strategies and the European Community

A company often becomes involved in exporting by accident. A one-off enquiry, a chance opportunity to get rid of surplus production which cannot be sold on the home market, speculative participation in a trade fair in the home country or abroad may start a company off on the export trail. Random factors - such as the nationality of the chairman's wife, the country where a manager has been on holiday, that another senior manager comes originally from Italy or Romania - may cause firms to look at a specific export market.

Whether ventures arising from these chance beginnings are successful or not, the effect on the company is often only marginal. If the venture fails, the cost is written off and the affair forgotten. If it is a success, then there is a point when the company has to decide whether to take seriously this initial export effort and expand it or invest in setting up a serious operation, perhaps with manufacturing facilities abroad. Service industries too are currently experiencing rapid cross-border growth in Europe and this chapter is equally relevant to them.

The Investment Decision

The investment decision affects functions of a business at many levels. It is perhaps the failure to realize this fully which accounts for some of the difficulties companies experience in developing overseas operations. Sometimes, for example, the personnel manager is the last to know about a projected foreign investment. Yet the task of finding qualified personnel, within the company or outside, and of training them in the appropriate skills to manage or coordinate the management of the venture, may require a much longer lead time than raising the finance for the operation.

It is more often the finance director than the personnel director who accompanies the chief executive on visits to the target country. The finance director must be aware of his responsibility for thinking about the investment from the viewpoint of other colleagues and functions, not just in financial terms.

Ways of Looking at Markets

There are a number of ways of looking at potential investment markets: by continents; country-by-country; regional areas; population centres; language; radio/TV area. These are considered below in turn.

Box 40: Total UK Exports by Area of Destination - 1988
£ million (seasonally adjusted)

<u>Developed countries</u>	
EC	40,932
Rest of Western World	7,412
US	12,623
Other	4,496
Total	65,462
<u>Developing countries</u>	
Oil Exporting Countries	5,021
Other	8,612
Centrally Planned Economies	1,614
Total	13,633

Continents

Some large companies have continental or regional operations. However, this continental approach breaks down when details of a company's operations or future operations are considered. It is rare for a company to be involved in all the countries of a continent, and if it is, then it probably should not be. Continents are not necessarily economic entities. Africa is a very diverse continent. The southern and central Mediterranean and the Arab African countries may not have enough in common to justify a

Box 41: UK's Top Export Markets - 1988

National exports go increasingly to other EC countries

Country	Exports £ million	% of total UK exports	Cumulative percentage
USA	10,544	12.9	12.9
FRG	9,522	11.7	24.6
France	8,270	10.2	34.8
Neths	5,583	6.9	41.6
Belg/Lux	4,252	5.2	46.8
Italy	4,106	5.0	51.9
Irish Rep	4,057	5.0	56.9
Spain	2,692	3.3	60.2
Sweden	2,195	2.7	62.9
Canada	2,038	2.5	65.5

Source - DTI Monthly Review of External Trade Statistics Annual Supplement No 10 1989

continental approach. However, with a population of over 300 million by the year 2,000 along the South Mediterranean littoral, this situation could well change. Europe is difficult to define too now that Central and Eastern countries have opened up.

One of the key points in the Betro Trust Report (Box 42) is the need to concentrate on key markets. These key markets can be seen to be increasingly European, as an analysis of the top 10 UK export destinations shows (Box 41). Over 50% of UK exports are today destined for European Community Member States. It is impossible to service adequately all the markets in the world - nor is it profitable. Only very large companies need world-wide operations. Many smaller companies need to concentrate only on a few targeted markets in a very limited number of countries.

Box 42: Concentration on Key Markets
Recommendations of the Betro Trust Report

(1) Concentration

Even the richest companies have only limited resources to deploy in the export markets. It is more profitable and conducive to faster progress to concentrate talent, effort and scarce cash resources in five or ten of the company's best key markets, for success comes from concentration.

(2) A new manpower policy

Let exports have an equal chance to that accorded to home trade. If a company sells half its output abroad and half at home, it cannot be right that it should have 50 salesmen in the home market and only one for all the export markets. Such a policy discriminates against exports and (even if highly profitable in the short run) will retard continued progress abroad. An investment in export manpower is the best investment British companies can make. The adoption of 'equality' could open an era of prosperity for most companies.

(3) Travel

Frequent personal contacts are by far the best way of solving problems and developing products and trade.

(4) Investment

This is the key to long-term prosperity. Investment, primarily geared to export, will reduce dependence on the static home market and ensure greater stability and faster growth. It is also the most effective answer to the perennial problem of long delivery dates and delivery reliability.

(5) The vital role of the accountant

The accountant's increasing involvement in exports is vital. He is a dispassionate and logical observer and his review of comparative home and export activities (e.g. pricing, profitability, manpower comparisons) could lead to a better appreciation of the advantages of exporting. In particular, the detailed study of comparative prices in the major markets can be most rewarding and should be given the highest priority. All the more so since pricing and investment policies are often interrelated.

(6) An approach to an export-led boom

Since 80% of exporters are looking abroad for expansion, this may be the right moment to look afresh at the four significant determinants of export success:

Concentration	Manpower
Pricing	Travel

If these were now to be given the priority accorded to them by our major competitors they would provide much of the funds and the justification for an export-led investment boom.

Source: the Betro Trust Report, Royal Society of Arts

Country-by-Country

A second method is to list a number of countries worth looking at and then to work out an appraisal system. For example, a company which manufactures, distributes and launders roller towels and work overalls decided to list and look at all the countries in the world. It proved an exhaustive if not an exhausting exercise. It found that the best three markets were several thousand miles apart. Because of this they could not all be exploited because of distance.

Regional Area

This approach is more promising, especially for a company which identifies areas that really have something in common. The European Community is an example, so is North America, Central America and other regional groups. The strength of these regional groupings needs to be assessed, as some are more integrated economically than others. The Middle East is often looked upon as a regional area, but from an investment viewpoint it divides up very easily into different countries: Israel and the Arab countries are divided; the North African countries differ from the Gulf countries, and Saudi Arabia differs politically from Iraq or Syria. Looked at closely it is difficult to see why the Middle East is considered a region at all from a business point of view, since it is diverse politically, economically, culturally, and even linguistically. The countries of the European Community are much more closely knit and doing business in all of them is increasingly similar as the Single Market becomes a reality.

Population Centres

This is a useful way of looking at markets. A company will say it is investing in France when perhaps it means it is investing in the Paris basin where the GNP per capita is much higher than the rest of France and where a large proportion of the population live.

Population centres will be of particular interest to companies selling to or manufacturing for mass consumer markets. While electronic components can perhaps be manufactured profitably in the south of Italy, it will pay to produce domestic paints closer to where they will be applied.

The roller towel company, mentioned above, eventually found that its best way of looking at the world was in terms of population centres. It needed centres of sufficient size to justify setting up an operation - where the population was growing both in size and wealth, and where labour bottlenecks were occurring. The traditional cheap laundering services in these areas would disappear or become expensive as semi-skilled labour was drawn into industry away from these services, thus creating a demand for roller towel and allied laundry services.

Language

Grouping countries by language or culture can be useful especially where knowledge of the language is important. It is cost effective to teach a manager a language that can be used in a number of different countries. For example, if a manager is taught classical Arabic then in a language sense the Middle East becomes a uniform area as classical Arabic can be understood in all of the countries. In the same way, French is useful in Luxembourg and parts of Belgium as well as Switzerland and former French colonies from Martinique to Lebanon. Packaging and advertising costs can be reduced by looking at the world in terms of language. As for the Community, English and French are the key languages. Indeed with these two languages a business executive has a good chance of being understood in most parts of the world. Cultural differences, however, are not appreciated sufficiently. An advertisement in one country may not be credible in another even though the language is the same in both.

Radio/TV Area

This aspect is important for marketing and advertising rather than for investment. TV programmes are increasingly crossing national frontiers and the number of television channels which will be available in a few years across Western Europe is growing at an exponential rate. High Definition TV will speed the process.

European-wide TV advertising will develop European-wide markets.

Investment Considerations

If a company has decided to invest in the Community, but is not sure in which country it should begin, on what criteria should it base its decision? The checklist approach is as good as any. A list of criteria can be compiled along the following lines, adding and subtracting criteria as appropriate for your company. You should write any points relevant to your company under each heading. At the end of the chapter there are suggestions for how to trade off opportunities in one country against those in another. It is a simple prioritization system which can work for you.

Political Stability

This is a key factor. A country which is politically unstable is an investment risk. But do not confuse political stability with the political leanings of the government.

Nationalization, Government Controls and Price Controls

Most governments in Europe have enough problems without contemplating nationalization. Most European countries encourage inward investment and this suggests that existing foreign investments will not be threatened by nationalization. Rather, in the changed political climate of recent years, privatization of previously nationalized industry sectors is the trend across the EC.

The threat, real or imagined, of government controls may present a problem. Export or foreign investment opportunities become less attractive if governments are inclined to impose controls without warning. The pharmaceutical industry has suffered controls, particularly on prices in some EC countries, making it difficult for foreign firms to take advantage of favourable exchange rates and to raise their prices. Non-tariff or technical barriers can also affect trade. In France, for example, the onus is on the company to prove that medicines do positive good, while in some Community countries, such as the UK, it is sufficient to show they do no harm. The Single Market is making non-tariff barriers and technical barriers a thing of the past but the pace of change in any specific case needs to be carefully monitored.

A government's attitude to foreign investment may be more relevant than where it lies on the political spectrum.

The main political consideration in any Community country is the effect of a political change on business confidence. New governments through new untried policies may have short-term effects on investment confidence but there is little if any correlation, in Europe, between the political orientation of the government in power and the profitability of companies.

Economic Outlook

There is advantage to investing in a country where the economy is growing. It is easier to obtain market share when the total market is buoyant. On the other hand, it may be easier and cheaper to find a good investment opportunity where the economy of a country is less strong. More businesses may be in difficulty, property prices may be lower and there may be greater labour availability. Part of the recent investment boom in the EC from firms outside the Community is accounted for by the opportunities of the Single Market but part also by the economic growth in Europe of the late 1980s.

Attitude to Foreign Investment

Government attitudes can make a great difference to investment plans. The recent surge of Japanese investment in the United Kingdom and Spain is a direct result of the positive attitude of these two countries to inward investment as well as the large national markets for consumer goods which they represent. Foreign investment is time-consuming and expensive. It is therefore necessary for a company to have a clear view of government attitudes so that time is not spent negotiating potential investments which will subsequently prove unacceptable. The Community's merger and competition policy and its relationship to those Member States may be relevant here, particularly where large takeovers or potentially dominant positions are involved. See Chapter 11.

Foreign Companies Expanding

This is a cheap form of market research.

It may be worthwhile for a smaller company to find out from embassies and trade missions abroad which companies are moving in or out of a particular country. Many smaller companies have made successful investments by going in on the back of, or following the trend set by, larger ones.

Corporate Forms

The kind of legal entity to be established will vary from one country to another. The Community is working towards making the process more simple. The European Company Statute and the European Economic Interest Grouping (EEIG) (Chapter 12) are likely to be increasingly relevant for companies wishing to operate across the EC. The EEIG came into force in June 1989 and enables companies to pool any number of different resources to work together: marketing - research - distribution, while retaining their own legal and financial reporting entities. These are the first attempts to help create pan-European business activity and will be useful to some companies. Others will prefer to be registered in one country for locational, fiscal or other reasons. The advantages of having a legal entity in one country of the EC rather than another are eroding as harmonization of company law legislation, and closer cooperation between the fiscal and economic authorities of Member States accelerates.

Patent and Trade Mark Protection

For this aspect of Community investment there is a growing Community level solution. There is a European Patent Office (EPO) in Munich. The EPO aims to avoid duplication in procedures for grants of patents by giving an applicant the opportunity to obtain patent protection in up to 12 states by means of a single application. The setting up of a Community Trade Mark protection office is a high Community priority. At present such matters are dealt with by Member States.

Remittability of Funds

The freedom of movement of capital, services, people and goods is written into the Treaty of Rome and now through Europe 1992 is becoming a reality.

Companies based outside the Community can remit funds from EC countries without difficulty as the freedom of movement of capital is intended not to be just EC-wide but worldwide. It is now inconceivable that Community countries would ever prevent funds from being remitted. This is not the case in many other countries where investment laws can change overnight with little hope of redress and the risk of considerable losses.

Taxes

At present these are the subject of much discussion as the Community countries debate the differing levels of direct and indirect taxation. Taxation changes and exchange rate variations can have a great effect on profits as they can, even in a year, amount to more than the expected rate of return on the investment. In comparing wage rates of one Community country with another, the incidence of indirect as well as direct taxation needs to be taken into account. VAT rates still vary although, either through EC legislation or through allowing market forces to approximate levels, there is a gradual move towards approximation of this tax. It remains one of the key as yet unresolved issues of the Single Market (see Chapter 18 on financial services and taxation).

Incentives

These are given only when governments believe that a certain region needs them. To invest in Bordeaux or the Mezzogiorno may seem to be advantageous given the incentives offered. But is skilled labour readily available? Do the incentives remain indefinitely or can they be changed from year to year? Careful financial accountants take any initial write-offs they can get. They do not add future incentives to cash flow and other projections unless they are absolutely sure that they cannot be changed by a new government policy.

EC policy on state aids is developing rapidly (Chapter 11). The Commission is demanding that any state aid is agreed beforehand and is 'transparent', that is identified clearly as aid. In a number of cases where Member States are suspected of Community law infringement, state aids are having to be repaid. The British Aerospace and Renault cases are recent examples.

Capital Sources

Many mistakes have been made over foreign financing in recent years because of inflation and violent exchange rate fluctuations. Cheap money may appear cheap from its interest coupon, but what about repayment? The rapid development of the Exchange Rate Mechanism of the European Monetary System in recent years has helped as has the growing use of the Ecu which is now the world's fifth most widely used traded currency in international transactions (Chapter 15). Capital sources in Europe are well advertized and yet availability of local finance is still an important part of the investment strategy decision-making process.

Personnel, Labour, and Social Considerations

Personnel issues should be higher up the checklist than they often are. It is more often than not the finance director and lawyer who accompany the chief executive when investments are being considered and yet many ventures succeed or fail as much on the quality of management and workforce as for financial reasons. Developing or hiring Euro-managers is a growing field of activity and there is already a shortage of well trained personnel who can move easily from one culture to another and one language to another in Europe.

The development of the Social Dimension of 1992 is now considered to be as important as the economic dimension. If goods, services, people and capital are to flow freely across national boundaries, there will be threats as well as opportunities for individuals and their requirements will need to be taken sympathetically into consideration during the next decade of quite dramatic change for a large number of companies in Europe. The implications for employers of the Social Charter and the Social Dimension are discussed in Chapter 16.

Efficient communications and closer understanding between unions at European level will make the investment decision more complex. Careful preparation and consultation with employees will be necessary. Companies will need to develop a personnel strategy both to train managers for foreign operations and, equally important, to operate from their home base and establish the boundary relationships with foreign managers in a subsidiary abroad.

An understanding of the different attitudes to business of the French or the Italians will be desirable for managers who will have contact with a new subsidiary in those countries. It may be equally as useful to understand the business culture as the language. It certainly takes less time. As regards language, the number of managers who are able to do business in a foreign language is very limited. You can learn to be polite, you can learn to communicate at a basic level, but there is no way you can learn to manage in a foreign language in a few weeks.

For someone with good linguistic ability, it will take at least six months of full-time study and a year to eighteen months in the country before he can hope to communicate and manage successfully. Before that time he may be managing through a bilingual secretary or a foreign adviser, which is a different form of management. The boundary between the home company manager and subsidiary foreign manager, wherever it is drawn, is always crucial. It is on this boundary that mistakes and misunderstandings occur.

As regards social considerations, the cost of laying off labour can be extremely high in Community countries. These costs need to be carefully checked out as part of the investment decision.

Box 43: The Importance of Languages in the Process of European Construction: Community Programmes

A foreign language policy, based on Europe's future needs, must have the objective of achieving diversification in foreign language teaching. The Commission has launched several programmes which maintain and strengthen the multilingual aspect of the Community by encouraging its citizens to communicate with one another in at least one language other than their mother tongue.

1. The Council of the European Community has adopted the Directive on the education of the children of migrant workers whose aim it is to contribute towards developing mutual understanding among cultural and language groups.

2. In December 1988 the Commission proposed the LINGUA programme to promote foreign language training in the Community.

Community action also involves: promotion of language training for young people, reinforcing initial training for foreign language teachers, promotion of language teaching in economic life and complementary measures to encourage innovation in foreign language teaching.

A knowledge of several languages by as many citizens as possible will help to make a living reality of the free movement of persons, goods, capital and services. Those who will have acquired foreign language skills will be able to participate more effectively in the opportunities which Europe 1992 offers.

Source: Languages in British Business, edited by Stephen Hagen, Newcastle upon Tyne Polytechnic Products Ltd, 1988.

Company Structure, Search Procedures, Trade Policy, Community Legislation

You need to consider whether to treat a European investment as part of your export market or as part of the home market. In what ways do you need to adapt company structure for an acquisition? It is all very well to say that the Community is a home market, but in practice it 'feels' to many of us very much like a foreign market in spite of its proximity and the Community ties. Establishing a search procedure so that no time is wasted is worthwhile (see Box 44). Current and future Community legislation needs to be monitored - the subject matter of part of this book - but so too does national legislation.

Exchange Rates

Exchange rate fluctuations can often make or lose more for the company than its operating profit or loss. The study of exchange rates and of invoicing, collecting and remitting, lending and borrowing in relation to them is a subject which has not, in the past, been accorded sufficient attention by senior management. The Exchange Rate Mechanism (ERM) of the European Monetary System (EMS) has brought considerable stability to most European currencies, and the growing use of the Ecu which has now become the world's fifth most traded currency, are both bringing more order to a complex European system (Chapter 15 - Economic and Monetary Union).

Evaluating the Investment Decision

Having made a list along the above lines, an investment decision needs evaluation. How do you decide between two or more investment opportunities? By the time the investment decision approaches, there is a battery of advice and advisers available within and outside the company. Many of them have their own particular interests and prejudices and a balanced assessment can be difficult to obtain. A simple weighting system as in Box 44 can be useful in deciding between options. Eliminate all but five or six of the variables of your checklist as they will not significantly affect the choice, even though they need to be considered. Give the remainder a weighting according to their general importance to the investment decision, as in column 1. The weights should add up to ten (or 100 if you wish to make a detailed assessment of the difference between the weights). Next grade each investment opportunity by country in columns 2 and 3. In the example Country A is considered politically very stable and is therefore graded 9. Country B is less stable and therefore graded 2. Cross multiplication shows that, in the example, Country A is preferred to Country B. This rough and ready approach has the advantage of fitting some simple numbers to subjective thinking about the strength of alternative investments. There are various complicated systems which can be developed from a simple approach. They are often too sophisticated and there is no

Box 44: The European Investment Decision

(1) A major step in the life cycle of a company involving *all* aspects of the business

(2) Ways of looking at markets:
Continents
Country by country
Regional area
Population centres
Language
Radio/TV area

(3) Investment considerations:
Political stability
Economic outlook
Attitude to foreign investment
Foreign companies expanding
Nationalization
Government controls
Price controls
Corporate forms
Patent and trade mark protection
Remittability of funds
Taxes
Incentives
Capital sources
Personnel
Labour

Trade policy
Social considerations
Company structure
Search procedures
Current and future Community regional legislation and trade legislation
Exchange rates
Time
Distance
Competitors

(4) A simple method of evaluating investment opportunities:

	1	2	3	4	5
	Weight (W)	Country A	Country B	1x2 (WA)	1x3 (WB)
Political	5	9	2	45	10
Taxes	2	2	6	4	12
Personnel	1	4	9	4	9
Economic	2	3	5	6	10
	—	—	—	—	—
	10	18	23	59	41

Note: Country 'A' preferred to Country 'B'

(5) Conclusions:

The past is not necessarily a guide to the future
Need for detailed analysis and research before decision about where, when and how to invest
Ideal investment opportunities will not necessarily be available
Need for method of trading off one opportunity against another
The role of chance in the investment decision

Source: J.S.N. Drew, London Business School, December 1985

evidence that they work any better. Investment decisions like most business decisions, once the necessary careful research and analysis has been made, are based then, to a large extent, on hunch or feel.

Once your company is operating in the European Community, it will need to monitor what is happening and keep track of

European legislation. The next chapter points to how this might be done.

10. Making Company Contacts in the European Community

In continuing to develop a 1992 audit or in monitoring its operations in the EC, your company will need to make contact with national and Community institutions. The key pressure points are listed in Box 45. Further information on them can be found listed in Section V. Trade associations and organizations such as, in the UK for example, the Confederation of British Industry (CBI), the Institute of Directors and the British Institute of Management are likely to be first ports of call. They will want to know your concerns, the better to get a common industry position together. They should also be able to help you draw up your company audit by providing their own commentaries on the 282 proposals of the White Paper. In the UK the key government department is the Department of Trade and Industry which is referred to in Section V. Although you are developing a European approach to legislation, it is the national government departments which will give you most practical support and advice. MEPs (Members of the European Parliament) will be interested to help your company activity. They will want to explain the importance of the Single European Act for the parliamentary decision-making process and to understand the issues of 1992 as they affect your company, especially if it is in their constituency. An invitation to visit you and possibly speak on 1992 is likely to be well received. 1992 committees have been set up by MEPs in some constituencies.

The Commission has offices in all Member States and in many countries around the world. They may have a special system for dealing with 1992 queries and sending you documentation. EC Business Information Centres have also been established in a large number of cities in the Community, with the specific intention of helping small and medium businesses develop their European dimension.

The Community institutions are at least as receptive to business views as national governments. Some knowledge of the decision-making process in the Community and of pressure points is required. A planned one day visit to Brussels by a well-briefed senior manager, from time to time, might do more for a company and its industry than a whole research department devoted to monitoring Community activity. This latter information can perhaps be bought in more cheaply, or be obtained from your trade association.

Lobbying in Brussels, by regular contacts on an individual company basis, or through a sectoral trade association, is also important. Get to know which are the relevant Directorates-General (Departments) of the European Commission dealing with the issues of particular interest to your company, for example competition law, public procurement, the service sector, banking legislation, telecommunications, grants and loans. You need to know the key officials involved. For newcomers, the national offices of the European Commission in the Member States are a logical starting place for this process.

It is often useful to obtain from acquaintances in one Community institution their opinion as to the best person to contact in another. MEPs are particularly helpful. In what follows the perspective of a UK business executive is used as an example, but the problems considered, and their solutions, have general application throughout the Community.

Pressure Points

In this chapter the pressure points themselves are considered - where the individual company can put over its point of view in a European context.

Suppose a company is not able to export a perishable product from one Community country successfully because of frontier delays, even though they should be by now abolished or the process speeded up. The company suspects that the delays are more than bureaucratic and in the nature of a non-tariff barrier. This problem can be raised with any of the contacts in Box 45.

Box 45: Contact Points in the European Community

To influence policy making or raise strategic issues, contact:

National trade associations - for industry-wide representation of views.

Relevant national government departments - at principal or assistant secretary level.

National government - your MP or a Minister - for quick action on urgent matters and for political lobbying.

The Commission - to obtain latest Community-wide thinking and to influence those who will draw up Community policies.

The European Parliament - your MEP - for quick action on urgent matters and for political lobbying at Community rather than national level.

The Economic and Social Committee - especially members representing industry.

European trade associations - for contacts and Europe-wide lobbying on behalf of your industry.

To arrange contacts with Community institutions refer to:

European Information Centres

The offices of the Commission in London, Cardiff, Edinburgh, Belfast or elsewhere for general information and contacts in Brussels of a general nature.

The UK Representation in Brussels (UKREP) - for briefing on latest Community thinking and introductions to the Commission.

For final appeal contact:

The Court of Justice - but usually through the Commission.

The media - if you have a good case, a newsworthy case and all other channels seem blocked.

European policies cannot be influenced, nor can non-adherence to Community law be investigated, until suggestions or information reach those officials whose task it is to collect views on existing and proposed legislation. Complaints addressed to the Commission are systematically followed up, if necessary, through the Court of Justice.

Some companies already have individuals, or even departments, dealing with Community matters. Other companies have ignored the Community almost completely and a few have paid for this with shareholders' capital. Even now costly mistakes are being made by companies which have failed to realize that Community legislation can seriously affect their operations. Heavy fines have been imposed for intentional or negligent infringements of Community competition law. This can amount to as much as 10% of annual sales and on occasion has risen to over a million Ecu. For example, United Brands had to change its pricing policy for bananas and the Distillers' Company marketing strategy was seriously affected because it ignored European Community legislation.

National Trade Associations

Trade associations play a useful part because they can align the force of their membership behind any representations. The problem is that some are poor, both in terms of money and quality of staff. If a merit table of effective trade associations were to be drawn up there would be a high correlation between the salaries of senior staff and positions in the table. Associations, such as the Food and Drink Industries Council and the Society of Motor Manufacturers and Traders (SMMT) in the UK are not only excellent sources of information on the Community but also powerful lobbies for the interests of their members. A letter setting out the problem of a suspected non-tariff barrier will enable the trade association to start investigation in the industry. It cannot act if it is not kept informed of a company's difficulties.

As well as the trade associations, there are national organizations such as the Confederation of British Industry (CBI), the British Institute of Management (BIM) and the Institute of Directors. The CBI in particular is a well-informed and powerful organization on the European scene and will become more so as it develops its resources in this field. CBI reports on different aspects of Community policies are excellently researched and presented. Similar organizations exist in most EC countries.

National Government Departments

In each government department, and particularly in the Department of Trade and Industry, there are a number of senior civil servants whose jobs involve monitoring, drawing up and negotiating policies affecting business in the Community. A telephone call, a letter or a meeting with one of these officials can be a useful way of influencing national and hence ultimately Community policy on specific issues. Government officials working in this area can often make representations or enquiries in Brussels personally, as many of them are frequent visitors. They will have direct links with their national Representation or embassy and, through it, with the Community. They will of course be involved with policy formation for the Government on Community matters.

Box 46: DTI Hotline

The DTI Hotline

The most useful telephone number for UK business in the Community:-

071-200 1992 - general information about 1992 (free of charge).

> The DTI 'Action Checklist' outlines the main issues a business will face. For further help, the DTI 'Enterprise Initiative' gives independent firms with fewer than 500 employees expert consultancy advice on marketing, design, quality, manufacturing systems, business planning and financial and information systems.
>
> For more information call 0800 500 200.
>
> The DTI's Single Market Unit has details of the many conferences and seminars which are being organized in every part of the country by chambers of commerce, trade associations and other organizations.
>
> For further information telephone 071-215 4770.

If your problem concerns a matter of policy then it may be advisable to contact a principal or an assistant secretary. An assistant secretary corresponds, approximately, to a senior middle manager in industry or a colonel in the army. He or she will certainly have access to top civil servants or the minister, if your problem warrants it. Occasionally it will be necessary to meet more senior civil servants, but the key official in most cases at the policy-making level is usually an assistant secretary.

A telephone call to the key working level official, once you have identified her or him, may have more effect than letters and visits to ministers which are time-consuming. In any case, letters will be passed on to officials for drafting and reply.

National Government

Lobbying MPs can be an effective way of influencing the European Community. An MP has the right to ask questions and obtain an answer from the government department concerned. This can be particularly effective when the problem is complicated and there is uncertainty as to which ministry to approach. It can also be a speedy one, as MPs' questions, whether asked in Parliament or written as letters to ministers or ministries, are very speedily dealt with. Companies may think that business-government relations and indeed business-Community relations, can be satisfactorily maintained by the chairman's dining with a minister from time to time, or a senior civil servant's being invited on retirement to join the board of the company. Both approaches have their merits, but neither is sufficient in itself. The level of the interface between the company and the government, the intensity of it and the kind of subjects discussed, should be considered carefully. Too often the interface is seen as the responsibility of one or two people on each side. Government contacts should be encouraged at a number of different levels within the company.

Representative Offices of the Commission in Member States

The Commission of the European Communities is represented in all Member States. In the United Kingdom there are four offices located in London, Belfast, Cardiff and Edinburgh.

The role of the Commission Offices is fourfold:-

(1) To represent the Commission and explain its policies.
(2) To communicate information about the European Community through the media and other channels to the general public as well as to specialized interest groups.
(3) To promote awareness of the direct effect of the European dimension on the lives and activities of UK citizens.
(4) To brief the Commission on the effects of its policies in the UK.

The London Office is at Jean Monnet House, 8 Storey's Gate, London SW1P 3AT. The Office includes a Media Office providing an extensive service for journalists, specialist writers, and radio and TV producers, and an Information Unit, comprising a Library and Data Room and supported by a network of 45 European Documentation Centres (EDCs). The External Relations Unit is responsible for the organization of specialized briefings, cooperation and support for local authorities and regional organizations through a regional campaign, and contributions to seminars and a wide range of European activities. You may also need to approach Euro-Info Centres or European Documentation Centres (Box 57 and Section V).

The National Representations in Brussels

The National Representation to the European Community in Brussels is worth visiting. It should rarely be necessary to see anyone more senior than a second or first secretary who will be an expert on your industry sector. You may also wish to meet the counsellor to whom a number of secretaries report. If you have only half a day in Brussels, telephone the relevant first secretary at least a week before to secure an appointment. He may suggest contacts in the Commission or elsewhere, and perhaps a meeting with colleagues in the Representation. If there is time to write beforehand, or the opportunity to visit the desk officer at the national Department of Trade or other relevant department, then your visit to Brussels will be even better prepared.

An alternative is to contact a Commissioner or Ambassador whom you know. There is nothing against high-level contacts and indeed much can be done through them, but usually not by them. If you ask a Commissioner how to appoint an exclusive agent for the Benelux countries, without falling foul of Article 86 of the Treaty, he will suggest an appointment with the Competition Directorate, and in particular the official dealing with exclusive agencies. In discussing exclusive agencies you may have wasted a good opportunity to talk with the Commissioner about more strategic matters. A direct telephone call to the appropriate official in the Commission Directorate-General IV, Directorate B, who would be only too pleased to help you, would have been more effective. It is not necessary to go to the highest level in Brussels for information or to express an opinion; on occasion it is a positive disadvantage.

Foreign Embassies

If your problem is connected with bilateral Community trade, the embassies in national capitals may help. Embassies have sections either attached to them or as separate organizations dealing with bilateral trade matters. Chambers of Commerce in national capitals may also be of assistance. This approach may be particularly useful if the problem is one where a national government can be of more help than the Commission. Making contact with embassies is simple. There is no need for introductions. A telephone call will suffice.

The Commission

Commission officials are very approachable. Their principal task is to propose and develop policies for European legislation. In drawing up legislation for industry they want to collect as many views as possible. The first step in getting to know the Commission is to meet officials dealing with your particular problem. A directory of the European Commission is readily obtainable and worth keeping on your bookshelf (Boxes 12 and 13). For those who need one, it is possible to get hold of an internal directory which contains direct telephone extensions of named individuals. If used effectively you can, from your desk, get in touch with officials throughout the Community. Bureaucracies within governmental or large private organizations are often more accessible by telephone in the first instance than by meetings. When did you last telephone a government official?

The European Parliament

European MPs can be contacted individually or through the parties to which they belong. You can meet them in their constituencies or, less frequently, in London. They will often be in Brussels attending committees or in Strasbourg when the European Parliament is in session. The further away from home they are, the easier it is to spend time with them. It may be more difficult to go to Strasbourg but once you are there, whether you are an MEP or have come to lobby one, there are fewer distractions than back in the United Kingdom or when sitting on committees in Brussels. Informal contacts with MEPs and officials of the institutions are perhaps more easily made in the buildings of the European Parliament than anywhere else in the Community.

The MEP is not only a useful contact and well-informed about what is going on in the Community, but he can also ask questions both written and oral on your behalf and take up your cause if you can persuade him that it is a good one. Many MEPs are businessmen and/or lawyers and, like national MPs, can and do have consultancy interests which are registered with the Parliament. (See Section V for contact telephone numbers.)

The Economic and Social Committee

Individual members can be useful interlocutors on your behalf. As about one-third of them are businessmen, they will be sympathetic to your problem, particularly if it has implications of a general Community nature. A list of members can be obtained from the Committee Secretariat. As most of them will be resident in their own countries, it may be easier to meet them in their home country rather than in Brussels where they will often be busy. The ESC has a growing interest in the Social Dimension, the environment and consumer interests.

European Trade Associations

Most national trade associations are affiliated to a European-wide association. Like national ones they vary in quality. They are often represented permanently in Brussels, are in regular contact with the Commission and other institutions, and are consulted by them regularly. In particular, the Employers Federation (UNICE) has an important role to play. It represents the combined strength of the CBI, the Patronat of France and employers' associations across Europe. It is useful to discover the strength of your European trade association in Brussels and the calibre of its representatives. They can be helpful not only directly but indirectly through the contacts they can obtain for you in the Commission and elsewhere. Secretaries-General of European trade associations have wide experience, a broad range of contacts and yet stand outside the official Community machinery.

The Court of Justice

Normally, there will be no need to consult the Court and indeed in almost every circumstance it would be best to approach the Commission first. In the last resort, of course, the Court of Justice can be petitioned by any country, company or individual on a matter of Community law and it is obliged to respond to petitions. It is also worth keeping a watch on judgements of the Court relevant to your industry.

The Media

If you have a good case and it is good news, then the media could be useful in furthering your interests. The correspondents dealing with Community affairs have very good contacts; they are well-informed and good lobbyists. The foreign press corps in Brussels is larger than in any capital except Washington.

There are then a wide number of channels through which business can become involved in the European legislative process. Lobbying involves action rather than inaction, and using time to good purpose. It is for this reason that it is worth considering using one of the growing number of consultancies which specialize in EC monitoring and advice.

The making of company contacts in the Community for reasons of information or for lobbying is a continuing process. Those involved tend to be specialists often from a corporate affairs or planning department, if not from the legal service. In smaller firms this task may fall to the Chairman or senior director. But strategy formation is too important to be left to the specialists. There must be a contribution from all parts of the company. Just as Europe 1992 is not a spectator sport, but something of concern to all those who work in a business, so strategy formation is a task to which all should contribute. It has been the purpose of this section to show how everyone can be involved in the process to some extent through seminars, briefings and written and audio material. The next section deals in outline with policies of the European Community of interest to business.

Section III: Community Internal Policies - Key Issues Affecting Business

11. Competition Policy

The competition policy of the Community is fundamental to business and has implications for nearly every other Community policy.

The Commission is responsible for developing and controlling the policy and has the power to inflict heavy fines on companies which infringe it. The principle of free trade is a cornerstone of the Community. The Commission's task is to ensure that it remains an integrated trading area in which prices are not distorted by trade restrictions, market sharing or monopolies.

Box 47: Summary of Articles 85 and 86 of the Treaty of Rome

Article 85 prohibits a number of agreements, associations or activities of undertakings which may affect or distort trade between Member States, for example those concerned with price fixing, the deliberate holding back of production and market sharing. Any agreements or activities caught by the above prohibitions are automatically void and unenforceable unless exempted by the Commission on the grounds that under Article 85(3) they are deemed to be contributing to improved production and distribution of goods or the promotion of economic and technical research. To clear your agreement you must either notify it to the Commission for an individual exemption, or see whether a Commission Group Exemption applies. In the second case, such as for exclusive distribution or patent and know-how licences, your agreement will be cleared providing its restrictions do not go beyond those permitted in the Group Exemption.

Article 86 concerns the abuse of a dominant market position within the Community wherever it is found to affect trade between Member States. For example, restricting markets or technical development to the prejudice of consumers, refusing to supply, or the application of dissimilar conditions to equivalent transactions.

Source: Treaty establishing the European Economic Community, Rome, 25 March 1957

The basic rules governing restrictions to trade are set out in Articles 85 and 86 of the Treaty of Rome (Box 47).

The Role of Competition Policy

Case law, which has developed considerably since the EC was first established, now allows companies to clarify aspects of competition without resorting to first principles and test cases. Competition policy is complex and large companies will need advice from legal experts with good contacts in Brussels familiar with latest Commission thinking as well as with the realities of

Box 48: The Objectives of EC Competition Policy

The Treaty of Rome which is the legal basis of the European Community stipulates that a system be set up to ensure that competition is not distorted.

The three principal objectives are:

- to create a single market for the benefit of industry and consumers. This is not simply a question of removing customs offices at the borders and enabling goods to travel unhindered throughout the Twelve. It is necessary to prevent companies from setting up 'invisible' frontiers through restrictive agreements and cartels;

- to prevent the abuse of economic power. When companies dominate a market, Community regulations ensure that they do not abuse their position;

- to encourage companies to rationalize and progress. By ensuring commercial rivalry, competition policy aims to encourage the competitiveness of European industry in world markets.

business. Cheap advice may be expensive. The presentation of a case to the Commission needs to be considered carefully so that the company's position is put in the best possible way.

Box 49: A Company Approach to European Competition Policy

1. Does our company have market shares in:
   a) the UK
   b) the European Community
   which might make us dominant in a market?

2. Do we operate formal or informal agreements which might distort or influence trade patterns in the EC?

3. Do we suspect competitors of either of the above?

4. Would exclusive agreements help us to get started in a particular market?

5. Are we the recipient of state aid or threatened by state subsidies to others?

6. Do we have any industrial property rights which protect or threaten us?

Concentration of industry is regularly monitored throughout the Community and each April a comprehensive report is produced by the Commission.

Box 50: The Commission View of Competition Policy and 1992

As the completion of the Internal Market by 1992 gathers pace, competition policy is coming more to the fore. This fact is widely reflected in the economic and industrial policies of the Member States and in the new emphasis on competition policy, even in Member States which hitherto did not have well-developed legislative and policy frameworks in the field of competition. There is an increasing awareness among the general public that the absence of an effective competition policy entails substantial costs since it is always the taxpayer who pays for unjustified State subsidies and the consumer who pays through higher prices and lower efficiency due to cartels, price fixing, abuses by dominant firms and other restrictive practices.

The future growth of the Community economy entails improving the allocation of production factors, and increasing market profitability and boosting innovation, in order to increase the international competitiveness of Community undertakings. Dynamic growth of supply is precisely the contribution that competition policy can bring to the economy of the Twelve. Much remains to be done in this field, both at international level, where protectionism - whether hidden or deliberate, general or selective - has flourished since the Tokyo Round, and within the Community itself. This is particularly relevant in those sectors where the anachronisms of market barriers and market partitioning remain prevalent.

The completion of the wider internal market means that the Commission must define a competition policy allowing both companies and consumers to draw maximum benefit from that achievement. The wider Single Market will be synonymous with rationalized production and stronger competition. The task of competition policy must be to give impetus to this integration by facilitating cross-frontier cooperation, for instance in the form of joint ventures.

Source: Introduction to the 17th Report on Competition, 1988.

The sources at the end of the book, in Section V, supplement the following brief treatment of competition policy and should be referred to by managers interested in more details of the implications of the policy for their business.

Exclusive Agreements - Either Distribution or Purchasing

Horizontal agreements between competitors as well as vertical agreements between manufacturers are prohibited if they restrict trade. A manufacturer cannot supply a single dealer exclusively in one specific part of the Community unless he can show to the Commission that it is in the consumer's interest. Although exclusive distribution and purchasing agreements may have detrimental effects for competition policy, they may at the same time have beneficial implications, improving efficiency and contributing to market unification. For example, a contract with an (exclusive) distributor/purchaser in a specific region may be desirable in the general interest to help a supplier entering a new market where there are linguistic and legal complexities with which he will have to deal.

Industrial Property

Industrial property rights include patents, copyrights, trademarks, performing rights, registered designs and models. 'Know-how' is not actually an industrial property right, but it is sometimes treated analogously. In order to implement the Single Market it will be necessary to agree Community-wide legislation for industrial property, to complement the application of these inherently national rights.

Articles 85 and 86 of the Treaty of Rome safeguard the free movement of goods. For example, a trademark holder in the United Kingdom can not use its UK rights to restrict imports of his marked product from Germany, if he has consented to the use of his mark there. Similarly, if an undertaking is in a dominant position in the EC, the improper exploitation of an industrial property right may be in violation of Article 86 (abuse of a dominant position).

In general, the tests for application of Article 85 (1) or exemption under Article 85 (3) are the same in industrial property rights as in other areas.

Merger Control

'We need to watch the spate of joint ventures, mergers and takeovers throughout the Common Market. When companies merge in order to become more efficient and competitive in European and world markets, we can warmly welcome it. When they simply seek to swallow up the competition and give themselves an easier ride, then it is the job of the European Commission to act - and we have substantial power to do so.'
Sir Leon Brittan, Commissioner for Competition Policy and Financial Institutions, September 1989.

The continuing wave of mergers with a Community dimension have made it necessary to look at merger rules at Community as well as national level. Major new proposals were made to strengthen Community merger control mechanisms in April 1989 at a meeting of the Internal Market Council. The Merger Control Regulation entered into force on 21 September 1990 and provides business with effectively 'one stop shopping'. A summary of Article 1 of the Regulation is set out below:

Mergers are subject to Community control when:

- the aggregate worldwide turnover of all the undertakings concerned is more than Ecu5,000m;
- the aggregate Community-wide turnover of each of at least two of the undertakings concerned is more than Ecu250m;

- one or more of the undertakings concerned does not achieve more than two-thirds of its aggregate Community-wide turnover within one and the same Member State.

The thresholds laid down above will be revised before the end of 1994. The Council will act by qualified majority voting on a proposal from the Commission.

Substantial progress on the merger Regulation was made at the Internal Market Council meeting in Luxembourg on 10 October 1989 although the question of future revision of the threshold remains unresolved. The question of Commission powers above the Ecu5bn threshold does not pose a problem and it was agreed that the formula for assessing mergers would reflect the clear competition policy considerations of Article 85 (3) of the Treaty of Rome. The sticking points, for the UK, Luxembourg and Germany in particular, are the provisions, insisted on by Italy, Holland and Belgium, allowing the Commission to intervene at the request of a Member State or on its own initiative below the threshold.

State Aids

Although there is no basic conflict between competition policy and industrial or regional policy, difficulties may arise where individual Member States provide unreasonable assistance to individual industries or firms, or improperly attract investment to specific regions through excessive regional aids. The Commission's power to control such measures may conflict with the internal affairs of Member States. Sometimes there are direct confrontations which, occasionally, can only be resolved by the Court of Justice which is the final arbiter in all competition cases. However, although all Member States dispense aid in one form or another to national business, they may only do so lawfully if the aid scheme has been notified in advance to the Commission and approved by it. As a rule this aid will fall under Article 92 (1) of the Treaty of Rome (see Boxes 51 and 52).

Box 51: State Aids: The Renault Case

In March 1988, the European Commission decided that French State aids to the car manufacturers, Renault, did not conform to regulations laid down by the Commission's competition policy and should accordingly be reduced to comply with Article 92(1) of the Treaty of Rome. In November 1989, considering that its decision had not been correctly executed by the French authorities, the Commission requested that the French government comply with the decision. It also stated that while proposals were being drawn up, the French government should recover Ffrs.12 bn from Renault.

A successful agreement between the Commission and the French government was reached and on 22 May 1990 the Commission decided:

- to halve the amount of aid to be repaid by Renault

- there should be no injection of capital by the State into Renault until after the end of 1990.

SMEs and Competition Policy

The Commission is particularly aware of handicaps faced by smaller firms in the context of the 1992 programme and of the importance to the Single Market of having a healthy and substantial network of small and medium-size firms. These contribute to economic growth and employment creation as well as performing an essential role in the maintenance of effective competition in the balanced economic and social development of the regions. This concern for the welfare of small and medium-size firms is reflected in the application of the State-aid rules.

Aid has been given to the small business sector at different stages of development - for example, via:

1. Grants, low interest loans or loan guarantees to help them get started.

2. Low interest loans or guarantees for investment by small businesses at reasonable terms.

3. Public support to encourage the flow of risk capital to the small business sector.

4. Grants for Research and Development (R & D).

5. Grants or low interest loans to innovation projects.

6. Grants towards the cost of improving small firms' management or sales policy, for outside consultants and for computerization.

Regional Development and State Aids

In 1987 there was a Commission Decision to adopt a method of application of Article 92 (3) (a). This Article concerns aid to less developed regions of the Community to promote the economic development of those areas where standards of living are abnormally low or where there is serious underemployment.

The above Decision aims to reduce regional disparities while not distorting competition. The provision of aid via this Article is compatible with the Single Market.

Box 52: Examples of the Latest Proposals Concerning State Aids

1. State aid to the motor industry. In view of the growing sensitivity of competition in the motor vehicle sector the Commission decided to introduce a framework for state aid in the industry in the form of measures based on Article 93 (1) of the Treaty of Rome.

   The aim is to establish full transparency of aid flows to the industry and also to impose stricter discipline to the granting of aids, to ensure that competitiveness of Community industry is not distorted by unfair competition. The framework foresees prior notification of all significant aid cases irrespective of objectives and annual reporting of all aid paid (as from 1 January 1989).

2. The enlargements of the Community have broadened the range of its regional diversity and new instruments are needed to regulate the granting of regional aid. Yet at the same time, Article 130 of the Single European Act aims to give impetus to greater economic and social cohesion to reduce regional disparity and disadvantage. The new arrangements will reduce regional disparities while not distorting competition.

Competition versus Cartels

Fair and open competition is the philosophy underlying Community legislation, but cartels still exist and sometimes for good reason. There are conflicting pressures, both economic and political, on the Community institutions and on Member States as the concept of open competition comes up against the reality of long-protected industries. The liberalization process continues but progress is not always as fast as the Commission might wish. There are conflicting policy issues both within the Commission, where Directorates-General have different responsibilities, and between countries depending on political and economic pressures put on their governments by different industries.

Air transport, traditionally one of the most protected industries, has recently come under scrutiny. The Community has laid down basic rules of procedure for setting fares and regulating government intervention in the industry. For example, a Community package designed to increase competition in the airline industry, notoriously closed to newcomers, includes two regulations adopted pursuant to Article 87 of the Treaty (which gives the Council the right to adopt directives to give effect to the principles set out in Articles 85 and 86). The first gives the Commission the same powers of investigation and sanction it enjoys in all other sectors of the economy in order to protect competition throughout the Community. The second enables the Commission to grant block exemptions to various categories of agreement and concerted practices including, in particular, the joint planning and coordination of capacity, the sharing of revenues, consultations on tariffs, fares and conditions where such exemptions are not considered to restrict competition in any way. The 1992 process very much favours an open and competitive economic system.

Concentration of Industry

In order to judge whether specific mergers or arrangements are compatible with the principles of the Common Market, the Competition Directorate-General monitors the progress of concentration trends through mergers and acquisitions on a country-by-country and industry-by-industry basis. Box 53 gives an indication of how concentration is monitored by the Commission. For example, between 1975 and 1986, the concentration of automobile production increased in Europe while the chemical industry saw a slight decline in the market share of the top fifteen firms.

An important new sector affected by Commission competition policy is that of audiovisual products and services. There are powerful economic forces encouraging enterprises to expand into adjacent product markets to take advantage of available economies of scale. In order to compete with the US and Japanese firms in the world audiovisual market, the European audiovisual industry must first overcome its present fragmentation and adapt its production and distribution structures, which are too narrow and insufficiently profitable.

Community audiovisual policy aims at developing coordinated action in this sector, geared to three issues: the establishment of the rules of the game, promotion of the programme industry and mastery of new technologies. These policies call for permanent monitoring of the market. Competition problems have arisen in three markets in particular:

(1) Production and distribution of cinema and TV films

Recommendations have been made in the application of

Box 53: National, Community and international mergers (including acquisitions of majority holdings) in the Community, 1984–88

Industry

Sector	National				Community				International				Total			
	1984/1985	1985/1986	1986/1987	1987/1988	1984/1985	1985/1986	1986/1987	1987/1988	1984/1985	1985/1986	1986/1987	1987/1988	1984/1985	1985/1986	1986/1987	1987/1988
1. Food	20	25	39	25	1	7	11	18	1	2	2	8	22	34	52	51
2. Chem.	25	23	38	32	23	28	27	38	5	6	6	15	53	57	71	85
3. Elec.	13	10	33	25	5	0	6	4	4	3	2	7	22	13	41	36
4. Mech.	24	19	21	24	4	3	8	5	3	7	2	9	31	29	31	38
5. Comp.	2	1	2	2	0	0	0	1	1	0	0	0	3	1	2	3
6. Meta.	13	14	15	28	3	1	4	9	1	2	0	3	17	17	19	40
7. Trans.	8	6	15	3	2	0	6	9	0	4	0	3	10	10	21	15
8. Pap.	10	18	17	24	5	4	7	6	3	5	1	4	18	27	25	34
9. Extra.	7	7	8	9	0	3	1	2	0	0	0	1	7	10	9	12
10. Text.	7	7	4	11	0	1	2	2	0	1	0	1	7	9	6	14
11. Cons.	14	12	13	21	1	2	3	12	0	0	3	0	15	14	19	33
12. Other	3	3	6	10	0	3	0	5	0	0	1	7	3	6	7	22
Total	146	145	211	214	44	52	75	111	18	30	17	58	208	227	303	383

Key:
Food: Food and drink.
Chem.: Chemicals, fibres, glass, ceramic wares, rubber.
Elec.: Electrical and electronic engineering, office machinery.
Mech.: Mechanical and instrument engineering, machine tools.
Comp.: Computers and data-processing equipment (in 1983/84 included under mechanical engineering).
Meta.: Production and preliminary processing of metals, metal goods.
Trans.: Vehicles and transport equipment.
Pap.: Wood, furniture and paper.
Extra.: Extractive industries.
Text.: Textiles, clothing, leather and footwear.
Cons.: Construction.
Other: Other manufacturing industry.

Source: Commission Report on Competition, 1989

competition law to the media, calling for the adoption of block exemption regulations or guidelines for certain agreements. The Commission is to draw up the guidelines.

(2) TV broadcasts

The Commission's main concern is to keep markets open and to prevent barriers to market entry.

(3) Satellite broadcasting services

The Commission guidelines will cover all types of aid, including tax incentives, taking into account the different characteristics of the audiovisual sectors. Given the importance the Commission attaches to the objective of maintaining pluralism while allowing and encouraging mergers, it may propose further legislation in this field.

Conclusion

Competition policy is the first of the policies outlined because of its immediate impact on many aspects of business in the Community and especially in the light of the Single Market. The policy is complex and companies likely to be affected will need expert advice. Further chapters deal with policies more briefly. It should, however, be clear from this section just how many aspects of business are now affected by Community policies. These policies are not something 'imposed by Brussels'. A Community policy or a Community Directive is agreed by Member States which undertake to apply it in their own territories, thus making it a uniform policy or law across the Community. The decision is made by the Twelve Member States, not 'by Brussels'.

12. Company Law

The attainment of a common market requires not only the free circulation of goods and services, but also an environment in which companies can establish themselves anywhere in the Community with the minimum of legal and tax problems. European Company Law Directives have been adopted to make it easier for companies to operate across the Community and to set up subsidiaries or branches in other Member States. These Directives are relevant to any company seeking to expand its activities in the Community. A brief description of some of the more important ones is given below. Harmonization of essential company law and accounting provisions has taken place slowly over the years and the process is continuing. The rules applying to small and medium-size businesses (SMEs) have been simplified in a number of cases in order to lessen the burden on them. Among the Directives are:

The First Directive (1968) lays down basic legal requirements for limited liability companies in the Community and also requires the disclosure of information on their memoranda and articles, company officers, paid up capital, balance sheets, profit and loss accounts, winding up, nullity and the appointment of liquidators.

The Second Directive (1976) lays down harmonized standards for the formation and maintenance of the capital of public companies with a view to protecting the interests of shareholders and creditors.

The Fourth Directive (1978) harmonizes contents, layout, and valuation methods used in annual accounts of all public and private limited companies. SMEs can draw up abridged accounts and be exempted from certain requirements such as mandatory audits.

The Fifth Directive (on which no decision has yet been taken in spite of several redrafts by the Commission) deals with the structure and management of public and private limited companies, provides for a mandatory system of employee participation and the introduction of a dual management and supervisory board system. The rules are less rigorous for firms with under 1000 staff.

The Seventh Directive (1983) lays down when and how consolidated accounts should be prepared and published. It complements the Fourth Directive which deals with the accounts of individual companies.

The Eleventh Directive This Directive was finally adopted in December 1989. It relates to conditions for setting up branches of limited liability companies in another Member State, regulating the types of disclosure required.

Box 54: Progress on Harmonization of EC Company Law

Directives Already Adopted		Proposed Directives
First -	14. 03. 68	Fifth
Second -	30. 01. 77	Ninth
Third -	20. 10. 78	Tenth
Fourth -	14. 08. 78	Twelfth
Sixth -	31. 12. 82	Thirteenth
Seventh -	18. 07. 83	
Eighth -	12. 05. 84	

Eleventh - a 'common position' was reached by the Council on 16 May 1989 (adopted December 1989).

Source: Directory of Commission Legislation in Force, 13th Edition, 1 June 1989.

With regard to the Fifth Directive, it is difficult to predict its exact timetable. The philosophy behind it, as with the 'Vredeling' directive (see Chapter 16), is the need for workers to be consulted and provided with information across national boundaries so that they can be in a position to assess the implications for their work of cross-frontier activities such as mergers or takeovers. The debate on the proposed Vredeling Directive has been at times stormy, with fundamental differences of opinion emerging between employer and employee representatives as well as between different governments. Some Member States are opposed to the introduction of compulsory measures of employee involvement at the European level.

Recently the principle of 'subsidiarity' has been invoked which demands that legislation should only be implemented at Community level if it cannot be drawn up more effectively at national level. Similarly, in the case of activities of firms, 'subsidiarity' has been interpreted to mean that decisions should be taken as near to the workplace as possible. During the early 80s there was considerable debate but, in view of the diametrically opposed views and the need for unanimity to agree the draft Directive, further discussion on the Vredeling draft was discreetly shelved. The Commissioner principally involved at the time, Ivor (now Lord) Richard, maintained throughout that the issue would not go away and in due course the Community would have to decide on the fundamental principles underlying the draft. There is still no agreement about how the debate will be resolved.

The proposed Statute for a European Company (Box 55) has been revived in recent years. There are still considerable reservations on the part of some Member States in spite of the fact that the proposals for worker representation are much more broadly drawn and effectively leave the precise form to national administrations.

Box 55: The Statute for a European Company

Societas Europaea

The European Company (Societas Europaea - SE) is designed to enable companies governed by the laws of different Member States to choose a structure for cooperation and restructuring suited to the dimensions of the Single Market to be achieved by 1992. It aims to free companies from the legal and practical constraints arising from the existence of 12 separate legal systems by offering them an alternative structure based on

Community law and independent of national laws where these have not been harmonized.

In June 1987, seventeen years after the first draft was put forward by the Commission, the European Council requested the institutions concerned 'to make swift progress with regard to the company law adjustments required for the creation of a European company'.

The text now proposed is in two parts:

(1) A Regulation concerning the creation and operation of European companies.

(2) A complementary Directive taking into account the diversity of national rules governing the above.

Finally, in order to make the form attractive to small businesses, the minimum capital requirement has been reduced from Ecu250,000 to Ecu100,000.

European Economic Interest Grouping

Since 1 July 1989, joint undertakings, formerly organized under the title of European Cooperation Groupings, are now regulated by a new instrument, the EEIG (European Economic Interest Grouping) (see Box 56). It is a simple, effective way for companies to collaborate across national frontiers without the legal expense and complication of a full merger. The collaboration can be limited to a specific field, for example R & D, market research, licensing or manufacturing.

The EEIG can best be described as a form of incorporated partnership at Community level. It has legal capacity; its formation depends on a contract drawn up by its members; there is no requirement for any capital. The liability of its members is unlimited.

The European Economic Interest Grouping aims to 'facilitate or develop the economic activities of its members and to improve or increase the results of those activities: its purpose is not to make profits for itself. Its activity shall be related to the economic activities of its members and must not be more than ancillary to those activities.' (Article 3 (1) of the Regulation.)

Adopted on 25 July 1985, the EEIG came into force on 1 July 1989. It is based on the successful experience in France which has had its own laws governing its 'Groupement d'Intérêt Économique' since the 1970s.

Box 56: Setting up an EEIG (European Economic Interest Group)

(1) An EEIG must have an address within the EC. Provision is made for the EEIG to transfer its address within a Member State and to change its registration to another Member State.

(2) The contract will give details of the EEIG's objectives and relations between its members, including shares of costs and revenue.

(3) There is no capital requirement .

(4) An EEIG may exist for the length of time its contract states.

(5) It is an entirely flexible means of cooperation aimed at maximizing the advantages of a wider market. Once the contract has been signed, the EEIG exists in a legal capacity as if it had a 'corporate personality'.

The most striking example of this sort of cooperation between European businesses is that of Airbus Industrie which has operated as a French GIE for the last 19 years. It could not become an EEIG since it employs over 500 people (for details of restrictions, see the Commission Background Report on EEIG - 22 May 1989 ISEC/B16/89). The GIE format enabled the aircraft industry to mount an effective challenge to the dominant global position of the American aircraft industry. EEIGs are now being set up across the Community in both the manufacturing and services sectors. Lawyers, architects and other professional groupings are using the EEIG as a vehicle for cross border collaboration.

Tax Directives

Tax Directives complement the Company Law Directives in the drive to harmonize national company law. A number of these Directives have already been adopted.

They deal with such matters as procedures for eliminating double taxation of associated firms, mergers, parent/subsidiary relationships and control of indirect taxes on raising capital. If you require information on Directives you can find it in the sources mentioned in Section V. Chapter 18 discusses taxation.

Other areas of harmonization of national laws with which the Commission is concerned, especially regarding public limited companies are:

1. duties and liabilities of directors
2. powers of general meetings
3. rights of shareholders
4. approval of annual accounts
5. functions and liability of auditors.

There is a wide ranging series of discussion papers, proposals from the Commission to the Council and draft directives at different stages of progress through the Community legislation and consultative process which will be relevant to your business.

Senior management needs to be aware of the Community decision-making process and should visit or invite Commission officials to meet with them, either through trade associations or directly with senior managers drawn from a spread of functions. The use of consultants needs to be considered especially if your interests relate to specific activities in the EC and may have legal implications.

13. Industrial and Sectoral Policies

Industrial Policy

The need for a Community industrial policy was not foreseen in the Treaty of Rome, although a number of attempts have been made to draw one up over the years. What the Community does have is a market philosophy based on the freedom of movement of goods and services, people and capital. The intention is to create conditions for an open industrial society where there is fair competition between firms within the Community. It is recognized that in some areas there will be need for coordinated Member State or Community support for high technologies, particularly at the pre-development stage. This has led to a series of European Community programmes such as BRITE and ESPRIT (see Box 61). Limited State or Community support for industries in crisis will also be required to rationalize and modernize them and to ensure that the workers affected by the restructuring are not disadvantaged, compensated for any loss of employment and trained where necessary for new employment.

Industrial tariffs were finally abolished in July 1977, since when goods have in theory been able to move freely from one country to another. There was a view at that time that once tariffs were abolished the Common Market would be in place. Only slowly did the Community recognize that non-tariff barriers were the real problem to the freedom of movement of goods. Preference for 'national Champions' and restrictive practices of different kinds prevented the opening of markets across national frontiers. The 1992 programme will redress this.

The specific problems of the world economic recession affecting individual Member States during the late seventies and early eighties slowed the impetus for the liberalization of European trade. It was not until the White Paper of 1986 was agreed and the Single European Act (SEA) signed in 1987 that the European Community set out on a path of wide-ranging reforms which would have a fundamental impact on the business sector (see Chapters 6 and 7). One of the primary objectives of the SEA is to create a Single European market in order to improve the competitiveness of European enterprises within and outside the Community. European business should benefit from a larger home market, economies of scale and the opportunity to specialize in areas of comparative advantage.

All firms, both large and small, will be affected by the three hundred measures set out in the White Paper. The European Commission is taking a number of initiatives to speed the process, including: the provision of relevant information about economic and national policies, regulations, markets and opportunities; the simplification of the legal and administrative environment; strengthening the commercial and financial framework for business; facilitating and funding cooperative projects; R & D; improved training and management schemes and the promotion of economic and social cohesion.

Industry, Competition and Pragmatism

Community industrial policy seeks to create an integrated economic base through a pragmatic process of adaptation to changing conditions and steady progress sometimes in one area of economic activity, sometimes in another, reinforced where necessary by Community legislation.

Industrial policy is particularly linked with competition policy which aims to create competitive conditions for Community industry by removing any arrangements which distort the free competitive market. Sectoral policies for industries in crisis have been developed but the intention is always to ensure that such industries ultimately stand on their own feet. State or Community subsidies are seen essentially as a transitional measure.

Businessmen will need to understand other aspects of the Community's work which affect industry and commerce. For example, the harmonization of Community company law (Chapter 12), the encouragement of mergers and pan-European activity through the European Company Statute and the activities of the Directorate-General responsible for Small and Medium-sized Industries (see below).

Small and Medium-sized Enterprises (SMEs)

The willingness of companies to adapt their strategy and organization to the larger market has increased dramatically in recent years thanks to the emphasis on the completion of the Single Market. A specific Community strategy towards SMEs was developed as a response to the difficulties faced by the European economies in providing full employment. Because of their potential for growth, SMEs can make an important contribution to job creation.

Box 57: New European Information Centres for Small and Medium-sized Enterprises

The Euro-Info Centre Project was launched as a Pilot Project two years ago by the Commission's Task Force for Small and Medium-sized Enterprises (SMEs), which became a Directorate-General early in 1989. Thirty-nine centres were opened in the Twelve Member States, including one in Scotland and three in England. The extension of the project follows the positive assessment of the pilot phase carried out by the Commission and Member States in autumn 1988. A new round of contracts was awarded following a public tender. The project now covers comprehensively the whole of the European Community. The new Centres were chosen by the Commission after consultation with the Member States. They are provided with all the same logistical support already granted to the first phase Centres. The Commission will also train staff, provide access to Brussels data bases and supply Commission documentation. A diminishing Commission grant is envisaged for subsequent years, and the intention is that Centres will become self-financing. The Centre organizers will provide the premises and staff for the Centres. The Euro-Info Centres provide a wide range of information and advisory services for small businesses and should be a first point of contact for SMEs looking to develop their EC business. See Section V for contact addresses.

Community Policy Towards SMEs

A specific strategy towards SMEs was developed as a response to the difficulties faced by the European economies in providing full employment.

The importance of promoting SMEs was illustrated by the designation of 1983 as the European Year for Small and Medium-sized Enterprises and Craft Industries and the setting up of an independent SME Task Force in June 1986. The Task Force grew with the increasing demand from European SMEs to participate in the creation of the Single Market. A 23rd Directorate-General was created to take over responsibility for dealing with the SME sector in Europe with the following objectives:

- to coordinate all relevant activities within the Commission (eg legal, easing of regulatory constraints, financing, services and analysis)
- to promote the approximation of national and Community policies
- to set up a system of liaison with organizations representing SMEs
- to help with the setting up at Community level of machinery for solving SMEs' practical problems and especially developing a communication and training strategy for SMEs to fulfil information needs and have well qualified staff.

General information or specific questions on Community SME policy should be referred to DG XXIII, Rue de la Loi 200, 1049 Brussels or to the Euro-Info Centres across the Community (Section V).

Industries in Decline

Helping companies and industries adapt to changing conditions is part of Community industrial policy. The economic recession of the 1970s placed increasing emphasis on supporting the 'crisis' industries such as steel, textiles, shipbuilding and footwear, while growing competition from developing countries has encouraged these industries to seek help from the Community and for Member States to provide Community funding.

The Commission's regulatory powers, as regards trade arrangements with countries outside the Community, can be advantageous to declining industries since they help protect them temporarily and enable them to restructure to face fierce international competition. This is a complex area as the Community is also committed to support continued free trade through the General Agreement on Trade and Tariffs (GATT) and the Organization for Economic Cooperation and Development (OECD).

Some Commission initiatives to improve recent crises in certain industries are:

Textiles

The basic objectives of the Multi-Fibre Agreement (MFA) are the expansion of trade, particularly for developing countries, the reduction of barriers to such trade and the progressive liberalization of world trade in textile production. At the same time it seeks to ensure the orderly and equitable development of this trade and to avoid disruptive effects in individual lines of production in both importing and exporting countries.

On 31 July 1986, after several months of intensive work, the General Agreement on Trade and Tariffs (GATT) negotiations on the renewal of the MFA (originally drawn up for a four year period between 1974 and 1977) for a further 5 years to July 1991, were concluded (see Box 58).

The renewal has helped European industry continue its large-scale restructuring and assisted developing countries in the expansion of their trade with the Community in textiles and clothing products.

The MFA does not jeopardize the management of Community bilateral agreements with other countries; moreover, the Community can continue its established practice of differentiating between certain non-Community countries with dominant trading positions by means of the growth and flexibility rates it applies.

Failure to respect intellectual property rights is for the first time recognized under the agreement, and compensation in case of evasion and fraud have been stepped up. The Community also secured acceptance of its proposal for special treatment to help the least developed countries.

Box 58: Current Negotiations in GATT on the Multi-Fibre Agreement

Trade within the textile sector may be considered a test case for the smooth functioning of the current Uruguay series of GATT negotiations for two reasons.

1. Textiles are the only industrial sector in which most countries participating in the GATT talks, including less developed countries, possess a considerable export potential and can participate in world trade.

2. They are the only sector where all participants in world trade may prove that there is potential for free competition in international markets.

Negotiations underway on textiles in the Uruguay Round have proved laborious. However, during the round of talks in June 1990, proposals were put forward by the EC for the progressive liberalization of the MFA (Multi-Fibre Agreement). The proposals aim to reduce the existing restrictions. The EC hopes to negotiate a list of products which might be integrated immediately into GATT without the need for a transitional regime. In other areas, a transitory period is foreseen in order to soften the blow of the initial removal of trade restrictions and access to markets. The proposals put forward by the EC during the GATT talks confirm its firm political will to push forward a collective and credible liberalization of world commerce in textiles.

October 1990

Footwear

The Community footwear industry provides about one-quarter of total world production of nearly 5 billion pairs of shoes. In 1986, Community production was estimated at Ecu15bn compared to the 1982 figure of Ecu13bn. Between 1982 and 1987 the number of pairs produced fell by 1.6% a year, partly due to strong pressure from imports. Wide variations in production exist between Member States. Italy is by far the largest producer, and together with Spain and Portugal, accounts for nearly 75% of total Community production.

In 1987, the top four exporters were China, Taiwan, South Korea and Hong Kong supplying nearly three-quarters of total extra-Community imports. Intra-Community production in 1982 satisfied 72% of the Community market, but had fallen to only 55% by 1987.

During the 1982-86 period the number of jobs in the European industry fell by nearly 3% a year and continued to fall in 1987. Investment in the industry is very unevenly distributed between Member States, most occurring in Italy, France and Germany (three of the richer Member States).

The outlook for 1990-91 is for similar trends with weak growth in the Community market being met by imports - partially explained by stagnant population trends and especially by changing consumption patterns.

Faced with growing competition from South East Asia, the Community industry is specializing in upmarket and fashion product ranges, developing brand policies and playing a larger role in distribution. The Community encourages all forms of R & D investment to improve competition by the application of new technologies to the industry.

Shipbuilding

1988 witnessed a sharp decline in the Community's merchant shipbuilding production from a peak year in 1976 of nearly 6m CGRT (Compensated Gross Registered Tonnage) to over 1.5m CGRT in 1987. This corresponds to a drop in Community share of world production from 27% to 19%. The main reasons for decline were continuing over-capacity in available transportation volumes in a globally declining market and growing international competition especially from Japan and Korea.

'RENAVAL' (Box 59) is a Community programme aimed at assisting the restructuring of areas badly affected by difficulties in the steel and shipbuilding industry. Adopted in July 1988 and with a total budget of Ecu200m, it pursues the same aim as that of 'RESIDER' (Box 60) in regions experiencing serious unemployment as a result of the crisis in the shipbuilding industry.

However, the decline in shipbuilding activity of recent years is expected to end in 1988-89 after which production should remain at 8-9m CGRT and increase in the 1995-2000 period to 17m CGRT annually.

Box 59: RENAVAL

The aim of RENAVAL is to renew the industrial fabric of the regions of the European Community hardest hit by the shipbuilding crisis and give workers from the industry a new start by finding alternative jobs - these are the twin pillars of the redeployment strategy which the Commission has proposed to the governments of the Twelve.

Over Ecu350m is to be channelled into the programme between 1987 and 1990. The Commission regards these urgently needed measures as the forerunners of a broader-based strategy in the years up to 1992. It is hoped to control, substantially reduce and make more effective use of State aid to shipyards, with the ultimate objective of concentrating on building technologically advanced vessels which the Commission sees as the only hope of maintaining a reasonable level of employment in the shipbuilding and allied industries.

Steel

With a gross steel output of 140 million tonnes in 1989, the European steel industry accounted for about 17% of world output compared to 13% for Japan and 11% for the US. But the steel industry has suffered serious set-backs in all industrialized countries since 1974 owing to reduced demand from steel based industries - hence considerable over-capacity and subsequent uncompetitiveness. Member States had to undertake restructuring operations which reduced production capacity by 18% between 1980 and 1986 while at the same time launching major productivity boosting programmes. A recent 4% increase in steel consumption between 1987 and 1988 shows restructuring policies have had some success.

In 1985 the Commission published a set of general objectives for the period to 1990 for domestic and foreign demand. The estimates were optimistic. Community companies have so far managed to develop production to remain competitive on the international market, although in a number of cases Community exports have come up against protectionist or restrictive measures especially from the United States.

Since 1982, Community steel products have had only limited access to the US market while a number of other countries have not been subject to such limitations. Community exports to the US have fallen substantially and the Community's share of the US market has been considerably reduced since 1982. In July 1989, the Commission agreed to examine the US proposals to extend the voluntary restraint arrangements in the steel sector until March 1992 with a view to defining the Community response. The US proposals include negotiations through the GATT Uruguay Round and bilaterally if necessary, to remove current trade distorting practices. Finally, in October 1989, the Commission approved the result of negotiations held with the US authorities regarding the liberalization of the steel trade. The Commission concluded that attempts to reduce government intervention in the steel industry, the assurance by the US of better Community access to their steel market - 7% as opposed to 6.68%, an increase of approximately 300,000 tonnes - and the agreement by both sides to work together to achieve a greater liberalization of the steel trade, represented a significant step forward. The Commission has since requested Council agreement to go ahead with negotiations.

Within the Community the restructuring effort will be pursued and will involve further reductions in capacity with serious consequences for the industry's workforce. Job cuts are a social and political as much as an economic concern, so that restructuring implies more than just reduced capacity. Funds for reconversion and retraining and encouragement for SMEs starting up in the steel sector are therefore necessary to take the burden off unproductive and unwieldy heavy industry.

Box 60: RESIDER

This programme is concerned with the regional aspects of the declining steel industry. It was adopted in February 1988 in order to assist the conversion of the steel area hit by reduced demand, The programme was set up with a total budget of Ecu300m aimed at backing up the restructuring of the steel industry. ERDF (see Chapter 19) assistance available under the programme aims to promote the creation of new activities and the development of small and medium-sized firms in regions where employment is heavily dependent on the steel industry and where, as a result, restructuring of the industry gives rise to particular difficulties.

Acting on a proposal from the Commissioner for Regional Policy, Bruce Millan, in April 1989, the Commission decided to include more employment areas in the list of regions eligible for assistance under the RESIDER and RENAVAL programmes. In the case of RESIDER the new areas involved are Asturias in Spain and the towns of Braunschewieg and Salzgitter in Germany.

Growth Industries

We have seen how the Community helps industries in decline but its main role is essentially a dynamic one of encouragement and sometimes direct involvement in new and emerging industries.

Information Technology (IT)

IT is the collective term for the office machinery, data processing and telecommunication industries, since these sectors have increasingly come to overlap in recent years.

The advances that can be achieved through deregulation and the setting of European if not international standards are significant in terms of growth prospects and international competitiveness. The IT industry will be further improved by the merging of office data and communications technology hardware. Annual growth in the Community software market should be consistently in double figures well into the 21st century.

The Community IT industry has gone through a period of rapid development. However, since production does not match demand, the share of imports on the market as well as the Community foreign trade deficit have grown enormously in the 1980s. Nevertheless, despite increasing competition, especially from Asian manufacturers, the Community industry has become more competitive and high growth rates can be anticipated in the coming years.

Telecommunications and Innovation Policies

Faced with the two-fold challenge of new technology and deregulation, the Community telecommunications industry has had to modify its structures and organization. The prospect of the completion of the Internal Market and a Community policy framework encourage the vigorous formation of alliances.

The Community telecommunications industry currently represents 31% of world production behind the US (33%) and ahead of Japan (17%). The Community will undergo two major changes as the result of deregulation and the completion of the Internal Market. Intra-Community trade will develop strongly and reach an annual growth in excess of 15% - the private market (professional and residential) not covered by 'Post Telegraph and Telecommunications' (PTTs) will constitute an important, but highly competitive, opportunity for European suppliers.

A number of IT and telecommunications programmes are being developed, essentially aimed at strengthening the Community's technological capacity through R & TD programmes (Box 61)

These involve cross-frontier cooperation between universities and industry.

Research and Development Projects

Although provisions for research programmes existed in the Euratom and ECSC Treaties, it was not a stated objective of the Treaty of Rome establishing the EEC. The Single European Act, signed in February 1986, finally closed this research policy 'loophole' by providing for a new sector 'Research and Technological Development' (R & TD) which sets out the objectives and details the implementation of research and technological development at the Community level. Today there is a large and increasing number of research programmes aimed at the technological development of European industries.

A common Community research policy avoids duplication of effort, allows savings to be made and enables the great but scattered resources of scientific and technical potential existing in Member States to be tapped. It is an efficient way of allocating scarce but vital funds to research projects to the benefit of all Member States.

Box 61: Research and Technological Development Projects

In the IT and Telecommunications sector, the ESPRIT (European Strategy Programme for Research and Development in IT) programme was established for pre-competitive research in 1984 after extensive consultations with the academic world and the industries concerned, both large and small firms. It was designed for a 10 year period (1984-1993). The projects must involve industrial partners from at least two Member States and all participants are linked by an electronic information network called Eurokom.

Similarly, the first phase of the RACE programme (Research in Advanced Communications in Europe) was completed in 1987. Its specific aim is to enable the Community to move towards higher technological telecommunications capabilities. Finally, standardization in the telecommunications industry is a vital aspect and a Community policy launched in 1985 is designed to encourage the harmonized application of international standards in the European context.

One of the most important of the programmes for new technology in traditional manufacturing industries is BRITE (Basic Research on Industrial Technology) which enables universities, research centres, and industrial companies to work together across national frontiers, making maximum use of European research capabilities within the industrial sector.

EUREKA is a Europe-wide framework for promoting collaborative projects in fields of advanced technology which was agreed between 18 countries and the European Commission in November 1985. EUREKA, although not strictly a Community policy but a collaboration between European States and business and government sectors, aims to improve competitiveness in world markets in civil applications of new technologies by encouraging industrial and technological collaboration within Europe.

Airbus

The Community aerospace industry has developed its civil aircraft and missile production over the last 10 years through large-scale European programes such as Airbus and Ariane, both resounding technical and commercial successes. Ariane does for European space research what Airbus does for aircraft. European industries have concentrated their efforts on the production of jumbo aircraft such as the Airbus A300 and A310. The launching of Airbus A320 which started delivery in 1988 should enable the European civil aerospace industry to maintain or increase its share of the world civil aviation market. Once the new Airbuses A330 and A340 start delivery in the early 1990s - which should break into the longhaul market - the European industry will cover the whole range of market sectors for commercial jets.

The main European aerospace companies involved in Airbus

production are Aerospatiale (France), MBB and Dornier (Germany), British Aerospace (UK), Casa (Spain), Fokker (Netherlands) and Sonaca (Belgium).

There are encouraging signs for the future, although with a number of production programmes in the military market having recently been completed (namely Tornado, Mirage F1 and 2000, and Harrier) there is likely to be a slack period in military collaborative efforts in the interim before production starts on a new generation of arms systems currently being developed. General prospects for growth are good - between 3 and 5% for 1989-90. However, with 60% of the industry invoicing in dollars, the industry is very vulnerable to fluctuations in US currency.

Conclusion

Preparing for 1992

The sluggish worldwide growth of the last 15 years masks the extent of changes in production structures. The third technical revolution is underway, even in Europe where growth of economic activity has been slower than in other regions. But in spite of significant growth of R & D efforts since the beginning of the decade, there remains a big quantitative gap between the Community on the one hand and the US and Japan on the other. Moreover, R & D efforts are still highly concentrated in three Member States, Germany, France and the UK which account for over 80% of the total. It is therefore important to move away from the 'sheltered' national projects resulting from individual Member States' defence concerns to the 'exposed' scientific culture evident in the US. The new and flexible forms of cooperation between private and public sectors which increasingly characterize the Community economy are an indication that it is moving in the right direction.

14. Customs Union and Common Commercial Policy

'The 1992 Operation means nothing less than putting into effect the four freedoms; the free movement of persons, goods, services and capital within the European Community without exception...The European Single Market will constitute a common area with uniform and equivalent rules where no discrimination will be permitted.'
Commissioner Frans Andriessen, 9 May 1989

Internal Trade

The Customs Union is fundamental to the Common Market. It has two objectives:

- The elimination of customs barriers between Member States

- The regulation of the Community Common External Tariff.

As regards the first of these, the idea of a single market goes back to the foundation of the Community itself. In the early years rapid advances were made, but progress during the 1970s slowed down and ultimately came to a halt. The main reason for this was the recession following the two oil price shocks, which awakened protectionist tendencies in the Member States and discouraged them from seeking further substantial progress towards a single market.

But it became clear that increased protectionism was not the answer to the economic problems facing Europe. In the 1980s, therefore, the Heads of Government turned their minds once more to the unfinished business of the Treaty of Rome. They called with an increasing sense of urgency for the completion of the Internal Market in order to break down the barriers that stood in the way of trade and industry and people operating on a Community-wide basis.

The Commission's White Paper

In June 1985 the Commission published a White Paper setting out a comprehensive and integrated package of some 300 proposals (condensed to 282 since then) aimed at removing completely the various barriers to trade within the Community. The suggestion was that the legislation should be agreed and implemented by Member States by the end of December 1992 *at the latest.*

The Single European Act

The programme for completing the Internal Market was endorsed by the Heads of Government in Milan in June 1985. It was further reinforced by the Single European Act of February 1986, which entered into force in July 1987. The Single Act improves significantly the Community's institutional framework by extending qualified majority voting in the Council of Ministers to some two-thirds of the proposals set out in the White Paper programme.

The Cecchini Report: The Cost of Non Europe

At the same time as the Commission drew up the White Paper which formed the basis of the 1992 Programme, it also commissioned a research programme to study the costs of the fragmentation of the European Community market and to estimate the potential gains of a market in which the freedom of movement of goods and services, people and capital was ensured.

This report is the result of a research programme conducted by Pablo Cecchini, a former Deputy Director General of the Commission, from 1986 to 1988 with a multi-national team of independent consultants (see Section V for details).

Its purpose was to provide a solid body of scientifically-assembled evidence as a means of judging the extent of market fragmentation confronting European business and community policy-makers.

It profiles the European Community home market in the 1990s, the cost of its absence today and gains on offer for the EC enconomy as a whole once costs are transformed into benefits.

The report analyses the costs imposed by frontier red tape, by protectionist public procurement, by conflicting national product standards and business laws and looks at the impact of these on specific sectors. 'Removal of market barriers' according to the authors 'will trigger a supply-shock to the Community as a whole'. With European market integration, costs will come down.

The report estimated that the potential gains for the twelve Member States expressed in 1988 prices were more than Ecu200bn or between 4.3% and 6.4% of Community GDP. It expected that employment would be increased by 1.5% – a net gain of 1.8 million jobs – and forecast that prices were likely to come down by 6%.

The estimated cost savings of implementing the Single Market have in retrospect been conservative, but Member States needed little further convincing of its advantages.

Over Halfway to 1992

A good deal has been achieved since the White Paper was published in June 1985. By 7 April 1990, 1,000 days before the 1992 deadline, all proposals were before the Council having been drafted and agreed by the Commission. By early 1991 over 200 of the 282 proposals presented to the Council had been adopted. The Commission which took office in January 1989 had, by mid-1990, just under two years in which to help drive through the remaining proposals. These figures show that the momentum has not been lost. The Internal Market programme will be completed on time.

The Single Market is very largely about the elimination of non-tariff barriers. They have proved much more difficult to abolish than the internal tariff barriers which have usually been eliminated according to a predetermined schedule and ahead of time. The countries which have recently entered the Community have yet to abolish all their tariffs, but if they follow the example of the earlier enlargements of the Community, these should disappear gradually over the next years with very few temporary exceptions or 'derogations', to use their official title.

The three areas where non-tariff barriers have yet to be eliminated are identified in the White Paper under the three headings of:

- Physical
- Technical
- Fiscal

1. Physical barriers to trade

These are the most tangible, visible barriers which anyone travelling in Europe will have experienced: the immigration controls, the passport checks, the occasional search of personal baggage carried out at frontier customs posts. These barriers not only slow down and inhibit the passage of the travelling citizen but are equally a hindrance to business. They impose an unnecessary burden on industry as a result of delays, formalities, transport and handling charges, thus adding to costs and affecting competitiveness. The objective of the White Paper and commitment by the 12 Member States to completing the Internal Market through the SEA is to do away with internal frontier controls completely.

Progress to date has been encouraging. The acceleration of the decision-making process is in part due to qualified majority decision-making and to the Commission's policy of combining mutual recognition and harmonization which has permitted agreements on technical regulations and especially recent decisions on cabotage, the elimination of veterinary controls, and on controls on means of transport. Important decisions have been made regarding freedom of capital movements and the abolition of road haulage quotas by 1992. However, progress in other areas is still insufficient. In particular, matters requiring the unanimity of the Council are falling behind schedule (about 19% of the Single

Market programme requires unanimity). Further, Member States are taking too long to transpose Community directives into national legislation and progress on eliminating border controls, specifically those concerning customs checks on goods and passport controls on travellers, is slow. It is imperative that these formalities and controls which apply either at the frontier or on intra-Community transactions are completely removed so as to free the crossing of frontiers from all hindrances. Problems also still remain concerning taxation and VAT procedures (Chapter 18).

2. Technical barriers to trade

The elimination of border controls does not by itself create a common market. Technical barriers to trade are those differences in product regulations, standards or compliance procedures which may hinder or even prevent a product which complies with one Member State's health, safety or environmental or other regulations, from being freely traded in another.

Goods and people moving within the Community should not find obstacles within the different Member States just as they should not meet them at the border. This does not mean there should be the same rules everywhere, but that goods as well as citizens should be able to move freely within the Community. The general principle is that if a product is lawfully manufactured and marketed in one Member State, there should be no reason why it should not be sold freely throughout the Community. If goods meet the basic requirements of national health and safety standards, they should not be prevented from circulating by national technical or other standards.

In eliminating technical barriers to trade, two principles then guide the Community:

- Avoidance of new barriers
  and the so-called
- New Approach to Harmonization

Avoidance of New Barriers

Member States have agreed that when introducing new standards, they will first submit them to the Commission which will have six months to attempt to develop a common Community-wide standard. Member States also agree not to introduce legislation which will widen rather than narrow existing differences in norms or rates.

The New Approach

The principle of harmonizing standards across the EC for each product has been replaced by the New Approach. This is based on a European Court of Justice ruling known as the 'Cassis de Dijon' case (see Box 62). The ruling stated that provided a product does not infringe the health or safety standards of the Member State to which it is exported, then it cannot be banned on any other grounds.

Box 62: The Cassis de Dijon Ruling

In 1978 a German company, REWE ZENTRAL AG importing the French liqueur 'Cassis', brought the 'Cassis de Dijon' case to the European Court of Justice against the German Federal Monopoly Administration for Spirits. It was protesting against a decision made by the Monopoly Administration not to allow the import of French Cassis on the grounds that it did not constitute a liqueur by German standards since its wine-spirit content did not reach the 32% minimum limit required. The French and REWE ZENTRAL AG argued that any liqueur considered good enough for the French home market was also good enough for the German consumer. The Court ruled that a product can be sold in any Member State so long as it respects the minimum health and safety requirements of that country.

To speed up the SEA and Single Market process further, it was decided that minimum levels of safety and performance targets, known as the 'essential requirements', would be set. These would be passed on to the European Standards Organizations CEN or CENELEC to draw up the detailed technical specifications. This system has been in force since 1985. The new approach also provides for mutual recognition of national standards.

3. Fiscal barriers to trade

Fiscal barriers constitute both tariff and non-tariff barriers since they can be levied both at customs posts and also within the various Member States. Differences in turnover taxes in particular are the source of serious distortions to trade.

Fiscal checks feature prominently among the functions carried out at the Community's internal frontiers. Consequently, the removal of frontier controls is bound to have inescapable implications for the Member States as far as indirect taxes are concerned.

Box 63: Commission Proposals for Approximation of Indirect Taxes

The latest modifications to the existing proposals in the field of indirect tax approximation of May 1989 are of a pragmatic nature although they do not alter the Commission's basic goal.

- The creation of a transitional phase lasting until the end of 1992 during which the Member States would be expected to make a positive commitment towards the alignment of their indirect taxes.

- Pragmatic solutions to certain problems in the field of VAT: amongst others, a standard minimum rate of VAT and no upper limit and maintenance of the zero-rate for a reduced number of products for those Member States which currently apply this system and wish to retain it, and the introduction of differentiated minimum rates for alcohol and tobacco products.

The Treaty of Rome provides that the Commission should make proposals for the approximation of indirect taxation. The adoption of a harmonized VAT system was given further impetus by the Council Decision in 1970 that the Community should be financed through an 'Own Resources' budget. Despite the integral role played by harmonization of indirect taxation in achieving a true common market, momentum was lost during the 1970s, due essentially to the impact of the recession on the economic policies of Member States. But since the SEA, progress has been resumed.

The Commission's proposed solution involves the abolition of zero-rating for exports to other Member States, and the approximation of VAT rates and excise duties across the Community. The objective is to avoid all distortions in competitive conditions of fiscal origin once the Internal Market is achieved.

There are considerable problems with the harmonization or approximation of indirect taxes, VAT not the least of them. Fiscal issues are dealt with in Chapter 18.

Common Commercial Policy (CCP)

The Common Commercial Policy of the EC is the mechanism adopted by the Member States which allows them to conduct formal commercial and trade relations as a single economic Community. Since 1979, the Community has been responsible for negotiating tariff agreements on behalf of Member States with other countries and the GATT. The completion of the Single Market will undoubtedly strengthen the position of the EC in international trade negotiations and lead to pressure for further liberalization of international trade.

External Trade Relations

Before the Community negotiates with a country, it needs to agree on a common position. This is developed by Member States through the Council of Ministers, on the basis of a Commission proposal. The Commission is then given a mandate to conduct the negotiations on behalf of the Community, but continues to take into account the interests of individual Member States. The work involved in negotiations is considerable and as some agreements are of limited duration or contain clauses for revision, there are regular renegotiations.

The Community has trade and cooperation agreements with over 120 countries. These agreements have been formed for trade, historical and geographical reasons. The agreements cover the EFTA countries, the Mediterranean countries, South American countries and the Asian, Caribbean and Pacific countries which are signatories of the Lomé Convention (Chapter 23). Although the details of these agreements may not be of direct interest to business, it is important to be aware, for strategic planning purposes, of the relationship between the Community and specific countries. If there are strong trade and commercial agreements, combined with a political commitment to develop trade and other relations, there are likely to be good business opportunities and the possibility of Community funds to support specific projects. A number of organizations now exist to help companies gain access to Community funds; some charge a flat fee as a retainer. The more dynamic charge a percentage of any funds which they obtain. Seeking funding from Community sources is a time-consuming task and should be seen in most cases as a bonus to a commercial venture rather than fundamental to it.

'Fortress Europe'

The completion of the Single Market will establish the EC as the largest integrated trading block in the world. The prospect of this has aroused fears in trading partners of a 'fortress Europe', entry into which of competitive goods and services will be restricted. These fears are unfounded. The Community has stressed repeatedly that 1992 will not lead to protectionism nor to any breach of multilateral or bilateral agreements already reached by the EC with third countries. As the largest exporter in the world, accounting for one-fifth of world trade and highly dependent on exports (10% of the EC GNP is represented by exports), the Community has a fundamental stake in the existence of free and open international trade. In the words of former Commissioner Lord Cockfield: 'the 1992 Europe will not be a fortress Europe but a partnership Europe'.

GATT

The Uruguay Round of the multilateral GATT negotiations began with the intention of reducing tariff barriers to trade, strengthening the bases of multilateral trade and redefining the role of the GATT. Unlike previous negotiations, the Uruguay Round negotiations include agricultural products as well as services, trade related investment measures and intellectual property rights. Progress has been made on the overall scale of new tariff reductions, on tropical products and on trade matters of intellectual property rights. However, the issue of agriculture has become the main blockage to progress. While the US has proposed the immediate abolition of subsidies to agriculture, the EC has supported a medium term, more gradual approach to the problem which can be reconciled with the Common Agricultural Policy and is claimed to be a more equitable approach. The issues of intellectual property, investment and services are also key issues in the current negotiations. It is estimated that $160bn a year is lost by intellectual property right owners alone. The tight series of meetings leading to a hoped-for agreement by the end of 1990 seem to be conducted almost permanently on the brink, with coercion and encouragement alternating. The negotiations are complex and difficult to follow, but a successful outcome is of inestimable importance to the development of world trade. In early 1991 talks were still continuing.

The Generalized System of Preferences (GSP)

The Community has always been concerned to introduce more fairness into economic relations with developing countries. It was first, in 1971, to introduce the Generalized System of Preferences which has been agreed at UNCTAD (United Nations Conference for Trade and Development). The GSP is a system of tariff preferences offered by most industrialized countries to less developed countries (LDCs) with the intention of creating a better balance of trade between the rich and poor countries of the world. It functions on the principles of:

(1) Non-reciprocity - The poorer countries do not offer concessions in return.

(2) Unilateralism - Preferences are granted without any negotiations.

(3) Non-discrimination - The preferences are granted to all developing countries.

(4) Generalized Preference - All industrialized countries are expected to grant preferences.

The GSP extended to 128 countries by 1987 and covered a wide spectrum of processed agricultural products, manufactured and semi-manufactured goods. Total tariff exemption is granted in some areas and the tariff reductions in others depend on the degree of sensitivity of the product. Where there is a quota restriction on a sensitive product, the total volume of preferential imports is divided up among all countries which want to export to the Community to give a share to all, not just those countries which make the products at the lowest cost.

The GSP marked a turning point in world trade and the formal recognition of the needs of developing countries. Considerable success has already been attained in the areas of agricultural products, certain industrial products and textiles. However, problems have occurred in terms of benefit distribution among the preferred countries. The more developed countries, such as South Korea and Brazil, have tended to gain more from the GSP than other LDCs. Nevertheless, the GSP remains one of the best means of working towards a more equitable distribution of the world's wealth.

Conclusion

This chapter has explained the framework within which trade flows are regulated both within the EC and in its relations with the rest of the world. The intention is to promote as wide and open a market as possible both internally and in external trade. The avowed intention of the EC is to create conditions for economic and monetary union and this is the subject of the next chapter.

15. Economic and Monetary Union

Introduction

At its meeting in Hanover in June 1988 the European Council recalled that 'in adopting the Single Act, the Member States of the Community confirmed the objective of progressive realization of economic and monetary union'. The Heads of State and Government therefore decided to examine, at the European Council meeting in Madrid in June 1989, the means of achieving this union. To that end they decided to entrust to a Committee of Governors of Central Banks, 'acting in their personal capacity', 'the task of studying and proposing concrete stages leading towards this union'. The Chairman of the Committee was the Commission President, Jacques Delors, acting also in a personal capacity.

The Delors Committee report represents the third attempt by the European Community to forge closer economic and monetary links. The Werner report of the early 1970s, shelved following the first oil shock, called for economic and monetary union (EMU) by 1980. It was also implicit in the creation of the European Monetary System (EMS), established in March 1979, which has shaped the relations of Member States in the economic and monetary field during the last decade.

Discussion of economic and monetary union in Europe involves not only the complete freedom of movement of people, goods, services and capital, but also irrevocably fixed exchange rates between national currencies, and finally, a single currency and a European Central Bank. These activities would lead to a common monetary policy and require a high degree of convergence of economic policies and consistency in a number of other policy areas, particularly in the fiscal field.

The development of competition policy to strengthen market mechanisms, an improved process of resource allocation to boost areas where market forces need to be reinforced, and macroeconomic coordination by governments and binding rules in the budgetary field would be other areas for Community action. The Member States still not part of the Exchange Rate Mechanism (ERM) - see below - would need to join. After the entry of the UK in October 1990, only Portugal and Greece are now outside the system.

Management of such a union would call for a new institutional framework. The Delors report proposes the establishment of a federal form of monetary policy-making through the 'European System of Central Banks' (ESCB), with the full status of an autonomous Community institution. In other words the members of ESCB Council (a sort of Board of Governors) should be independent of national governments and Community authorities. Accountability should be in the form of an annual report submitted to the European Parliament and the European Council.

Steps Towards Economic and Monetary Union

The Committee agreed that the creation of an economic and monetary union should be viewed as a single process. In other words the decision to enter upon the first of three stages should be a decision to embark upon the entire process. For example, it would be a strong expression of commitment if all members of the Community became full members of the European Monetary System in the course of Stage 1 and undertook the obligations to formulate a convergent economic policy within the existing institutions.

However, there should be a clear indication of the timing of the first stage, which should start no later than 1 July 1990 when the Directive for the full liberalization of capital movements came into force.

Stage 1

Stage 1 represents the initiation of the process of creating an economic and monetary union. It aims at a greater convergence of economic performance through the strengthening of economic and monetary policy coordination within the existing institutional framework.

Stage 2

This stage could begin only when revised Treaty obligations came into force. The basic structure of the economic and monetary union would be set up - most importantly the ESCB or 'EUROFED' would be established and would absorb previously existing institutional monetary arrangements.

Stage 3

The final stage would commence with the move to irrevocably locked exchange rates and the attribution to Community institutions of the full monetary and economic consequences. In the course of the final stage, national currencies would be replaced by a single Community currency.

The Committee was of the opinion that the European Currency Unit (Ecu) has the potential to be developed as a common currency. Once the exchange rates were irrevocably fixed, it could be transformed from a basket of currencies into a genuine single currency.

The momentum of the Delors report proposals was maintained during 1988 and 1989 by widespread discussion across the EC at government and central bank level and in academic and business circles. It led to the agreement for an Inter-Governmental Conference (IGC) to be held in Rome in December 1990 with a view to amending the Treaty of Rome to bring about economic and monetary union. Stage 1 came into force in July 1990, stage 2 is proposed for January 1994 and Stage 3 in 1997 at the earliest.

Business throughout the Community is strongly in favour of a single currency. The benefits of further integration of the European economy, which has been growing at a high (three to three and a half per cent a year) and steady pace, are clear. Most countries of the Community wish to accelerate the pace of European economic and monetary integration. A minority have reservations about the economic effects. There are also political reservations about the transfer of decision-making to an autonomous central bank, expressed by the United Kingdom. Events seem to be gathering a momentum of their own and while the outcome at the time of writing is uncertain and the downturn in the world economy and the Gulf war have made it even more so, the trend is towards further monetary union in the European

Community.

Alternative approaches to EMU include discussion of a Common, or 13th, Currency to be available in parallel with existing currencies in Stage 2, known as the 'hard Ecu'. This suggestion by the UK government could lead at a later stage to a Single Currency. Member States are discussing differences over the timing of Stage 3, whether the Central Bank will be independent of Member States and when and how a proposed Common Currency would be replaced by a Single Currency. The EMU Inter-Governmental Conference which began in December 1990 is set to resolve these issues during 1991.

The European Monetary System

The EMS was created on 13 March 1979 with three objectives, namely to attain a zone of internal and external monetary stability (with both low inflation and stable exchange rates), to improve economic policy coordination (and so increase economic convergence and boost growth and employment) and to provide a pole of stability in world currency markets. It was a more pragmatic attempt to advance monetary integration than the 1970s 'Snake' which collapsed because it was too rigid. The role of the EMS in the further development of the Community was formalized in the Single European Act in 1985.

After ten years of existence, the EMS has been successful in promoting lower inflation and more stable exchange rates. It has proved flexible against a background of a changing monetary and financial environment and yet strict enough to maintain effective monetary constraint and bring about a general convergence of economic policies and performances amongst its members.

Britain's decision in autumn 1990 to complete its membership of the European Monetary System (EMS) by joining the Exchange Rate Mechanism (ERM) should prove to be of concrete and lasting benefit to British business and industry by making a climate of stable exchange rates in which receipts for goods exported to the Community can be planned in sterling terms. This will be particularly important for smaller businesses which do not have access to expensive techniques for financial hedging and selling foreign currency which are available to big businesses.

In the past, a 15% movement of exchange rates has been known in a year or less and this can make the difference between a profit and an unsustainable loss. It is interesting to note in this context that intra-Community trade over the past 15 years has grown twice as rapidly as trade with the rest of the world.

The developing internal market is a major explanation for this, but so too is the zone of monetary stability which the EMS system provides. The UK operates with a 6% margin of fluctuation. However, the Government has said that when circumstances are right, it will join most other countries which operate within a 2.25% margin.

Box 64: The European Currency Unit

The Ecu is a basket of fixed amounts of the currencies of each of the Member States. These amounts, which may be revised, are not, of course, identical for all currencies, but have been chosen in such a way as to reflect the relative economic importance of each Member State within the Community. On 19 June 1989, the Commission announced the inclusion of the Spanish peseta and the Portuguese escudo in the composition of the European Currency Unit (Ecu). Use of the Ecu as a private unit of accounting has greatly increased for settling international transactions.

Independent of the official use made by the central banks in the context of the EMS, the Ecu gradually developed a 'private' market. Indeed, today the Ecu has become a major currency unit, in 1985 ranking 5th after the dollar, deutschmark, Swiss franc and the yen in terms of bond issues and banking transactions on the international market. The use of the Ecu by private individuals shows that together with banks and business, they could play an active role in promoting what could become a single European currency in a few years time.

The Ecu (European Currency Unit) is central to the EMS and is becoming a currency in its own right. The official use of the Ecu as a reserve currency has been disappointing, although the private sector has made extensive use of the Ecu because of its stability. There is currently an upsurge in the use of the Ecu and a growing number of companies are now invoicing and carrying out their internal cross-frontier accounting in Ecu.

If you are involved in doing business in Europe, the progress towards economic and monetary union is of importance as perhaps the clearest indication of the pace of European integration. The other indication is the rate of growth of the EC economy. Forecasts to the end of the century show that economic growth is likely to turn out even more favourably than the estimates of the Cecchini Report (see Chapter 14). Certainly the pace of EMU has changed during the last two years and the prospects for a single European currency and an independent European central bank are good. You will need to track carefully the development of the Inter-Governmental Conference on the EMU which began in December 1990 and the implications of its decisions for Stages 2 and 3 of Economic and Monetary Union.

16. The Social Dimension and the Social Charter

The Social Dimension and 1992

Social policy is concerned with people and their welfare both at work and in the home. It seeks to ensure that all sectors of society are supported including the young, the old, the handicapped and the unemployed. The Commission has a Directorate-General for Employment, Social Affairs and Education, and Box 65 shows its activities. Social Affairs covers specifically the freedom of movement of people, employment, living and working conditions, involvement of the social partners, health, social security, housing, and the environment.

The objectives of Community social policy are:

(1) Full and better employment throughout the Community.

(2) The improvement of living and working conditions.

(3) The involvement of both sides of industry in economic and social policy decisions.

The Treaty of Rome says so little about social policy that nearly all developments have depended on the political will of the Member States. Some progress was made under the Commission's Social Action Programme of 1974, but it had slowed significantly by 1976 as Community activities came under pressure from world recession.

It was not until the Single European Act (SEA) was signed in 1987 and the guidelines laid down at the European Council by the Twelve Member States in June 1988 in Madrid that the Social Dimension of the Community gained impetus. It was agreed that the social aspects of the implementation of the 1992 programme were equally as important as the economic aspects.

The Commission, under the Social Dimension of the SEA, aims to ensure:

(1) Freedom of movement of people from one Member State to another and the freedom of establishment (that is, the right to live and work in another State).

(2) Measures designed to help long-term and youth unemployment with special support for vocational training.

(3) Provision of development and adjustment funds for less developed regions of the Community and for those suffering from industrial decline.

(4) Health and safety protection of workers in the work place.

(5) Mutual recognition of diplomas and occupational qualifications.

(6) European standards for the protection of workers.

The Commission, on behalf of the Member States, is committed to the implementation of these programmes. It encourages the development of a dialogue between the two sides of industry at the European level; it is working on the proposal for a European Company Statute (see Box 55) and a European Charter of Social Rights was agreed in December 1989.

Box 65: Directorate General V of the Commission

EMPLOYMENT, INDUSTRIAL RELATIONS AND SOCIAL AFFAIRS

Directorate A
Employment

(1) Employment and labour market policy.

(2) Social aspects of industrial policies, new technologies and industrial relations.

(3) ECSC readaptation and social aspects of iron and steel policies.

(4) Action on employment and equality for women.

Directorate B
Living and Working Conditions and Welfare

(1) Social Security and social action programmes.

(2) Freedom of movement, migration policy, and social security for migrant workers.

(3) Measures for the disabled.

Directorate C
European Social Fund

(1) Coordination, planning and administration.

(2) Member States I : France, Luxembourg and Portugal.

(3) Member States II: Denmark, Ireland and UK.

(4) Member States III: Germany, Greece and Spain.

(5) Member States IV: Belgium, Italy, Netherlands.

Directorate D
Public Health

(1) Industrial, medicine and hygiene.

(2) Toxicology and safety in work.

(3) Mines and extractive industries.

(4) Finance and administration.

Directorate E
Health and Safety

(1) Medicine and safety at work.

(2) Radioactive effluents and nuclear safety.

(3) Public health and radiology protection.

(4) Security of work.

TASK FORCE FOR HUMAN RESOURCES, EDUCATION, TRAINING AND YOUTH (now separate from DGV)

Educational cooperation, ERASMUS and youth activities including relations with the Youth Forum.

COMETT programme, and university-industry cooperation in advanced training.

Education and training for technological change.

Training and continuing training, and vocational qualifications.

Strategic planning, evaluation and links with other Community policies.

The Community Charter of Fundamental Social Rights

Following the European Council meetings at Hanover and Rhodes, it was agreed in Madrid in June 1989 that in the context of the Single European Market the same importance should be attached to social as to economic aspects, and that they should be developed in a balanced manner. This led to the Social Charter, a declaration of intent, setting out the main areas to be covered by Community legislation.

Social Action Programme

The Social Charter was agreed by all Member States with the abstention of the United Kingdom at the Strasbourg meeting of the European Council in December 1989. It is important for two reasons. In the first place it lays down a reference framework for action in the social field and from it the social action programme stemmed (see below). Secondly, it underlines the principle of subsidiarity in legislation which has become an important approach to EC law-making (see page 218). The principle of subsidiarity is that legislation is enacted at the lowest possible level within the Community. As an example, the representation of the workforce in a company does not necessarily have to take the

Box 66: The Social Charter Objectives - Summary

(1) The right to freedom of movement within the Community: for example, equal treatment, free choice of occupation, no discrimination on grounds of nationality, social protection, freedom to subcontract services.

(2) Employment and remuneration: measures concerning the basic wage, contracts, access to public placement services free of charge.

(3) Right to freedom of association and collective bargaining - any employer/worker may join any professional organization or association/union of his/her choice and be able to conclude collective agreements freely and legally. The right to strike (with a small number of exceptions).

(4) Rights of men and women to equal treatment.

(5) Right of workers to information, consultation and participation.

(6) Protection of children and adolescents - maximum working hours for a child under 18 is limited to 40 hours per week.

same form across the EC although it should be equally effective. Whether there are works councils, worker representatives on the boards of companies or other forms of consultation, these will depend on national or even regional practice. What is important is to ensure that such representation exists. The EC might will the ends, but the means are up to national and local laws, custom and practice. Member States differ in their attitude to social legislation not so much on the ends as on the means.

In November 1989, the Commission drew up its social action programme intended to implement the general principles contained in the Social Charter which was subsequently adopted in Strasbourg in December 1989. The action programme relates to the concrete implementation of the rights defined in the Charter. It contains 47 new initiatives, relating principally to the social security of migrant workers; freedom of movement; employment and working conditions; vocational training and the improvement of the working environment (Box 67).

Member States are committed to mobilizing all necessary resources to guarantee the fundamental social rights of the Charter and the full implementation of social measures indispensable to the effective operation of an internal market, either through legislation or through collective agreements between both sides of industry at national, regional, sectoral or company level. The draft directives to implement the Programme will be presented by the Commission to the Council of Ministers during 1991 and 1992.

Box 67: Table of Initiatives Proposed in the Social Action Programme

Labour Market

* 'Employment in Europe' report
* 'Observatory' and documentation system on employment
* Action programmes on employment creation for specific target groups
* Revision of Part II of Regulation 1612/68 on the

clearance of vacancies and applications for employment and the related procedural decisions (SEDOC)
* Monitoring and evaluation of the activities of the European Social Fund

Employment and Remuneration

* Opinion on the introduction of an equitable wage by the Member States
* Directive on contracts and employment relationships other than full-time open-ended contracts

Improvement of Living and Working Conditions

* Directive for the adaptation of working time
* Council Directive on the introduction of a form to serve as proof of an employment contract or relationship
* Revision of the Council Directive of 17 February 1975 (75/129/EEC) on the approximation of the laws of the Member States pertaining to collective redundancies
* Memorandum on the social integration of migrants from non-member countries

Freedom of Movement

* Revision of Commission Regulation (EC) No 1251/70 of 29 June 1970 on the right of workers to remain on the territory of a Member State after having been employed in that State
* Proposal for a Regulation extending Council Regulations (EC) No 1408/71 on the application of social security schemes to employed persons, to self-employed persons and to members of their families moving within the Community and Council Regulation (EC) No 574/72 (laying down the procedure for implementing Regulation No

1408/71) to all insured persons

* Proposal for a Community instrument on working conditions applicable to workers from another State performing work in the host country in the framework of the freedom to provide services, especially on behalf of a subcontracting undertaking
* Proposal for a Community instrument on the introduction of a labour clause into public contracts
* Communication on supplementary social security schemes
* Communication from the Commission to the Council on the living and working conditions of Community citizens residing in frontier regions and of frontier workers in particular

Social Protection

* Recommendation on social protection: convergence of objectives
* Recommendation on common criteria concerning sufficient resources and social assistance in the social protection systems

Freedom of Association and Collective Bargaining

* Communication on the role of the social partners in collective bargaining

Information, Consultation and Participation

* Community instrument on the procedures for the information, consultation and participation of the workers of European-scale undertakings
* Community instrument on equity-sharing and financial participation

Equal Treatment for Men and Women

* Third Community programme on equal

opportunities for women
* Directive on the protection of pregnant women at work
* Recommendation concerning child care
* Recommendation concerning a code of good conduct on the protection of pregnancy and maternity

Vocational Training

* Proposal for a Community instrument on access to vocational training
* Updating of the 1963 proposal for a Council Decision on the general principles for implementing a common vocational training policy
* Communication on the rationalization and coordination of Community action programmes in the field of initial and continuing vocational training
* Proposal concerning the joint programme for the exchange of young workers and youth exchanges
* Comparability of qualifications

Health Protection and Safety at the Workplace

* Proposal for a Council Directive on the minimum health and safety requirements to encourage improved medical assistance on board vessels
* Proposal for a Council Directive on the minimum health and safety requirements for work at temporary or mobile work sites
* Proposal for a Council Directive on the minimum requirements to be applied in improving the safety and health of workers in the drilling industries
* Proposal for a Council Directive on the minimum requirements to be applied in improving the safety and health of workers in the quarrying and open-cast mining industries
* Proposal for a Council Directive on the minimum safety and health requirements for fishing vessels
* Recommendation to the Member States on the adoption of a European schedule of industrial

diseases

* Proposal for a Council Directive on the minimum requirements for safety and health signs at the workplace
* Proposal for a Council Directive defining a system of specific information for workers exposed to certain dangerous industrial agents
* Proposal for a Council Directive on the minimum safety and health requirements regarding the exposure of workers to the risks caused by physical agents
* Proposal for a Council Directive amending Directive 83/447/EC on the protection of workers from the risks related to exposure to asbestos at work
* Proposal for a Council Directive on the minimum safety and health requirements for activities in the transport sector
* Proposal for the establishment of a safety, hygiene and health agency

Protection for Children and Adolescents

* Council Directive on the approximation of the laws of the Member States on the protection of young people

The Elderly

* Community initiative for the elderly (communication and proposal for a Decision)

The Disabled

* Proposal for a Council Decision establishing a third Community action programme for disabled people (HELIOS) for the period 1992-96
* Proposal for a Council Directive on the introduction of measures aimed at promoting an improvement in the travel conditions of workers with motor disabilities

People's Europe

Whereas the Social Dimension of the Internal Market aims at securing better working conditions for Europe's workforce, the concept of a People's or Citizens' Europe aims to give people a firmer sense of European identity through measures such as the introduction of the European passport, driving licence, flag, anthem and the reduction in border controls. It recognizes that the European Community will not progress unless it is a process desired and encouraged by all its citizens.

It was in June 1984 that the Fontainbleau European Council decided to give the European Community a new dimension to bring it closer to its citizens. The Addonino Committee was instructed to draw up two reports to identify measures which would bond the inhabitants of the Community more closely. The two reports were finally agreed in 1985 at the Brussels and Milan European Summit meetings and a number of practical measures were proposed including:

1. The right to live and work unhindered and for an extended period of time in the country of one's choice - formalities should be minimized.

2. The right to travel and shop unhindered; greater cooperation within the Community on immigration formalities for nationals of non-member countries, on the battle against drugs and crime, on the recognition of Community-wide or various national standards for products and the approximation of VAT.

3. General recognition as a citizen of Europe. For example, the right to take part in European elections on equal terms. For inhabitants of frontier regions (some 48 million citizens) the right to be consulted if a neighbouring country is to take measures affecting them, for example major public works, transport, ecology. The right for the holder of a European passport to seek help from the embassy of another Member State.

4. Working together to help the Third World.

5. Young people, the first citizens of Europe: exchange programmes, language learning, European themes to be taught in class, vocational training.

6. Europe - a daily experience. A number of proposals are under consideration including: health protection, sport, town twinning, broadcasting, European lottery to help finance Community cultural activities, promotion of the Community flag, emblem and anthem.

In short, People's Europe is designed to affect the daily concerns of the citizens of Europe in such a way as to bring them closer together and to unite them in the common purpose of developing the European Community beyond 1992 into a closer form of economic and political union.

Progress to Date

Among the most significant measures have been:

- a European passport issued since 1985-6.

- the mutual recognition of professional qualifications since December 1988.

- an agreement by the Community Institutions on the use of the European flag and anthem.

- the COMETT programme to give a European dimension to cooperation between higher education and industry to improve training in the new technologies.

- the adoption in May 1989 of the ERASMUS programme to promote student mobility and collaboration between universities in different Member States.

- the Youth for Europe exchange programme for young people within the Community.

- Community aid to television and cinema co-productions.

Further measures not yet adopted but 'in the pipeline' include:

- the simplification of checks at internal frontiers.

- a joint approach to repairing damage caused by terrorist acts.

ETUC - European Trade Union Confederation

Founded in 1958 (although the present name was only adopted in 1973), it represents and defends economic, social and cultural interests of workers at the European level, particularly with regard to institutions, and aims to strengthen European democracy, and further economic and social progress. Its Congress is held every 3 years when it elects an Executive Committee and Officers. It has a number of affiliated organizations including a youth organization, and has consultative status vis-à-vis a number of other European and world organizations. Its membership includes national trade union confederations. Monthly ETUC information and press releases are published which should be consulted for more detailed information of its activities. It deals, for example, with vocational training, women in training and reports of public opinion regarding unemployment which, according to a Eurobarometer survey published in the ETUC publication for the beginning of 1989, is currently viewed by 97% of European citizens as the most pressing issue on the Community's agenda.

Status of Company Law Directives

Minority Rights

Companies in Europe need to be fully aware of progress of European legislation regarding employee rights, such as those concerning women, equal opportunities, and children.

Women and Equal Opportunities/Pay

Within the European Community there are three bodies working to promote equality between men and women:

> The Office of Equal Opportunities (part of the Employment, Social Affairs and Education Directorate of the Commission)
>
> The Advisory Committee on Equal Opportunities

Women's Information Service

The European Parliament set up a Committee on Women's Rights in 1981 in order to support Commission efforts and this has been followed up by a series of reports and debates. The debate on women's rights involves further debate on equal opportunities and equal pay which have a direct effect on a European company.

The Commission, as 'Guardian of the Treaty of Rome', has a duty to ensure that Article 119 of the Treaty - equal pay for equal work - is respected. Since 1975, five Directives aimed at ensuring equality for women and men at work, proposed by the Commission, have been accepted by the Council of Ministers. However, the law alone has proved insufficient, and two Action Programmes for Equal Opportunities set up by the Commission have sought to eradicate inequalities resulting from the exclusion of women from better paid jobs with good prospects. The Programmes seek to identify the fields in which women are still disadvantaged - mainly training in new technology, local employment, child care, family responsibilities and especially women belonging to ethnic minority groups. Direct Commission support has been focussed on these areas and has so far met with success.

Children

As set out in the Community Charter of Fundamental Social Rights, the protection of children and adolescents will also have an effect on employment conditions for firms operating within the European Community. For example, amongst other clauses, it is stipulated that 'young people over 16 who are in gainful employment must receive equitable remuneration'. Similarly, young workers under the age of 18 may not work more than 40 hours per week.

The European Social Fund (ESF)

Set up in 1960 to assist in combating structural causes of unemployment, the Fund does not reimburse national governments for money they would spend in any case. The funds are intended to be additional to them. It attempts to encourage governments to disburse more than they would normally do when helping to train and place workers in the right jobs. The sums themselves are often only a fraction of those spent by national administrations in the same policy areas. Nevertheless, the functioning of these funds, and the ways in which the moneys are used, has provided a useful European framework for cooperation.

The ESF contributes to the financing of two types of measure:

(a) vocational training operations, accompanied where necessary by vocational guidance.

(b) subsidies towards recruitment into newly created stable jobs and toward the creation of self-employed activities.

These aim to combat long-term unemployment of persons aged over 25 and facilitate the occupational integration of persons under 25 from the age at which compulsory schooling ends. There are measures which come under regional priorities designed to promote stable employment and to develop new employment opportunities for the unemployed. There are a number of categories of application for funds, the majority reflecting ideas and action programmes of the Community to promote the insertion of young people into working life.

An example of aid from the ESF: in Italy a framework project is being carried out in Sardinia in favour of 370 long-term unemployed over the age of 25 in the context of the protection of the environment. The beneficiaries will receive training in one of the following skills - operation and management of modern waste handling centres, monitoring of pollution levels and evaluation of the possibilites for the development of agro-tourism.

Involvement of Both Sides of Industry in Decision-making and Participation - the European Company Statute

The European Company Statute is summarized in Chapter 12, Box 55, but what especially concerns us here is the Fifth Directive and its relation to the 'Vredeling' proposal concerning worker participation and representation on supervisory boards of companies.

The Commission has been active in encouraging the 'social

Box 68: European Social Fund

The amounts committed by the Commission under the European Social Fund for each Member State for the 1988 and 1989 financial years are in Ecum:

	1988	1989
Belgium	46	49
Denmark	31	34
Federal Republic of Germany	176	193
Greece	243	318
Spain	496	618
France	373	448
Ireland	214	240
Italy	592	593
Luxembourg	2	3
Netherlands	70	91
Portugal	331	355
United Kingdom	607	656
TOTAL	3,179	3,597

As regards 1990, in accordance with the recent reform of the Structural Funds, the commitments for each Member State will be made on the basis of operational programmes which are now being drawn up and adopted in compliance with the Community support frameworks.

The figures for 1990 are not yet available (April 1991). However, the total amount allocated to the European Social Fund for 1990 is Ecu4,075m.

Source: Answer given to the European Parliament by Ms Vasso Papandreou, Commissioner responsible for Social Policy on behalf of the Commission, February 1990.

partners', as the two sides of industry are called, to come together to develop common European policies. There have been three major developments on employee participation. The first was the draft statute for a European company, the second, the Fifth Directive proposal and the Green Paper produced by the Commission on Employment, Participation and Company Structure. The third is the so-called 'Vredeling' proposal of October 1980 on information and consultation of workers employed in companies with subsidiaries in several European countries. A fourth proposal is that of January 1991 for a Directive on the establishment of European Works Councils (see below).

1. **The European Company Statute** sets out an industrial relations framework for companies which might wish to opt for European status when a European company form is finally accepted. The idea of a European company grew out of the realization that cross-frontier mergers in Europe were desirable, but that a major obstacle was the problem of different legal requirements in the Member States which made these mergers difficult, if not impossible. In June 1987, seventeen years after the first proposal was put forward by the Commission, the European Council requested the institutions concerned 'to make swift progress with regard to the Company law adjustments required for the creation of a European company'.

2. **The Fifth Directive**, one of the few remaining Company law Directives not to have been adopted, is concerned with worker participation and creating the opportunity for employees to be represented on supervisory boards of companies or their equivalent. It should not be confused with the 'Vredeling' proposal, which requires firms with European subsidiaries to provide workers with full information about their financial

situation and activities.

The purpose of the Fifth Directive is to further the process of harmonizing company law within the Community since differences in company structures and procedures hinder cross-national business cooperation and the status of employees varies from country to country. Problems have arisen not only over the differing interests of trade unions and employers but from differing customs and labour legislation (or the lack of it) in the twelve Member States.

3. **The Vredeling proposal** was approved in draft directive form by the European Commission in October 1980. It required multinationals and Community firms which have subsidiaries, to follow procedures for informing and consulting with their employees. The reasons for the Commission's proposal were (a) widespread concern over current and projected levels of unemployment throughout the EC; (b) a desire to improve industrial relations through improved disclosure and consultation; and (c) a view that the voluntary codes regarding disclosure, such as the OECD guidelines, were not being supported.

The proposal was widely debated during the 1980s and was the subject of intensive industry lobbying. Progress could not be made with the result that it has remained a draft only. The Community is looking to alternative methods of ensuring that workers are kept informed of developments across Member State borders likely to affect their employment.

4. **European Works Councils Proposal**. In January 1991, the Commission proposed a Directive on the establishment of European Works Councils for the purpose of informing and consulting employees in those companies operating across the Community. It was designed to cover European groupings where total staff exceeds 1000 persons and which are established in at least two Member States with over 100 employees in each. It is estimated that although the Directive would only apply to 1% of companies, they employ over 28% of the Community workforce. The Directive would allow workers representatives to decide whether or not they wanted a European Works Council. This new proposal follows the Vredeling draft Directive which did not gain sufficient Member State support and also the proposals for worker consultation contained in the proposed 5th Company Law Directive and the Statute for a European Company. In March

1991, the Economic and Social Committee gave a favourable opinion on the draft for a European Works Council although this was opposed by its Employers group thereby presaging a lively debate in the European Parliament and recognizing that the rights and responsibilities of workforces operating across Member States are by no means yet clearly defined.

17. Environment Policy

In a survey taken of Community citizens between 1982 and 1987, the protection of the environment was rated fourth in a list of the ten great causes for which people would accept sacrifices. It followed on from world peace, human rights, and the fight against poverty, coming above defence of country and even individual freedom. Business in Europe now recognizes the need to take seriously this vitally important but complex issue. The cost of environmental protection is vast and will need to be shared also by governments through taxation and by consumers through higher prices.

Box 69: Objectives of a Community Environment Policy

'The aim of a Community environment policy is to improve the setting, the quality of life, the surroundings and the living conditions of the peoples of the Community. It must help bring expansion into the service of man by procuring for him an environment providing the best conditions of life and to reconcile this expansion with the increasingly imperative need to preserve the natural environment.'
Commissioner for the Environment, Carlo Ripa di Meana.

The broad lines for achieving the above objectives:-

- to supplement and enforce Community legislation
- to integrate environmental policy with other Community policies
- to step up Community action on an international scale

Public awareness of environmental issues has grown significantly over the past decade. Concern over the affects of global warming, the greenhouse effect, carbon dioxide and sulphur dioxide emissions and nuclear radiation is widespread and the implications for companies, although recognised by the larger firms, have not yet been fully explained to electorates where important resource allocation decisions have to be made.

Action to be Taken

Community legislation on the environment concentrates on a few major lines of action: first, the public must be given a clearer perception of the value of a Community policy, and secondly industry must be provided with a frame of reference enabling economic growth and technological development to be reconciled with environmental protection.

The cost, in ecological terms, of neglecting the environment needs to be taken into consideration, but the severe cost consequences for industries, regions and industrial sectors cannot be ignored.

Progress to Date

Approximately 200 directives, regulations and decisions for the protection of the environment have been implemented in the Community. There is now a firm link between the Single Market and environmental considerations and the Community participates in a number of international conventions.

During December 1988, at the **Rhodes Summit**, the Twelve stressed the urgency of taking measures regarding the destruction of the ozone layer, the greenhouse effect, water resources, soil erosion, the harmful effects of chemical waste and the destruction of the tropical rain forests.

In March 1989, at a meeting of the Environment Council, Member States agreed to eliminate all production and consumption of CFCs by the end of the century and achieve an 85% reduction as soon as possible.

In June 1989, the Commission proposed the creation of a European Environment Agency (Box 70).

Box 70: Proposed European Environment Agency

'The purpose is to provide the Commission and Community with the scientific and technical means to assess, monitor, and forecast the various factors which make up the Ecosystem.'
Carlo Ripa di Meana, Commissioner for the Environment

This agency would be responsible for gathering data on environmental problems and membership would be open to concerned European nations outside the Community - Sweden, Norway and Switzerland have already asked to join and the Soviet Union, Hungary, Poland and Czechoslovakia have expressed interest although it is less likely they will join.

Since the Madrid Summit in July 1989, environmental issues have been discussed at a number of meetings of European institutions in Paris, at the so called Summit of the Arch of the Group of 7 in 1989 where environment issues were for the first time a major topic of discussion, and in Strasbourg at the European Parliament.

A Eurobarometer survey in June 1989 concluded that 9 out of 10 Europeans think the Community should lay down joint rules for decisions for the protection of the environment.

The Commission's determination to solve the problems of European pollution is evident in its dealings with the UK government concerning the quality of the country's drinking water. In July 1989, it was decided by the Commission that if a satisfactory solution was not found to the problem of compliance with the EC Directives on drinking water within two months, then the matter would be referred to the European Court of Justice and the government could find itself subject to heavy fines.

Conclusion

Europe's citizens are now more aware of environmental issues and there is no issue more popular with the electorate for Community-wide action. The Community possesses the necessary advanced technology and scientific knowledge.

Business will need to take the issue seriously because of popular support for the protection of the environment. There will be a need to balance costs and benefits. The costs of environmental protection are potentially enormous and they will need to be apportioned between government agencies, fiscal authorities and commercial interests. The difference between a successful commercial operation and one which is not economically viable could depend on getting the company response right to environmental policy in Europe.

18. Financial and Banking Services and Taxation

The financial services sector is of growing importance to the European economy. In terms of output, it now accounts for about 7% of gross domestic product (GDP) for the Community as a whole and nearly three million jobs. The sector ploughs nearly half of total profits (from credit and insurance institutions) into the Community through reinvestment in other industries. However, the dismantling of barriers in financial services has been slower than in manufacturing industry.

The Community programme for financial services is closely linked to the liberalization of capital movements. The aim is for residents of any Member State to have access to the financial systems of the other Member States and all the financial products available. There should be no restrictions on capital transfers and no distortion of the market for services for reasons of different fiscal regimes. The aim of the Community is to break down national regulatory barriers which obstruct freedom of establishment and free trade in services. Common rules for the supervision of financial operators are being drawn up to ensure that business does not move to those sectors or countries where supervision is the least rigorous. Equivalent standards for the protection of the investor are being drawn up. The Commission White Paper of 1985 proposed the liberalization of all capital movements. On 1 July 1990 the first stage of EMU began. It implements, with certain derogations for some Member States, the freedom of movement of capital. The intention is that by 1 January 1993 the liberalization of financial services will also be achieved.

Based on the Treaty of Rome, the Single European Act and the Commission White Paper on the Completion of the Internal Market, the Community's policy aims at the creation of:

- a single banking market in which a bank can establish branches anywhere in the Community and offer its services in any Member State. This is to be achieved by means of mutual recognition and a single licence for banks and other financial institutions which would be valid throughout the Community.

- an insurance market where insurance can be bought on the most competitive terms and provide Community-wide cover. Insurance and investment firms will have the right to establish branches and to provide their whole range of services throughout the Community.

- a securities and capital market with enough capacity to meet European industry's financing needs and capable of attracting investors from all over the world.

Some 40 directives will be needed to create the Single Market in financial services. The Second Banking Directive was adopted on 15 December 1989 (Com 98/646/EC). The Second Directive aims to create freedom of establishment for banks, free provision of services, harmonization of banking, securities and insurance laws and to establish the principle of home country control. Harmonization, mutual recognition and home country control (set out below) are the three guiding principles behind activities in the financial services sector.

Main Lines of the Commission Financial Services Programme

1. Harmonization of Financial Regulations

Widely diverging national financial structures and regulations could cause considerable distortions of competition in a common banking market. One example of the problem is illustrated in the German insurance case taken to the European Court of Justice in 1986, when several Member States maintained they were entitled to require insurance companies to be legally established on their territory in order to conduct business with their residents. Several Member States still restrict advertising for deposits by foreign banks. For such reasons and for the protection of the consumer, the Court confirmed that the harmonization of financial laws was a 'prerequisite of mutual recognition'. The main instruments of such harmonization have been legal directives although these have not always been complied with by the Member States. It is necessary for Community laws not only to be agreed, but for them to be applied and enforced.

2. Mutual Recognition of Financial Standards

This approach represents a significant breakthrough in the progress towards financial integration by 1992. It has already been used in conjunction with technical standards and professional qualifications to good effect. This is based on the well-known 'Cassis de Dijon' case and the 'New Approach' to harmonization of standards. In the case of financial services, they should be regarded as acceptable (see Chapter 14 and Box 62) to the entire Community as soon as they are considered to comply with the standards in one national market. Articles 30 and 59 of the Treaty of Rome, governing harmonization and mutual recognition, thus apply to financial products and follow the principle of home country control.

This mutual recognition is reflected in the Directive known as UCITS (Undertakings for Collective Investment in Transferable Securities) which came into effect in October 1989. It involves mutual recognition of investment projects by means of the approximation of supervisory laws and structures of investment funds. It will enable unit trusts to be marketed freely throughout the Community.

3. Home Country Control

Although financial institutions may have branches and subsidiaries in other Member States, in the absence of a single Community supervisory authority, it is necessary for control to be at national level, i.e. financial institutions will be supervised by the competent authorities of the Member State of their origin. The principle of home country control is of great importance. It means that once a company is legally established in any Member State, it is free to trade across the Community and does not have to set up companies in every other Member State in order to trade.

Taxation

VAT

Most Member States, with the exception of Denmark and the UK, currently apply at least two VAT rates. These can differ widely from country to country - an unacceptable situation in a single market. One rate is probably unrealistic and multiple rates would be unmanageable, so the Commission has proposed to introduce two bands, a standard rate of 14-20% and a reduced one of 4-9%. The most recent VAT proposals were made in May 1990. The new proposals, according to Mme Christine Scrivener, Commissioner responsible for taxation policy, 'would allow Member States to continue collecting VAT until 1996 in the country where goods are consumed'. The Community will have, first, a transitional system after 1992 ensuring the abolition of all checks at intra-Community borders on a temporary basis, with the VAT collected in the country of destination. Secondly, after the transition period, and not later than 31 December 1996, the collection of VAT will take place in the country of origin.

The Commission has put forward three proposals; the first establishing a transition taxation regime which will last till not later than 31 December 1996, the second introducing a new instrument of administrative cooperation, and the third adopting statistical reporting, over the transition period, on the trade of goods between Member States. However, a common system of VAT has been slow to develop due partly to the number of derogations granted to enable countries to make the necessary adjustments to accommodate new levels of taxation over a transitional period. However, after many failed attempts, a proposal made in 1984 to abolish more than 50% of derogations and move towards a system more compatible with the Single Market was finally adopted in June 1989. It is known as the 18th VAT Directive.

Two important new proposals were made in May 1989 concerning the closing of loopholes in attempts at fiscal harmonization and a common market for financial services. These two proposals, the essential complement to the free movement of capital which came into effect on 1 July 1990, are not intended to bring about complete harmonization of the taxation of savings. That, according to Mme Scrivener, Commissioner with special responsibility for taxation 'is something which is neither necessary nor desirable at the moment'. They are designed primarily to deal with the increased risks of avoidance or evasion which will be a direct result of the final phase of the liberalization of capital markets throughout the Community.

The agreement on the three outstanding corporate taxation directives (abolition of withholding tax for subsidiaries to parent companies in another Member State, deferral of capital gains tax for companies taken over in cross-border mergers, establishment of compulsory arbitration procedures in transfer pricing disputes for companies operating in more than one Member State) finally reached by Finance Ministers, is seen as an important step forward in one of the most difficult fields in the run-up to the Single Market in 1992. A favourable first reception has also been given to the revised proposals on VAT.

Excise Duties

The approximation of indirect taxes within Europe is a sensitive issue because of its important role in national budgets. While the approximation of VAT rates is a delicate issue itself, that of excise duties is even more so. This is because VAT is calculated on the price of goods including the excises and it is therefore not possible to envisage the same flexibility for excises as for VAT without the risk of exceeding the existing and proposed VAT bands. The Commission has been guided by a concern to create as little disturbance to national fiscal systems as possible. It has made specific proposals for each product individually, in certain cases also taking into account non-fiscal requirements such as the fight against cancer in the case of tobacco excises.

Community VAT bands and excise duties should enter into force no later than 31 December 1992. Member States will be encouraged to work towards these bands in the intervening period. In mid-May 1991 there was still considerable work to be done before a VAT and Excise regime acceptable to all Member States was agreed.

Tax and financial services issues in the EC are complex, but harmonization at the Community level and mutual recognition at national level now interact to provide a more cohesive approach to this aspect of the Single Market. Specialist advice should be sought from firms which can draw on a wide variety of expertise and up-to-date knowledge. The shape of fiscal and financial Europe is fast-changing and a coherent framework is essential to the success of the Single Market. This area has proved, along with the freedom of movement of people, to be among the most difficult issues of the Single Market to resolve.

19. Other Policies: Energy, Transport, Regional and Consumer

ENERGY POLICY

At the Rhodes Summit meeting of December 1988, the Heads of Government urged the Community to intensify its efforts in respect of 1992 in all areas where progress has not been sufficient. Energy was explicitly mentioned as one such sector.

To meet the challenge of setting up a true European internal energy market, it was agreed there should be a permanent dialogue between the Member States and industry, the producers and distributors of energy, and also with all those who use energy and for whom the Internal Market will undoubtedly have positive effects. The establishment of a Community internal energy market will need extreme care and respect for other sectors such as the environment, and regional and social policy.

The emphasis on an internal energy market is already clearly expressed in the Commission's working programme for 1989 and will be translated into a comprehensive package of measures. Two proposals for Council Directives - COM (89) 334 and 336 Final - were published in September 1989, outlining a package of proposals to look into the exchange of gas and electricity between Member States' networks.

Increased Competition

A European energy policy will create conditions for increased intra-Community trade, encourage market forces and lower energy prices for industry, thus increasing worldwide competitiveness for European companies. Europe's limited energy resources would be better allocated and security of supply would benefit from increased integration and greater flexibility of the energy system.

National governments are coming to realize that the energy market needs to be opened up and driven by market conditions. It cannot remain subject to constraints that force some consumers to have to buy national energy when it is available at lower prices elsewhere in the Community. As regards electricity prices, the Commission is taking action (May 1991) to erode the state energy monopolies that dominate gas and electricity production and prevent cross-border trade in these commodities.

Box 71: Major Guidelines for Community Energy Policy

An end to the twelve separate national viewpoints and a rationalization of the European market through a new approach to energy infrastructures. Complementarities and economies of scale are to be encouraged if the Member States are to profit as much as possible from Europe's continental dimension.

Need for a revision of the concepts of self-sufficiency and security of supply.

Redefinition of priorities for setting up power distribution networks.

Approximation of fiscal conditions and trade patterns.

Joint efforts which will lead to a new momentum in promoting research and development useful to both the producer and consumer.

Source: European File, The Community Energy Policy, 2/87.

Public Procurement

In October 1988, the Commission published its proposals, including a draft Directive to extend EC public procurement rules to the energy sector (amongst others) in order to open up national markets to Community-wide competition and hence reduce industry's costs and increase competitiveness. The cost of being required to buy energy from national sources is estimated at over Ecu20bn per year.

Although purchases of energy by contracting entities in the energy sector are not covered by the Directive, the Commission is addressing the issues, especially the removal of barriers to increased transfrontier electricity trade.

Price Transparency

Price transparency is one of the first areas to be addressed in the framework of the internal energy market to create conditions for the free flow of energy supplies. Comparative energy prices are published and available to actual and potential consumers. For example, a draft Directive concerning transparency of natural gas and electricity prices charged to industries and end-users was published on 18 September 1989 (COM (89) 332 Final). This will help choices between fuels and suppliers and help to open markets.

Energy and the Environment

In September 1989, the Commission presented to the Council a comprehensive study on energy and the environment known as 'Energy 2010: How to ensure economic growth, secure energy supply and environmental protection'. The main objective of the study is to identify the 'major themes' in energy which could determine the direction of policy in the early to mid-1990s.

The study addresses the question - can Europe have reasonably priced and secure energy supplies without destroying its environment? It aims to contribute to the global discussion now taking place and envisages a future in which consumers have more money, more free time and are increasingly concerned with environmental protection. It concludes that because of environmental considerations, greater penetration of the market by more energy efficient technologies will be required. A new transport infrastructure with more passengers and freight being carried by rail and the greater use of electricity generated by nuclear power and gas are further recommendations. Discussions with the Soviet Union continue and the dream of European self-sufficiency in energy of the sixties could come close to reality in the nineties. The exploitation of Soviet natural resources by EC companies with perhaps Japanese capital is a distinct possibility.

TRANSPORT POLICY

According to Karel van Miert, the Commissioner responsible for Transport Policy, the two main dimensions of Community transport policy are: internal market/competition and social/environmental issues. Not only is there the need to develop a genuine free market for road, rail, air and maritime transport and the corresponding infrastructure. The policy also needs constantly to bear in mind safety, consumer aspects and environmental protection.

The Single European Act heightened the need to introduce full freedom of movement for transport as attempts since 1973 to convince other Member States of the Community to liberalize their systems have had little effect. This is now a high Community priority after a decade of relative inaction in this field. Some 30 major proposals were adopted by the Council of Ministers in 1989-90 and a further 40 Directives and Regulations will be put forward before 1 January 1993.

Road Transport

Most goods are moved between Member States by road. At a Council meeting of 20 June 1988, the EC Transport Ministers agreed to gradually phase out truck quotas and permits for the movement of goods by road by the end of 1992.

The question of congestion is also being considered, especially in countries such as the Netherlands, Belgium and the United

Kingdom where the problems are far greater than elsewhere. The Community has witnessed France and Italy moving towards electronic toll collection to save labour and the Netherlands moving towards road pricing to deal with congestion, so that drivers travelling around Europe could be faced with having to stick a number of different cards on their windscreens. An EC group has been set up arguing the benefits of electronic tolls all over the Community. The Commission aims to introduce at least limited 'cabotage' by 1992 and it is hoped that such liberalization will lead to a more economic use of lorries by reducing 'empty running'. Some Member States are still restricting the freedom of movement of goods by not allowing trucks carrying goods across national frontiers to take return loads or pick up part loads.

Tax Harmonization

Although no formal proposal has been made, the Commission intends to introduce a tax based on the territoriality principle, so that vehicles pay taxes according to the country whose roads they use, instead of the current situation where tax is paid in the country where the vehicle is registered.

The Commission also wants to propose a ban on systems of refunds of vehicle excise duty according to toll mileage or age of vehicle/fleet size, which currently operates in France and Belgium respectively.

Speed Regulations

A Directive on standard levels of drivers' hours came into effect on 1 January 1989. The Commission has also approved proposals to introduce a Community-wide speed limit of 80 kmph (50 mph) for lorries with trailers on motorways and A-roads, a considerable slowdown for British trucks.

External Considerations

To maximize the benefits of the Single Market, agreement needs to be reached with the major non-Community countries through which Community freight passes. The countries are Switzerland,

Austria and Yugoslavia, all of which apply some constraints on transit traffic. The Commission is currently negotiating with them to resolve these problems.

Rail Transport

There is a strong case for adopting a Community approach to rail transport and for making better use of the railways in the run-up to 1992. Europe's railways have been greatly handicapped by their strict division into national networks and by delays in modernization. A policy needs to be established in the Community to take maximum advantage of the technical and environmental benefits offered by the railway network, including the High Speed Train network and important developments such as the Channel Tunnel.

The problem of government reluctance to spend more on the railway network could be solved by charging railway operators for their use of the rail infrastructure just as road users have to pay for using toll roads.

Maritime Transport

Two major obstacles to the Single Market remain in this sector in the shape of maritime cabotage restrictions and state aid to ports. In some Member States, access to coastal shipping is limited to the country's national lines. In addition, subsidies given to Community ports are considered as distorting free competition and although the Commission is investigating these issues, progress is slow. The Council recently adopted (1991) the principle of cabotage, and proposals for setting up a European shipping register (EUROS) will be put forward.

Air Transport

'The aim for 1992 is to secure the greatest possible freedom for airlines to provide the services they consider commercially appropriate. Governments should interfere only to curb anti-

competitive behaviour. This means that economic regulation must indeed be confined to economics. The politics of patronage and protection belong to the past. They will have no place in the Community of 1992.'
Sir Leon Brittan, Commissioner responsible for Competition Policy, June 1989

In December 1987, the Council of Ministers agreed a package of proposals aimed at opening up market access and removing constraints on capacity. The package came into effect on 1 January 1989. Abuse of dominant position has been particularly evident in the airline industry. Since April 1989, the Court of Justice allows national courts to rule on illegal agreements and abuse of dominant position in the airline industry Previously, in August 1988, the Commission introduced block exemption regulations which applied the Competition Rules to air transport. The ultimate aim is to phase out altogether the block exemptions granted to various airlines. The opening up of air transport to competition is a current major preoccupation of the Commission and slow but steady progress is being made. Two liberalization 'packages' have been adopted and a third during 1991 will establish a genuine European policy on fares, cabotage, standards, safety, airline establishment, pilot training and air slots.

Transport and the Environment

'Any benefits we reap from achieving the 1992 objective will be shortlived if in the process we damage our environment.'
Karel van Miert, Commissioner responsible for Transport Policy

In the aviation sector, the Commission has already made proposals on noise emissions and these need to be kept up as growth in air transport continues and air traffic expands. There are also safety aspects which are being studied at Community level relating to such issues as cross-border bus and coach travel. Transport policy, having been ignored for over a decade, is now an important part of the integrated approach to the opening up of the EC market. It has important implications for business both in the costs it helps to reduce and because of its influence on location decisions.

'Transport in a fast changing Europe'

Group Transport 2000 Plus was established in 1989 to examine the future of European transport and its report is blunt and unambiguous. Urgent action is required to ensure cohesion of national regulations to avoid potentially disastrous barriers to efficiency and quality. The word 'crisis' is used in virtually every one of the reports 75 pages and is not used lightly.

REGIONAL POLICY

In every country of the European Community there are disparities between the levels of development and prosperity of different regions. These disparities, caused by an unequal distribution of economic activity, are much more pronounced when the Community is taken as a whole.

The regions considered to have the most serious problems can be divided into two principal groups; underdeveloped regions whose economy still depends to a large extent on agriculture, with low income and often high unemployment, and regions whose former prosperity was based on industries now in decline such as coal, textiles, steel and shipbuilding. The recession of the early 1980s compounded the difficulties of these regions and unemployment increased at widely diverging rates between these areas and their more prosperous counterparts.

Regional disparities in economic performance impede economic and social cohesion within individual countries as well as in the Community as a whole. For this reason, national governments have developed policies to stimulate economic progress in regions in difficulty. In an attempt to make such policies more effective, an effort at Community level became desirable. Under the Treaty of Rome, the Community has the task of promoting a harmonious development of economic activities throughout its territory, as well as an accelerated raising of the standard of living in regions in decline. The Single European Act gives the Community responsibility to help reduce disparities between regions and support the least developed regions.

With these objectives in mind, the Community has set about analysing the state of the various regions of the Community and their progress, and regularly updates reports detailing their economic and social situation. It then works to contribute to the coordination of the regional policies of Member States. To reduce disparities between the regions requires close collaboration between the Member States to determine in which regions state investment aids are most necessary. Regional development programmes are also set up in which Member States must indicate where aid is to go and how priorities are to be set. In order to maximize the efficiency of such programmes, the Community is increasingly involved in linking regional policy to other sectors of the economy, for example the moving of agricultural land away from crop production (thus reducing pressure on the CAP) towards tourism (thus promoting small and medium-sized enterprises). Finally, and probably the Community's most obvious contribution to regional policy, are the various financial aids, particularly those from the **European Regional Development Fund** and from the **European Investment Bank**. There are other structural aid facilities such as the **European Coal and Steel Community**, the **European Social Fund**, the **Guidance Section of the European Agricultural Fund (EAGGF)** among others. The Community thus has a whole range of budgetary and lending instruments which, though they are geared to different policy areas, have the same objective.

Changing circumstances, brought about by the completion of the Internal Market, led to major reform of the Structural Funds, the main instruments of EC regional policy. Since 1 January 1989, new principles and guidelines have governed the allocation of the Funds and the total budget is being increased so that by 1993 it will be twice the 1987 figure.

A number of factors combined to bring about the reform of these Funds:

- The enlargement of the Community to include Spain and Portugal.

- The growing regional disparities brought about by the addition of these two countries (a doubling of the population of the least-favoured regions).

- The 1992 programme - many of the gains to be made from the completion of the Internal Market, outlined in the Cecchini Report, were based on the expectation of structural adjustments reducing the regional disparities.

- Some Member States made reform of the Structural Funds a precondition of their signature of the Single European Act and their acceptance of the 'objective 1992'.

- The grave problems faced by traditional industries such as steel, shipping, coal and textiles.

- The increasing need to resolve the Community's perennial financial problems and set the budget on a sound footing.

The main objectives of the reform, which has linked the three funds (above) more closely, are set out under five headings:

Objective 1
To promote the development and structural adjustment of less-developed regions. Ecu38bn will be spent between 1989 and 1993.

Objective 2
To assist the transformation of regions or parts of regions seriously affected by industrial decline. Ecu7.2bn will be disbursed from 1989 to 1993.

Objective 3
To combat long-term unemployment among those over the age of 25.

Objective 4
To integrate young people into employment.

Ecu7.5bn is available for objectives 3 and 4.

Objective 5
(a) Improving structures in agriculture and forestry - i.e. production, processing, marketing.
(b) Promoting the development of rural areas. Both of these objectives are geared to the reform of the

Common Agricultural Policy.
Ecu6.2bn will be spent from 1989 to 1993.

Including certain innovative actions, Ecu60bn is available for these objectives during the period 1989-1993.

Member States submit plans outlining their priorities and intentions concerning the use of the Funds. Although the Commission then scrutinizes them in the light of agreed Community policies, it is ultimately by a process of negotiation that the parties concerned arrive at a decision, rather than through directives issued by the EC. The aim is to encourage decentralized management which will be more sensitive to local needs. Businesses will benefit by being able to negotiate directly with the regional or national authorities in eligible areas without necessarily having to seek further approval from the Commission. However, the greatest bonus to industry throughout the Community is in the form of the overall doubling of the Funds' budget from Ecu7.2bn in 1987 to Ecu14.5bn in 1993. The liberalization of public procurement will make it easier for firms to tender for contracts financed by the Funds. The principle of additionality has recently been invoked by the Commission to ensure that Community funds are genuinely additional to funds provided by Member States or their agents to resolve problems of regions or industries with restructuring programmes. It has lead in some cases to the witholding of Community funds until such conditions are complied with.

CONSUMER POLICY

'My aim as chairman of the National Consumer Council will be to get away from the image of consumers and their representatives as moaning minnies and impress on government, industry and others the importance of always consulting and involving consumers and their representatives when crucial decisions affecting their everyday lives are made. If more of this had been done in the past, probably fewer things would have gone wrong.'
Lady Judith Wilcox, Chairman, National Consumer Council

Consumerism, like environmental protection, is of growing interest to legislators and business people alike although until the SEA of 1985 it was not recognized as a fully fledged Community policy. With the establishment of a Single Market without frontiers, the choice of goods and services will grow further with the elimination of barriers to trade. In the preamble of the Treaty of Rome, it is affirmed that the essential objective of the Treaty is the constant improvement of the living and working conditions of the people. Article 100 (a) 3 of the Single European Act adds this specific dimension with the words: 'the Commission in its proposals concerning health, safety, environmental protection and consumer protection will take as a base a high level of protection.'

Although the Community has been working on consumer policy since 1961, the first consumer programme was not adopted until 1975. It was not until 1981 with the adoption of a second programme that the policy began to develop seriously. Since then the programmes have become a regular feature of normal Community business. November 1989 saw a further effort to intensify activity in the field of consumer affairs (Box 72).

Box 72: Resolution of Future Priorities for a Relaunch of Consumer Policy - November 1989

1. **Consumer Representation**

   The decision by the Commission to establish a Consultative Council gives a lead in consumer representation and affords a better and more effective system of involving consumers in the various policies being established at Community level.

2. **Consumer Information**

   A number of action information services have been set up by the Commission, supporting local initiatives of three pilot projects: (1) European consumer information and advice centres,(2) promotion of cooperation between consumer organizations and education systems in exchanging teaching materials, (3) collaboration with youth information and awareness programmes. Transparency is an important concept in consumer information; maximum transparency is sought, for example, in banking and insurance. Labelling of food to support quality products is being pursued, while comparative testing throughout the Member States is designed to protect the consumer from sub-standard produce and ensure that the highest quality is available.

3. **Consumer Safety**

Much harmonization of legislation in the Community has been proposed and adopted already on a sector by sector basis. However, there is still the need to take account of developments in technology and cover sectors not addressed by existing legislation. The draft Product Safety Directive should be adopted speedily to be implemented effectively in time for the completion of the Internal Market. Standards setting by CEC/CENELEC is taking longer than envisaged, but every effort is being made to achieve this goal.

4. **Consumer Transactions**

When purchasing goods or services from other Community countries, consumers have had to battle with the problems of different laws and languages. The protection of consumers is a future priority, particularly in relation to new selling techniques such as those used in the selling of timeshare holiday homes. The Door Step Selling Directive 85/577 provides for a 'cooling off' period to allow for cancellation of a purchase order after reflection.

The construction of the Internal Market is expected to advantage the consumer, and manufacturers will need to pay careful attention to Community legislation and its relation to national standards. The 'subsidiarity' principle will apply widely. Much consumer protection activity will be at the national or even regional level. Future Commission activity will involve a series of legislative texts on comparative advertising, cross-border purchase and distance selling. There will be new major proposals on product safety and liability for services and further support to European consumer information agencies.

Competition Policy and Consumers

Competition policy can provide significant benefits for the consumer by ensuring a deregulated and open market.

Examples are air transport and telecommunications. The Commission has worked out guidelines to ensure that interlining (giving tickets validity on other airlines on a particular route) is not denied to smaller companies for full price tickets. It has also proposed emergency measures which will allow intervention when an airline is using predatory practices to undermine smaller competitors (swamping a route with new services, pricing below cost, granting special inducements to travel agents, abusing loyalty benefits).

Moves toward a common air transport policy intensified in June 1990 when EC Transport Ministers reduced the amount of capacity sharing that a Member State can demand of a national carrier from 40% to 25% beginning in April 1993. They also reduced government scope to block new tariffs.

The Commission is vigilant in telecommunications - an area of growing significance to consumers. It is a field of rapid technological change, expanding at speed, but still largely controlled by national telecommunications authorities. The Commission is concentrating on:

- liberalization of services, to limit the exclusive rights of the monopoly providers of telecoms services.

- ensuring that price cartels are not used between telecoms authorities to fix charges - the European Committee of Posts and Telecommunications has already changed its practices as a result of intervention.

- international call charges, which are being examined to see whether they have been fixed under agreements incompatible with the EC rules.

Conclusion

This section has covered in outline a wide range of Community policies and indicated how they may be of concern to industry. It should be stressed that Community laws and policies are the agreed policies of Member States and are not separate or different from national policies, except in that they are applicable to all Member States. The objective of Community legislation is to simplify rather than complicate matters. It is easier for business to deal with a uniform set of policies and laws than to find them different in different countries. This simplification is the rationale behind the Europe 1992 process to implement the Single Market.

Section IV: Community External Policy: Key Issues Affecting Business

20. The United States and the European Community

Although there is no formal agreement setting out a general framework for economic relations between the US and EC, consultations between officials, frequent visits to the US by ministers and European Commissioners and close contacts through the Commission Delegation in Washington and the US Mission in Brussels have grown steadily over recent years. In early 1990, President Bush and the Irish Prime Minister (Ireland was holding the Presidency of the European Council at that time) agreed to formalize meetings to ensure that there were official talks between the US and the EC during the course of each six-month Presidency. There are frequent suggestions that there should be a formal treaty arrangement to ensure a more general framework for discussions and to avoid specific trade issues being given undue importance. The bulk of trade and investment in both directions is, however, unaffected by these disputes.

The Western economic triangle of trade between the United States, the European Community and Japan has been of fundamental importance to the world economy during the last two decades. While the EC's relationship with Japan has perhaps received more public attention, the underlying trade and investment relationships are most developed between the US and the EC.

Trade and Investment Statistics

The United States is the Community's biggest supplier and also its biggest customer. Cross-investment statistics show the same interconnection of the economies. In 1990 US exports to the EC are expected to reach $100 billion and sales from US subsidiaries in the EC to amount to $400 billion. A deficit of $20 billion in 1987

Box 73: EC - US Trade (Ecubn)

	1986	1987	1988	1989*
EC imports from the US	57	56	68	63
EC exports to the US	75	72	72	57
Surplus/deficit	+18	+16	+ 4	-6

* estimated figures

US investment in the EC (1987)	$160 billion
EC investment in the US (1987)	$122 billion

The US and the EC together account for over:
- 30% of world trade
- 40% of world gross domestic product
- 35% of world steel production
- 55% of world automobile production
- 70% of world aircraft production

Source: Eurostat

changed to a $10 billion surplus in the US trade balance with the EC in 1990. Sixty per cent of US exports to the EC go to the UK, Germany and the Netherlands.

For reasons of history, shared values, common approaches and mutual interest, there has been an intertwining of the economies of the US and the EC and the process looks set to continue. The strategy for US companies operating in the EC does not differ significantly from that of companies investing or exporting from any other part of the world. The relations developed by US companies in the EC have, however, over time, been so close that many of the larger ones are often seen as European companies in all but name.

The tendency for multinational companies (MNCs) to manufacture, source, research and invest on an increasingly global scale, makes their contribution of fundamental importance to the world economy. The attempts to integrate their operations in the countries in which they operate both economically, socially and environmentally have major implications for governments and individuals whether workers, consumers or investors. The encouragement and, at the same time, effective regulation of the MNC is a continuing major activity and interest of the Community. Much of the 1992 programme is of relevance to the MNCs wherever their home base.

Box 74: Reviewing US Corporate Strategy in Europe in Fast Changing Times

Reviewing corporate business strategy in Europe at a time when events are shaping policies, and when no-one can look ahead with confidence more than a few weeks, is a challenge both for the multinational company and the small business operating into Europe. There are opportunities to be grasped, but it could be costly to be too far ahead of the game. Here are some suggested guidelines to which company specific ones might be added from Section II to form a framework for strategic thinking:

(i) The European Community is two-thirds through the 1992 process, which will be completed on time. Goods, services, people and capital will then flow freely across the Twelve Member States. The process is creating faster economic growth than expected and this steady progress looks set to continue from now until the end of the decade at least. The forecasts of the Cecchini Report (Chapter 14, and references in Section V), considered rather bullish by some commentators when produced in 1985, are now thought to be on the low side.

(ii) The Community will give priority to the deepening of its relations with existing Member States. The widening process - the developing of relations with other countries - will be restricted to trade, association and other agreements. In spite of a lengthening queue of applicant countries and those considering applying, the Community will complete the Single Market before considering new applications to join the Twelve. When there is a choice, therefore, business should, other considerations being equal, be developed within the existing Community rather than outside because of the greater market access it guarantees.

(iii) The unification of Germany is happening at a pace unforeseeable a year ago. Business opportunities in what was East Germany are there to be seized and there is no time to waste. The unification of Germany means that East Germany (the Democratic Republic) has become part of the European Community. It will cost billions of Ecu to bring East Germany up to EC standards - environmental, health and safety, for example - and to apply in a very short period of time the directives and regulations of the EC to its economy. This process will be underwritten by the Federal Republic. This underpinning effectively guarantees a security of investment and economic growth not to be found in the other Central and Eastern European countries. If you are looking eastwards for business opportunities, the five Länder of what was formerly East Germany must be the safest place to start. Working from a non-German based operation could be an additional advantage. Some East German companies will want to make a fresh start and not always be told how and what to do by their fellow countrymen in the Western part of the country.

(iv) There are considerable grants and loans for doing business in East and Central Europe, both from the EC and from national Know-How (consultancy and training support) and other funds. There is also good advice to be had from US embassies and consulates in Eastern Europe. They have traditionally been supportive in their help to business because of their experience in working the state system. Their help can still be invaluable in the changed circumstances and they should be a first port of call for advice and information. The major US accounting firms are well established now in Eastern and Central Europe and have effective consultancy divisions.

(v) The EFTA countries - Austria, Switzerland, Sweden, Norway, Finland, Iceland, Liechtenstein - are working with the European Community to create a European Economic Area. Negotiations are due to be completed during 1991 so that the new relationship can begin in 1993 (see next chapter). The difficulties are that the EFTA countries want to have a maximum say in the decision- making process, while the EC points out that this role is principally reserved for full members. There is a growing body of opinion in these countries held with differing degrees of conviction that full membership is the best way ahead. Austria has already applied to be a full member; Norway is interested. Sweden was expected to apply in the summer of 1991.

(vi) The European Community is moving towards economic and monetary union. The two Intergovernmental Conferences which opened in Rome in December 1990 are expected to take decisions amending the Treaty of Rome and leading to further political integration as well as laying down the timetable for the move towards economic and monetary union, the first phase of which came in on 1 July, 1990 (Chapter 15).

(vii) In developing a European strategy, the open frontiers between Member States, the size of the market – 340 million compared to 220 million – in the US, the progressive harmonization of standards, and of fiscal and financial arrangements make it possible for the first time for corporations outside the EC to look at the EC market as a whole rather than as a collection of different European states.

Source: The European Business Journal Vol 2, Issue 3 1990.

The EC takes over a quarter of US exports which in 1989 amounted to over $63 billion, slightly more than US exports to Canada and over twice the exports from the US to Japan.

The importance of the trading relationship has been accentuated by the EC drive to complete the Single Market by the end of 1992. It has led to renewed interest in the prospects for the EC economy in the United States and increasing concern to ensure that the US can continue to develop its long standing trade and investment activities within the EC States without fear of discrimination.

Fortress Europe or Europe, World Partner?

During recent years there has been widespread comment in the United States that the Single Market could mean the EC puts up barriers against the rest of the world and the US in particular. The phrase 'Fortress Europe' was coined and many fears raised in the United States of a Europe no longer open for business. The European Community denied this intention and coined its own phrase 'Europe - World Partner'. Both sides have shown concern and expressed this on occasions quite vociferously.

The facts and allegations of protectionist actions or tendencies cannot be discussed here in detail. The background is, however, of steady growth of two-way trade and investment over three decades. The EC can never seek to cut itself off from the rest of the world as it is not a continental economy. It needs to import raw materials, fossil fuels and, increasingly, technology. In order to pay for these, it needs to export goods and services and therefore has no interest in developing a siege economy. Even when the disputes over steel and textiles, soya and pasta, citrus fruit and cereals, airbus, semi-conductors and hormones are analysed and put into context, all but a minute percentage of trade flows freely across the Atlantic in both directions and will continue to do so.

The current Uruguay Round of the GATT negotiations are crucial and their successful outcome is the top trade policy objective of both sides. The Community sees that the best way to work towards a multilateral stable trade environment is by pursuing a triple strategy based on:

- effective market opening
- reinforcement of the multilateral system
- the extension of the GATT rules and disciplines to new areas particularly in services

The Community sees the 1992 'Europe without Frontiers' programme and GATT negotiations as two closely-linked and parallel processes. The success of both is vital to the EC. The Uruguay Round is the eighth multilateral round of trade negotiations under the auspices of GATT. The seven previous rounds, of which the Kennedy Round in the sixties and the Tokyo Round in the seventies were the most important, helped greatly to stimulate world trade which rose in value from some $60 billion in 1948 to around $3,000 billion today. The 107 participants including the EC, USA, Japan and a large number of developing countries are in the final stage of the negotiations which are proving very difficult (June 1991).

The Uruguay Round is the greatest and most complex trade negotiation of all time. With its heavy dependence on international trade, the Community is vitally concerned that it should succeed. Protectionist pressure and practices have been building up in recent years. For the EC this negotiation is the final test of whether or not multilateralism with stronger common rules and disciplines will triumph over unilateralism.

The monitoring of developments in EC legislation will be of growing importance to US companies as this legislation will increasingly affect the business environment, complementing and taking precedence over Member States' national legislation in trade and other fields. The public affairs aspects of doing business in Europe will need careful integration into corporate strategies.

21. Japan and the European Community

Community Policies Towards Japan

There have been three main thrusts to policies in recent years:

1. The opening up of Japan's domestic market

The first is to encourage Japan to open up its domestic market by eliminating a wide variety of trade barriers. The sectors targeted in recent years include motor vehicles, medical equipment, cosmetics, wines and spirits, and the Kansai Airport construction projects. There has been particular pressure put on the need to recognize standards, norms and test-data to improve market access for EC products. During the last two years, emphasis has been in the fields of pharmaceuticals, agricultural products and the protection of intellectual property. There has been recourse to GATT procedures for specific products such as wine and spirits, leather goods and the US-Japan semi-conductor agreement. In order to encourage EC companies to enter Japanese markets, the EC has established a number of initiatives such as the Export Promotion Programme (EXPROM), the EC-Japan Centre for Industrial Promotion and Information Policy Initiatives. This latter aims to create a permanent information infrastructure throughout Japan to encourage the recent interest in the internationalization of the economy.

Box 75: EXPROM (Export Promotion Programme)

Since 1979, the Commission has been actively helping European firms to enter the Japanese market by providing management training, market studies, logistic and financial help for trade missions and other trade promotion services.

At the centre of the programme is the Executive

Training Programme (ETP) through which the Commission has sent more than 200 young executives from export oriented firms to Japan for eighteen months of intensive language and business training. The success of the scheme is confirmed by the fact that a number of ETP graduates have since reached leading positions in the management of their companies' Japanese subsidiaries.

EXPROM, the Export Promotion Programme, may also have a wider influence. For example in the case of alcoholic beverages, when a comprehensive market study revealed evidence of discriminatory fiscal treatment of imports, the Commission was able to persuade the Japanese authorities to modify certain dispositions and to pursue the matter in the GATT on those points that were not resolved bilaterally.

The projects to which the Commission gives its support have to benefit a representative group of European firms located in more than two or three Member States. EXPROM also undertakes market studies and a census of European investment in Japan. It provides a directory of European firms in Japan which are ready to help newcomers, and is also now preparing an inventory of major construction projects in Japan with a view to facilitating European firms' participation.

Source: COM(88) 136 II March 1988

One of the main growth areas of the next decade is High Definition Television (HDTV) in which the EC and Japan both have considerable interest.

Box 76: High Definition TV

The overall EC aim with regard to High Definition Television is to ensure the compatibility of High Definition TV with existing equipment. There should be one production standard throughout the world to facilitate the exchange of programmes and the development of the European broadcasting industry, and especially exports. This is also relevant to the future of cinema, video, colour printing and advertising.

The new Japanese HDTV system (developed by NHK - the Japanese broadcasting authority - and certain electronics companies) is incompatible with existing broadcasting systems and the issue of whether compatibility is essential or not will be hotly debated.

Several European companies funded by the EUREKA Project are researching an alternative, more advanced system which would have the advantage of compatibility with existing world systems, including the European 'D Mac' satellite broadcasting standard.

The Commission's remit is to spread information, strengthen understanding of the European proposal and seek agreement with interested parties in Japan, the US and other countries with a view to a single world production standard.

Source: Relations between the Community and Japan: COM(88) 136 II March 1988

2. EC pressure to reduce Japanese dependence on exports

The Community has encouraged the Japanese government to reduce dependence on exports and to stimulate internal demand. This involves increased imports of manufactured goods and processed agricultural products, while at the same time encouraging Japan to restructure its economy. It will need to increase its imports in order to reduce the trade surplus. While the growth of international trade is good for world economic growth, it is not desirable or perhaps even possible for one major player to continue over decades to amass export surpluses. There must be a pendulum swing over time as there has been with trade between the United States and the EC. The EC has supported the US structural impediments initiative and in particular made sure that any favourable results would apply worldwide.

Box 77: EC - Japan Trade (Ecubn)

	1986	1987	1988	1989*
EC imports from Japan	33	34	41	35
EC exports to Japan	11	14	17	16
Surplus/ deficit	-22	-20	-24	-19
EC exports as a % of imports	33%	41%	41%	45%

* the first three quarters of 1989

Source: Eurostat

3. Moderation and monitoring of exports

From 1983-5, the Community has had an arrangement under which Japan 'moderated' her exports of sensitive products such as automobiles, video-recorders, TV sets, motor cycles and machine tools. However, since 1986, imports have been monitored with bi-annual reviews to assess developments. There have also been closer cooperative links in science and technology in an attempt to strengthen this weakest side of the Western economic triangle - US-Japan-EC.

Recent Growth in Economic Activity

There has been a very rapid growth in economic activity in recent years. Trade has increased from Ecu19bn in 1980 to Ecu67bn estimated in 1989. The EC takes some 18% of Japanese exports and 19% of its direct foreign investment. At the beginning of 1990 there were about 450 Japanese companies in the Community employing over 150,000 people. In 1987, the Japanese government, in response to pressure from the US and EC, initiated an economic stimulation package which led to EC exports increasing, admittedly from a low base, by about 20% in 1987 and again in 1988. As regards exports to Japan, the deficit is still considerable - a deficit of Ecu19.1m in the period January to September 1989.

EC exports would need to grow more than two and a half times as fast as Japanese exports to the Community to reduce the deficit significantly. In May 1990 it was announced that the European Commission and Japan would set up a joint committee to speed up the correction of this imbalance in the context of the Uruguay Round. Another recent change largely on account of the yen/dollar/Ecu exchange rate has been Japanese diversion of exports from North American markets towards the EC. Japan-EC trade has grown from 33% to 50% of Japanese-US trade in the last four years.

Foreign Investment into Japan

The investment imbalance (16-1) is a cause of some concern and the Commission is currently working on measures to help EC firms willing to invest in Japan. The problem is no longer so much Japanese government restrictions, but the inherent complexities and difficulties of doing business in Japan. Differences in social economic structures and trading practices hinder investment in Japan. In 1988 there were more than 300 Japanese mergers and acquisitions in Europe compared to less than twenty by the EC in Japan. There is considerable difficulty in changing the situation. It has become an important issue in the Uruguay Round of the GATT (Chapter 14) where trade related investment measures (TRIMS) concerning conditions imposed by host countries on foreign direct investments which distort or restrict trade are being discussed for the first time.

Japanese Direct Investment in the EC

Japanese direct investment in the EC has been increasing sharply in recent years and reached a cumulative total of $28 billion by 31 March 1989. The greatest increase was in banking and insurance partly because of the yen exchange rate, but also because of the increasing interest of Japanese firms in investing in the EC as the 1992 programme became a reality, a threat and an opportunity.

Of Japan's cumulative direct foreign investment, 18% goes to the EC, which is nearly as much as the amount going to Asian countries. The US share is 39%. Japan puts a heavy emphasis on non-manufacturing industries. In 1989 nearly 80% of its investment in the EC was in finance, insurance and commercial activities.

Indications are that while direct Japanese investment in the services sector has been undertaken for trade related reasons, manufacturing investment is rather more defensive to counter perceived or real attempts at market protection by Member States. Adding value locally by assembly, production and even research activities is a developing strategy which is encouraged by some Member States, the UK and Spain in particular.

Japanese direct investment in the EC provides employment, may transfer technology, management skills and more flexible labour relations and also helps to integrate the Japanese economy in regional economic systems. On the negative side, it may sometimes take the form only of assembly operations, it may be on greenfield sites giving comparative advantage over older established firms and it can lead to Member States and regions outbidding one another over aid and attractive conditions, all of which may distort competition. It is generally considered that for most Member States, the advantages seem to outweigh the disadvantages.

Financial Services

Problems faced by European exporters to Japanese markets are compounded by the situation facing European banks in the commercial banking sector.

Although the Japanese authorities continued the liberalization programme set up since the Yen/Dollar Ad Hoc Committee Report in May 1984, progress has been too slow and difficulties still remain in the commercial banking sector. The profitability of European banks working in Tokyo remains low because of high funding costs which is in turn due to interest rate regulation and lack of a true interbanking market in Japan.

The Japanese decision to liberalize interest rates on deposits of Yen100 million and over from spring 1987 has been criticized by the Commission which demands a far lower level - in the region of Yen10 million. The Commission has also pressed for the creation of a liberalized and competitive interbank market. Substantial progress has been made in the securities sector, but as regards the deregulation of interest rates and the interbank market, neither the Ministry of Finance, nor the Bank of Japan was prepared to give a firm commitment nor a precise timetable for further liberalization.

The Commission has also proposed to the Japanese authorities an arrangement for improving import financing by Community banks operating in Tokyo, thus helping European exporters interested in selling to Japan. Japan's replies were not very positive but they were at least prepared to be flexible on a case-by-case basis.

Box 78: Main Economic Indicators 1987-1991 - UK, EC, US and Japan GDP at constant prices (% change on previous year)

	1987	1988	1989	1990*	1991*
UK	4.7	4.1	2.3	1.5	2.25
EC	2.9	3.8	3.4	3.0	3.0
USA	3.7	4.6	3.0	2.0	2.25
Japan	4.2	5.7	4.8	4.25	3.25

Source: EUROSTAT Monthly 1989-90. * Forecast

Conclusion

The Commission is committed to opening up the Single European Market to all-comers. It is concerned to achieve a broad multilateral balance of economic advantage rather than a strict sectoral reciprocity of advantage, and is pursuing this end in the forum of the GATT trade negotiations in the current Uruguay Round. Future relations between the Community and Japan will largely be determined by the outcome of these negotiations. A joint declaration between Japan and the EC modelled on the statements signed by the EC with the US and Canada was expected to be signed in June of 1991. In its relations with Japan, the Community seeks a developing relationship based on fair trade, free investment patterns, competition, equal terms and cooperation.

22. The EC and Central and Eastern Europe

The pace of change in Central and Eastern Europe during 1988-1990 was on an historic scale. The European Community is very deeply involved in this continuing process of economic and political change. The countries involved differ considerably in their economic and political maturity and in their capacity to move from command economies to those combining differing mixes of capitalism and socialism.

The signature of the Joint Declaration by the EC and the Council for Mutual Economic Assistance (COMECON) in June 1988 marked the formal recognition of the EC and enabled the states of Central and Eastern Europe to develop bilateral relations with the EC for the first time. Some of the key developments are in Box 79.

The European Community is a magnet for Central and Eastern Europe. The responsibilities and burdens that have been put on it, and the high expectations the emerging democracies have of it, underline its achievements during the past five years. The EC is of particular relevance for three reasons. Firstly, it is a uniquely successful experiment in collaboration and common decision-making between independent democratic countries. In the second place, it offers a centre of gravity and political stability in Europe which is urgently needed during these times of rapid change. Third, it offers a mechanism for immediate common action to help the countries of Eastern Europe to build the competitive economies which will be needed to sustain their new political freedom.

Eastern Europe comprises some 140 million consumers before taking account of the 200 million Soviets west of the Urals, and could, according to some experts, become the most exciting region of the world for business opportunities over the next twenty years (see Box 81).

Box 79: EC Relations with Central and Eastern Europe: Some Key Events

1. 25 June 1988 - formal recognition by COMECON of EC - Joint Declaration of Luxembourg.

2. August 1988 - by this time, six out of seven COMECON members had established diplomatic relations with the EC.

3. Over the next 18 months, bilateral trade and commercial and economic cooperation agreements concluded by the EC with individual countries.

4. July 1989, Western Summit leads to European Commission's being entrusted with the task of coordinating economic aid to Poland and Hungary and subsequently to others on behalf of the 24 OECD countries.

5. December 1989 - decision taken to establish the European Bank for Reconstruction and Development (EBRD) for the financing of productive and competitive investment in Central and Eastern Europe.

6. January 1990 - negotiations begin with East Germany (GDR).

7. January 1990 - Community expresses readiness 'to promote the process of liberalization in Central and Eastern Europe', but underlines that 'the Community's own integration process is of central importance in any consideration of the future of Europe'.

8. February 1990 - the Group of 24 (12 EC members, EFTA members, Canada, US, Japan, Australia, New Zealand and Turkey) examine the memoranda presented by Bulgaria, Czechoslovakia, the GDR, Romania and Yugoslavia in the light of progress towards the implementation of political and economic objectives.

9. German monetary union or the 'Staatsvertrag' took place on 2 July 1990. It involved the immediate introduction of monetary union (with transfer of sovereignty to the Bundesbank) and the gradual integration of the German Democratic Republic into Germany.

10. 5-6 July 1990 - NATO Summit and London Declaration. A far-reaching package of measures, known as the London Declaration, which signalled the end of the Cold War, was approved by NATO leaders at the final session of the historic two-day summit in London. President Gorbachev was invited to address this summit at which measures decided upon included the maintenance of an integrated military structure, the retention of America's forces in Europe, a united Germany in NATO and a continued nuclear element in defence strategy.

11. 3 October 1990 Germany reunited.

The breaking down of barriers draws attention immediately to the fact that the countries are very different one from another. Some, such as Hungary and Czechoslovakia, are much nearer to Western living standards than others - even though in all of them there is no prospect of catching up to the same level as the EC countries' average in the next five years. The situation of what was the German Democratic Republic is different from the other countries. When Germany re-united, the GDR became part of the European Community with all the advantages and responsibilities this entails. The application of EC law and the length of the derogations required were the subject of considerable discussion. The former GDR was always known as the 13th State of the EC as goods have been freely imported into the EC through the FRG since the Community was first formed.

Box 80: Imports-Exports EUR 12 - Total (Ecubn)

	Imports		Exports	
	1977	1987	1977	1987
Eastern Europe	13	24	13	19
EFTA	24	82	27	90
US	28	56	22	72

The latest figures for trade with Eastern European countries for the year up to September 1989 show an increase on 1987: imports to the EC from Eastern European countries for the 9 months totalled Ecu21bn and exports totalled Ecu18bn.

Complications of doing business and the fast-changing situations make market research and desk research prior to visits of above average importance. Because of the high up-front investment costs, the markets of Central and Eastern Europe are for those developing long term strategies . Consultants and middlemen are likely to have an important role and it is of interest to note how many of the major consulting firms are now establishing themselves across Eastern Europe. Embassies and trade missions of the Member States have a key information and market research role and the European Community is establishing missions in the countries as well as extending the Euro-Information Business Centres (Box 57) to these countries.

Box 81: Doing Business in Central and Eastern Europe

1. Each country is a different market - need to prioritize - see Boxes 42 and 44.

2. Long term commitment

3. Importance of up to date market research because of fast-changing economic and political climates

4. Role of consultants and middlemen

5. Skills shortages may necessitate heavy training investment

6. Financing issues

7. Technical know-how problems

8. Selection of joint-venture partners

9. Language and culture issues

10. Assessment of EC programmes such as PHARE and Member State programmes to seek out potential sources of aid (see Box 82)

There are enormous management training and development issues to be resolved as well as the need to develop technical skills. Trained managers will be in very short supply for a long time. There will be much to be said for training younger people to operate on Central and Eastern European affairs. They will need to learn languages as well as do business and for reasons of cost and flexibility there will be great opportunities for the younger generation.

Financing operations will be complex because of the unresolved issues of currency convertibility and the reluctance of the banks to lend as willingly as they did to Third World countries over the last two decades.

There will be considerable opportunities to sell licences and know-how although many countries being short of hard currency will want to develop joint venture operations involving high up-front investment rather than buying know-how and developing it themselves. The opportunities will be considerable, but the pay-back period will not be short term.

There are funds available and opportunities to become involved with EC programmes for Central and Eastern Europe. As the programmes are proliferating and the time from conception to implementation is often very short, it will be worth while obtaining information as to the latest state of play from the European Commission in Brussels or from its offices in Member States.

Box 82: The PHARE and TEMPUS Programmes of the EC

One of the most important recent developments in trading relations between the EC and the Eastern European countries has been that of the PHARE Programme - Poland/Hungary: Aid for Restructuring Economies.

Also, the Paris Summit 14-16 July 1989 (Heads of State and Government of the Seven - Germany, France, Italy, UK, Canada, Japan, US and the European Commission) decided that along with other interested countries they should give coordinated economic aid to Poland and Hungary. This would provide both moral and material support to the Hungarians and the Poles and encourage them in their efforts to achieve democratic reform. The Commission was given the task of coordinating this operation.

The main activities include food aid to Poland, investment promotion (creation of joint ventures), improved access to Western markets, cooperation in environmental protection and vocational training. The first coordination meeting was held between the Group of 24 (12 EC members, EFTA members, Canada, US, Japan, Australia, New Zealand and Turkey).

A review meeting on 22 May 1990 between the G-24 nations was able to look back over a year of progress, improved access to Western markets and projects identified in priority areas of agriculture, training, environment and investment. The inclusion of Romania in the scheme in January 1990 now means that, alongside Poland and Hungary, four other countries have been added - Czechoslovakia, Bulgaria, Yugoslavia and Romania. The PHARE programme for

1991 is Ecu800m with a further Ecu500m proposed for the Soviet Union.

In the context of economic aid for Central and Eastern Europe, the Trans-European Mobility Scheme for University Students (TEMPUS) and a European Training Foundation were set up in May 1990. The scheme aims to cover initial and continuing vocational training as well as retraining for young people and adults, including in particular management training. The Commission will be responsible for the implementation of the TEMPUS scheme, supporting 'Joint European Projects' through mobility grants to encourage young people to study in universities and/or companies in Central and Eastern Europe and the EC. Teaching staff and employees in industry will also be eligible for these grants.

Past statistics and past experience will be very little use as a guide to the future, especially as regards the growth sectors. There will be business opportunities in virtually every sector with emphasis on those with export or import substitution potential. Joint ventures or other forms of collaboration, in agriculture and food processing, in packaging and distribution, in energy saving and pollution control will develop rapidly. There will be opportunities for smaller firms to supply to contractors running major schemes and indeed going in on the backs of larger companies could be an important risk-reducing strategy for SMEs.

For many companies, the opportunities for business in Central and Eastern Europe are easier to talk about than act upon. The great changes planned are going to take some years to become reality and in the meantime, there are plenty of advisers, plenty of opportunities, but also plenty of risks. How can a business manager be sure that those he is doing business with are underwritten by either the state or a bank? What about the legal issues when there are not even property registers in many cities? What are the problems of doing business with companies and countries where there is an acute shortage of hard currencies?

For the smaller company it will be necessary to resort to all the traditional methods of doing business in such countries - barter trade, irrevocable letters of credit, joint venture activity where both sides clearly contribute and have something to gain as well as something to lose. Larger companies will require to spread their risks carefully, to work with other companies, to ensure guaranteed access to markets for goods and services produced or provided from local manufacturing or sales bases. While EC governments may not underwrite business totally, there will be significant support from know-how funds and similar incentives to encourage the development of these markets both at Member State level and through Community funding.

The business and trade framework being established in Central and Eastern Europe will be high on the list of priorities of the EC during the next decade, but other regions of the world such as the Mediterranean countries will continue to attract attention and it is these other parts of the world that are the subject of the next chapter.

23. European Community Relations with Other Parts of the World

In previous chapters of this section business and trade issues between the European Community and the two other corners of the Western Economic Triangle have been covered. As well as the chapters on the US and Japan, there has been discussion of relations and business with Central and Eastern Europe. This chapter describes, with a few examples, the relations of the Community with the rest of the world.

The development of the Community's external relations is a continuing task and over 144 countries have diplomatic relations with the EC. In the GATT negotiations (see Chapter 14) the Member States give the Commission a mandate to negotiate on their behalf, once they have arrived at an agreed approach. In the United Nations, the Twelve Member States vote together on most issues, and through the growing development of the political cooperation procedure, they develop common approaches and policies on an increasing number of international issues. The current Inter-Governmental Conferences will develop common foreign, security and economic policies still further.

The moral and political, not to mention economic, power of the Community is more effective when combined in one policy representing the Twelve Member States and their 340 million inhabitants. Relations with a number of regional groupings are described below in outline, but they would all require a book to themselves to do justice to the wide range of activities and actions which they cover. In 1986 foreign trade (and that excludes intra-EC trade) represented about 10% of Community GDP compared to 7% for the US and 8.5% for Japan.

Box 83: The Foreign Trade of the Community (Ecubn)

Intra-Community trade	540
EC trade with rest of the world	387
of which the major trading partners are:	
EFTA	90
US and Canada	76
OPEC countries	31
Mediterranean basin	30
Latin America	23
ACP (African, Caribbean and Pacific) countries	17
ASEAN (Association of South East Asian Nations)	12

Source: European File 1989

The European Free Trade Area (EFTA)

Over 25% of EC trade is with the EFTA countries - Austria, Finland, Iceland, Norway, Sweden, Switzerland and Liechtenstein. For this reason alone, relations between EFTA and the EC are taken seriously. The proximity of the countries, the similarity of their political and economic systems and the fact that some of these countries at least are likely to join the EC during the next decade make relations of even greater importance.

Since 1973 there has been a free-trade area in manufactured goods between the two organizations. Efforts to develop closer relations began in 1984 with the concept of a 'Single Economic Space' (now more aptly called in English 'Single Economic Area'). In 1989 sufficient common ground was identified to begin negotiations for an agreement on a single market where goods and services, people and capital would move freely - along the lines of the Single Market of the original Twelve Member States. Certain flanking policies such as research and development, competition policy, consumer protection, working and social conditions and the environment were also to be subjects of scrutiny to see how close the EFTA countries could come to the EC without actually becoming members. This implied that the EFTA countries would have to accept the 'Acquis Communautaire' - the accrued series of laws and regulations which go to make up the EC legal base - for those matters to be covered by the agreement.

Both sides have considerable political interest in bringing this about and the intention is to finalize negotiations so that the agreement will be in place at the end of 1992 at the same time as the completion of the Single Market. Negotiations are inevitably difficult as the EC wants to give as few derogations - that is agreements to delay application of specific rules - as possible, while the EFTA countries want to have as much influence on the Community decision-making process as they can while not actually becoming members. A tight series of high level meetings took place in the autumn of 1990, the outcome of which will have a profound effect on future relations and, in particular, on the likelihood of other EFTA countries following Austria in applying for full membership. The EC view is that the deepening of the Community, that is the implementation of the Single European Act and the 1985 White Paper, must have priority over the widening of the Community to include other members although the widening of the EC is of growing importance.

Box 84: The Lomé Convention

Essential Features

The Lomé Convention, a comprehensive cooperation agreement between the European Community (EC States) and the ACP Group of African, Caribbean and

Pacific countries, was first signed in 1975 and renewed, after fresh negotiations, in 1979, 1984 and 1989. An example of North-South dialogue in practice, it offers:

- a partnership in which the political, social, cultural and economic options of each partner are respected;

- secure and lasting cooperation based on a freely negotiated and legally binding contract;

- permanent dialogue, through 3 joint institutions:
  ACP-EC Council of Ministers
  ACP-EC Committee of Ambassadors
  ACP-EC Joint Assembly;

- overall, flexible cooperation using the full range of aid and trade development instruments.

Aid and Trade

Aid
The European Development Fund (EDF) provides grants and risk capital, and the European Investment Bank (EIB) provides loans, for national and regional development programmes. Also included in the EDF are five specific funds:
- Stabex - for cash transfers to offset serious losses on agricultural exports
- Sysmin - for mining industries in difficulty
- Emergency aid - for disaster relief
- Refugee aid - for serious refugee situations
- Structural adjustment aid - for countries undergoing economic reforms

Trade
The main arrangements are:
- duty and quota-free access to the EC market for almost all ACP exports
- guaranteed purchase by the EC of up to 1.3 million tonnes of ACP sugar at EC prices
- funds for trade promotion and development

Lomé IV

Duration
10 years (1990-2000)

Membership
12 EC States
69 ACP States, including three new members: Dominican Republic, Haiti and, after independence, Namibia

Financial Resources

	Ecum
Lomé I (1975-1980)	3,450
Lomé II (1980-1985)	5,700
Lomé III (1985-1990)	8,500
Lomé IV (1990-2000)	12,000
Financial protocol (1990-1995) made up of:	
European Development Fund (EDF VII)	
Grants for national and regional programmes	6,215
Structural adjustment	1,150
Stabex	1,500
Sysmin	480
Emergency aid	250
Refugee aid	100
Interest rate subsidies	280
Risk capital	825
European Investment Bank (EIB)	
Loans for national and regional projects	1,200

Of the total amount of Ecu12,000m (EDF + EIB), 1,250 million are set aside for regional cooperation.

Source: The Lomé Convention, European Commission, DG for Information, Communication and Culture, 1990.

The Mediterranean Policy of the Community

The 12 countries of the Community have 340 million inhabitants while the 14 non-EC countries in the Mediterranean have 200 million. By 2025 the EC will have the same population while that of the 14 will have grown to 400 million. They are the third most important customer of the EC and the fourth largest supplier. Relations are of key importance and yet there are problems of resource allocation, of a deteriorating environment, and of economic and political stability.

Because of their important relationship with the EC, Commissioner Abel Matutes, responsible for Mediterranean policy, called in 1989 for a new initiative for these countries based on:

- the need to keep EC markets open and improve market access

- support of economic reforms and technical assistance

- the need to act swiftly to address basic food shortfalls.

In late 1989 a new Community action programme was proposed to the Commission - PROMED. The intention was that it would start in 1990 and be fully implemented in 1991. It was in six parts, which would deal with measures to support economic adjustment, encourage private investment, increase financial aid especially from the Community, improve access to Community markets, involve more those countries with the 1992 Single Market process and ensure closer economic and political dialogue.

The activities of the Community in external relations and trade are extensive. Three partial examples are given below and the Lomé Convention is described in Box 84. For those doing business in countries of the world which have commercial treaty relations with the EC, and that is virtually all of them, it is worth investigating the nature of these agreements. Many contracts for training, joint projects and technical assistance stipulate that the supplier of goods and services should be from the EC. If your company is EC-based, such contracts may present business opportunities.

Aid to Asian and Latin American Countries (ALA)

Aid is intended to support rural development operations, mainly food related, to promote regional cooperation and to help reconstruction projects in the wake of disasters. In 1989 the budget appropriation was nearly Ecu300m.

Cooperation Agreement with the Arab States of the Gulf

In November 1989 a Cooperation Agreement was signed to strengthen relations between the EC and the GCC (Gulf Cooperation Council) countries to broaden economic and technical cooperation in a large number of industrial sectors. It established a Joint Council for GCC/Community cooperation. Following the Gulf war, a new role for the GCC will probably be developed.

Relations with ASEAN (Association of South East Asian Nations)

The Community has not traditionally had the same special relationship with the developing countries of South-East Asia (Brunei, Indonesia, Malaysia, Philippines, Singapore and Thailand) as it has had with the Lomé Convention countries, but there has been cooperation in the trade, economic and development areas. Between 1976 and 1988, the Community allocated Ecu357m to aid projects in the region. During the eighties, trade between the EC and ASEAN has doubled from 12.5 to nearly Ecu25m.

Conclusion

From this chapter, which gives only a glimpse of the wide range of commercial and trade and aid activities of the Community, the conclusion is clear. The EC is open for business in both directions; it will not and cannot become a fortress. It has widespread concerns, and plans to work with developed countries as well as to work with and aid the developing regions of the world.

Section V: Sources of Further Information

24. Information Sources

The structure and the working of the various institutions of the European Communities generate an enormous quantity of documents. Indeed, the continuing progress of political and economic integration of the European Communities has increased the amount of information and documentation. Many documents may well remain internal documents, but others later develop into policy, information or communication documents and are made available to the public.

When the institutions' documents reach the public, they may be in the form of the broadly known documents such as the Commission COM documents or the Official Journal of the European Communities. These are read by a wide spectrum of professional, commercial and political organizations. They may, however, take the shape of specific articles on specialized Community topics. The Office of Official Publications in Luxembourg is very conscious of the increasing task of meeting the needs of the public and providing concrete and timely information on a wide variety of specialist sectors.

Once a document has been drafted, it receives a different status and the logical but sometimes painstaking path the document will follow very often confuses the information seeker. This applies whether the document is a communication from the Commission, the final text of a proposal, a further step in a policy-making process, or the work of one of the other institutions. The confusion is often compounded by the various channels of distribution. All official publications are ultimately available from the Office of Official Publications in Luxembourg. However, each member state also has one or two sales agents and, in addition, it is possible to obtain other documents free of charge from the Offices of the Commission or the Parliament, or from the Institutions themselves.

This chapter contains names and addresses of organizations and short explanations of their functions and relevance to those doing business in Europe. It also gives a comprehensive source of publications and explanations of how best to use them and how to interpret them. They are published by both the European Community institutions and by external authors to provide further and more in-depth information on specific sectors. Updates of documents are published regularly and you should check when ordering that you have the latest edition.

The Offices of the Commission in Member States

- They represent the Commission and act as a point of contact with national authorities and organisations
- They inform different audiences about the aims of the European Community in general, its institutions and its policies, and about the aims of the Commission in particular
- They communicate Commission views through relations with the national, regional and specialist press, radio and television
- They report regularly to the Commission on developments relevant to policy making at the European level

The Offices are in all European Community capitals, many important regional cities, and in many other parts of the world.

UK addresses are:

Jean Monnet House
8 Storey's Gate
London SW1P 3AT
Tel: 071 973 1992
Telex: 23208 EURUK G
Fax: 071 973 1900

4 Cathedral Road
Cardiff CF1 9SG
Tel: 0222 371631

Telex: 497727 EUROPA G
Fax: 0222 395489

7 Alva Street
Edinburgh EH2 4PH
Tel: 031 225 2058
Telex: 727420 EUEDIN G
Fax: 031 226 4105

Windsor House
9/15 Bedford Street
Belfast
Tel: 0232 240708
Telex: 74117 CECBEL G
Fax: 0232 248241

DG XXIII Enterprise Policy and Small and Medium-sized Enterprises

The SME Task Force was established in 1986 to implement the SME Action Programme. Its role is to develop policies for small and medium-sized businesses and to identify and resolve any practical problems they might encounter in the application of Community policies and access to Community funds and programmes. It is now integrated into DG XXIII and is responsible for the development of the European Information Centres, the Business Co-operation Network and EURO/INFO Bulletin.

'EC Measures to Help', published by the Directorate-General, is an indispensable guide to the opportunities that exist for businesses in the European Community.

DG XXIII is located at:

80 rue d'Arlon
1040 Brussels
Tel: 02/236 16 76
Telefax: 236.12.41
Telex: 61.655 BURAP B

Postal address:
Commission of the European Communities
200 Rue de la Loi
1049 Brussels
Belgium

The Business Co-operation Network

The Business Co-operation Network (BC NET) is a computerized system involving 250 business consultants located in all member states. It permits the rapid identification of potential partner firms in other member states or regions, in response to specific offers of cooperation, thus helping to open up new markets for SMEs.

In the first two years, more than 100 cooperation agreements between firms (commercial and technological agreements, joint ventures and licences) have been concluded.

For further information contact DG XXIII.

European Business Information Centres

The creation of a new channel for direct and permanent communication between what goes on at Community level and the world of enterprise and entrepreneurs is the aim of the Centres of European Business Information.

Established in cooperation with existing organizations which already advise firms, each centre has a specially trained staff which provides SMEs with information on all aspects of Community affairs likely to interest local business. The Centres keep SMEs abreast of opportunities for Community research and development support, regional aids, training etc. They represent an intermediary between the businessmen of the region on the one hand and the European Commission on the other. Following the success of the pilot scheme, the number of centres has been increased across the Community. They will also be established in Central and Eastern Europe.

Addresses of European Business Information Centres in the UK:

Scottish Development Agency
Euro Info Centre
21 Bothwell Street
Glasgow G2 6NR
Tel: 041 221 0999

Birmingham Chamber of Industry and Commerce
PO Box 360, 75 Harborne Road
Birmingham B15 3DH
Tel: 021 454 6171

Northern Development Company
Bank House
Carliol Square
Newcastle-upon-Tyne
Tel: 091 261 0026

Department of Employment
Small Firms and Tourism Division Limited
Ebury Bridge House
Ebury Bridge Road
London SW1W 8QD
Tel: 071 730 5874

Local Enterprise Development Unit
Ledu House
Upper Galwally
Belfast
BT8 4TB
Tel: 0232 491031

Federation of Sussex Industries and Chamber of
Commerce Euro-Info Centre
Seven Dials
Brighton
East Sussex
BN1 3JS
Tel: 0273 262825

Bristol Chamber of Commerce and Industry
16 Clifton Park
Bristol

BS8 3BY
Tel: 0272 737373

Exeter Enterprises Limited
University of Exeter
Hailey Wing, Reed Hall
Exeter
EX4 4QR
Tel: 0392 214085

Euro Team
Euro-Info Centre
University of Leicester
Leicester
LE1 7RH
Tel: 0533 554464

Kent European Information Centre
Kent County Council
Springfield
Maidstone
Kent
ME14 2LL
Tel: 0622 671411

Manchester Chamber of Commerce and Industry
Euro-Info Centre
56 Oxford Street
Manchester
M60 7HJ
Tel: 061 236 3210

Norwich Chamber of Commerce and Industry
112 Barrack Street
Norwich
NR3 1UB
Tel: 0603 625977

Euro-Info Centre
Farraday Building
Highfield Science Park
Nottingham
NG7 2QP
Tel: 0602 222414

Welsh Euro-Info Centre
UWCC - Guest Building
P.O. Box 430
Cardiff
CF1 3XT
Tel: 0222 229525

Chamber of Commerce and Industry
Thames-Chiltern
Euro-Info Centre
Commerce House
2-6 Bath Road
Slough
SL1 3SB
Tel: 0753 77877

Shropshire Chamber of Commerce and Industry
Euro-Info Centre
Industry House
16 Halesfield
Telford
Shropshire
TF7 4TA
Tel: 0952 588766

The Southern Area European Information Centre
Central Library
Civic Centre
Southampton
Hampshire
SO9 4XP
Tel: 0703 832866

Directorates-General III, IV, VI, VII, XI, XV, XXI and XIII of the Commission

The European Commission is divided into 23 Directorates-General (DGs) and other services, each of which is sub-divided into a number of directorates with responsibilities for a specific area of Commission policy. Many of the DGs are of relevance to business. Some key ones are:

DG III

- responsible for the ***internal market and industrial affairs***

It is divided into directorates responsible for:

- Industrial economy, services industry, non-member countries, raw materials
- Internal market and industrial affairs
- Approximation of laws, freedom of establishment and freedom to provide services
- Steel
- Public procurement

DG IV

- responsible for ***competition policy***

It is divided into directorates in charge of:

- General competition and co-ordination
- Restrictive practices, abuse of dominant positions and other distortions to competition
- State aids

DG VI

- responsible for ***agriculture***

- Its directorate B-II is in charge of quality and health aspects of agricultural produce

DG VII

- responsible for ***transport***

It is divided into directorates in charge of:

- Maritime transport; transport economics; tourism; legislation
- Inland transport; market analysis; transport safety; research and technology
- Air transport; transport infrastructure; social and ecological aspects of transport

DG XI

- responsible for ***environment, consumer protection and nuclear safety***

It is divided into directorates in charge of:

- Nuclear safety, waste management, prevention and control of pollution
- Protection of water and the air, and conservation
- Protection and promotion of consumer interests

DG XV

- responsible for financial institutions and company law

It is divided into:

- Financial institutions: banks, insurance and stock exchanges
- Company law, company and capital movements, taxation

DG XXI

- responsible for the *customs union and indirect taxation*

It is divided into directorates in charge of:

- External tariff questions
- Customs union legislation
- Indirect taxation including elimination of fiscal frontiers

DG XXIII

Has a Directorate responsible for *enterprise policy and small and medium-sized enterprises*

It has divisions dealing with:

- Policy development and improvement of the business environment
- Information for SMEs and relations with the Community institutions and trade associations. Also Euro-Info Centres
- SME cooperation and transnational development and the Business Cooperation Centre
- Cooperatives

They can be contacted at:

Commission of the European Communities
Rue de la Loi 200
1040 Brussels
Tel: 010.322.235.11.11
Telex: 21877 COMEU B

The European Parliament

The European Parliament has a legislative role in respect of most Community legislation on the internal market (see Chapter 4).

The Parliamentary committees principally concerned with the achievement of the internal market are:

- Economic and Monetary Affairs and Industrial Policy
- Legal Affairs and Citizens Rights
- Transport
- Social Affairs and Employment
- The Environment, Public Health and Consumer Protection

Documentation and information on the MEPs involved in this committee work can be obtained from:

European Parliament Information Office
2 Queen Anne's Gate
London SW1H 9AA
Tel: 071 222 0411
Fax: 071 222 2713

European Committee for Standardization (CEN)

Its aims are to promote standardization at the European level with a view to facilitating the exchange of goods and services by eliminating obstacles caused by technical requirements. It develops technical, scientific and economic procedures necessary to give effect to standardization activities, by harmonizing national standards of Member States and implementing international standards.

European Committee for Electrotechnical Standardization (CENELEC)

Its aims are to ensure uniform implementation of international standards in fields of electrical technology, telecommunications and information technology, telecommunications and information technology at national level by the member countries in order to promote European trade and to prevent trade barriers.

Conference of European Postal and Telecommunications Administrations (CEPT)

Its aims are to establish closer relations between member Administrations and to harmonize and improve their administrative and technical services.

The three above organizations can be contacted at:

Rue Bréderode, 2
1000 Brussels - Bte 5, B
Tel: (322) 519 68 11
Telex: 26257
Fax: (322) 519 68 19

British Standards Institution (BSI)

BSI is the recognized authority in the UK for preparing national standards which are in use in all industries and technologies, in trade and in the home. BSI has developed a wide range of commercial services related to standards in order to help British Industry and to ensure customer satisfaction.

2, Park Street
London W1A 2BS
Tel: 071 629 9000
Telex: 266933 BSILON G
Fax: 071 629 106

The European Investment Bank (EIB) - The EC's Bank for Long-term Finance

Established by the EC Treaty in 1958, the EIB is the European Community's bank for financing capital investment promoting the balanced development of the Community.

The EIB can finance up to half the gross investment costs of a project or group of schemes, with loans normally beginning at about £1.5 million - no absolute maximum.

Total lending by the EIB in 1987 came to Ecu7.84bn, of which nearly Ecu400m went to projects outside the EC as part of the Community's development aid under specific financial co-operation or association agreements.

Further information can be obtained from:

UK Liaison Office
68 Pall Mall
London SW1Y 5ES
Tel: 071 839 3351

EIB Headquarters
100 Boulevard Konrad Adenauer
L-2950 Luxembourg
Tel: 352 4379-1

ECOSOC/ESC

The Economic and Social Committee of the European Community (ECOSOC) is an advisory body consisting of representatives of employers, trade unions and consumer groupings. The Economic and Social Committee is required to express its opinion formally on a range of issues put before it by the European Commission. It publishes reports regularly and is a sounding board for the Commission and the Council of Ministers, in view of the broad spectrum of experience covered jointly by the corporate experience of its members. (See Chapter 5.)

2, rue Ravenstein
B-1000 Brussels
Tel: 010 322 512 3920
010 322 513 9595

The Department of Trade and Industry (DTI)

The DTI is the main department in the British Government handling commercial and industrial issues. It is responsible for trade and industrially related matters both domestically in the UK and the rest of the world. Recently, a unit has been created in the DTI concerned with the provision of information for British industry and commerce during the years leading up to 1992.

For further information, contact:

DTI - 'Europe Open for Business'
1 Victoria Street
London SW1H 0ET
Tel: Freephone 0800 500 200
or local DTI Office

Chambers of Commerce

These represent commercial interests in their areas and provide a wide range of services to local businesses. Firms can gain from them information and advice about European internal market issues and export services.

For further information, contact

The Association of British Chambers of Commerce
Sovereign House
212a Shaftsbury Avenue
London WC2H 8EW
Tel: 071 240 5831
Telex: 265871
Fax: 071 379 6331

The Confederation of British Industry (CBI)

The CBI is a body representing a wide range of industries. It has long experience and expertise in coordinating and representing British industry's views and enjoys a close working relationship with the government.

It lobbies actively at national and Community level, has a well established office in Brussels and is an influential member of UNICE, the European Federation of employers organizations. A comprehensive briefing pack on the major internal market issues is available called 'Europe Sans Frontieres'.

London:
'Europe Sans Frontieres'
Confederation of British Industry
Centre Point
103 New Oxford Street
London WC1A 1DY
Tel: 071 379 7400
Telex: 21332
Fax: 071 240 1578

Brussels:
Confederation of British Industry
40 rue Jospeh II
Bte 14
Brussels B 1040
Tel: (010 322) 231 0456

European Documentation Centres

European Documentation Centres - EC
Depositary Libraries -DEP
European Reference Centres - ERC

If you cannot come to the Commission Offices and are unable to consult by telephone or mail, you can obtain assistance at one of the 45 EDCs set up in various parts of the UK. European Documentation Centres are housed in university libraries and public libraries. The status of EDCs is conferred subject to certain rules laid down by the EC in Brussels. The centres play a positive role in stimulating the development of the study of European affairs in the academic institutions they serve and, in an increasing number, supply a specialist information service to the local community. Addresses can be obtained from Commission Offices.

25. The Office for Official Publications

The Office for Official Publications of the European Communities publishes in 9 Community languages for:

- The European Parliament
- The Council
- The Commission
- The Court of Justice
- The Economic and Social Committee
- The European Centre for the Development of Vocational Training
- The European Foundation for the Improvement of Living and Working Conditions
- Other Community bodies

It is possible to obtain free of charge from the Offices of the Commission of the European Communities a general catalogue entitled 'The European Community as a Publisher - 1990'. Most publications are available for sale in the United Kingdom.

Whenever possible, the ISBN and the price of the publication will be mentioned. So far as possible this will be in £ sterling but Commission policy is now to quote in Ecus. When publications are available from another source, this source will be explicitly mentioned. Ecu1 = approx. £0.70.

Addresses

The Office for Official Publications of the European Communities
2 Rue Mercier
L2985 Luxembourg
Tel: (010 35 2) 49928-1

H.M.S.O. Publications Centre
51 Nine Elms Lane
London SW8 5DR
Tel: (071) 873 9090

(sub-agents)
Alan Armstrong Ltd
2 Arkwright Road
Reading
Berkshire RG2 0SQ
Tel: (0734) 751771

A. BREAKDOWN OF EUROPEAN PUBLICATIONS BY INSTITUTION

I. The European Parliament

1. The European Parliament
   1987, (20pp)
   AX-47-86-777
   available free from the European Parliament Information Office

2. European Parliament - Rules of Procedure
   July 1989
   free from the E.P. Information Office
   (explains the way the European Parliament conducts its affairs)

3. European Parliament - List of Members
   October 23 1989
   free from E.P. Information office
   (also known as the 'Grey List', referring to the colour of the cover)

4. Fact Sheets on the European Parliament and the Activities of the European Community
   1989
   ISBN 92-823-0163-X
   Price: Ecu17.50

5. Europe's Parliament and the Single Act
   1989
   free from the E.P. Information Office

6. Progress Towards European Integration: Survey of the Main Activities of the European Parliament
   published annually
   free from the E.P. Information Office

7. Ten Years that Changed Europe - 1979/1989
   February 1989
   free from the E.P. Information Office
   (well-documented publication covering all areas of E.C. policy)

8. Official Journal of the European Communities - Annex: Debates of the European Parliament
   monthly
   annual subscription running from March until February Price: £83.00
   (verbatim reports of the sittings constituting a monthly session of the European Parliament)

9. Minutes of Sittings of the European Parliament, irregular, published in the 'C' series of the Official Journal
   (diaries of the business conducted during the sessions of the Parliament)

In addition, it is possible to register on a mailing-list in order to receive the following publications on a regular basis free of charge:

1. European Parliament News
   monthly
   newspaper covering the debates and activities of the European Parliament

2. European Parliament - Briefing
   diary of items to be discussed during the sessions and summary of some reports

3. European Parliament - The Week
   summary of the week's proceedings, comes

out half-way through the following week

4. European Parliament - Press Releases
   irregular
   produced by the London Office of the European Parliament
   cover specific items of news

Addresses:

European Parliament
Directorate-General for Information and Public Relations
Publications and Briefings Division
L - 2929 Luxembourg
Tel: (010 35 2) 430 01

European Parliament Information Office
2 Queen Anne's Gate
London SW1H 9AA
Tel: (071) 222 0411
Fax: (071) 222 2713

European Parliament Information Office
43 Molesworth Street
Dublin 2
Tel: (01) 719 100

II. The Council of Ministers

When the Council adopts a proposal put forward by the Commission, the final text of adoption is published in the Official Journal of the European Communities series 'L' while other items relating to the work of the Commission appear in the series 'C' of the Official Journal (see section B).

It is also possible to obtain extracts of the Minutes of the Meetings of the Council of Ministers from the United Kingdom Offices of the Commission. The minutes give a good summary of the meetings.

On a more general level, two publications are of direct value to the information user:

1. Guide to the Council of the European Communities - I/1988
   Secretariat of the Council, 1988
   ISBN 92-824-0546-X
   Price: Ecu6.50

2. 38th Review of the Council's Work
   1990
   annually
   ISBN 92-824-0600-8
   Price: Ecu8.50

Address

Council of the European Communities
Secretariat for Information, Publications and Documentation
170 Rue de la Loi
B 1048 Brussels
Tel: (010 32 2) 234 6111

III. The Commission

The Commission produces a wide range of documents, some of which are working documents and as such not generally available to the public. The Commission documents are:

1. Working documents published by the Directorate-Generals of the Commission

   They are internal documents and their numbering indicates their provenance - e.g. document III/134/89 refers to the 134th document issued by DG III (Internal Market) in 1989. These documents form very often the basis of proposals for legislation, do not represent official Commission policy and are as such not available to the public. Sometimes a DG's documents represent reports written by independent experts who have been invited to help the DG in formulating policy guidelines.

2. The COM document

   The final DG documents are then submitted to the Secretariat General of the Commission for consideration by the 17 members of the Commission and are re-issued by the Secretariat-General of the Commission bearing a COM document No. - e.g. COM (89) 205 represents the 205th document issued by the Secretariat-General in 1989. The documents can be amended several times before they become COM final.

3. The COM final document

   Once approved by the Commission as a College, the COM document receives the word 'final' at the end of its numerification - e.g. COM (89) final. This distinction is important to grasp as it means that the document is now finalised and therefore available to the public from the sales agents or from the Office for Official Publications in Luxembourg.

   COM documents can be either proposals for legislation or communications/memoranda.

   They can be obtained on an annual subscription basis (selective subscriptions by subject are possible) or as single copies.

4. The SEC document

   These are less formal documents issued by the Secretariat-General. Their aim is to provide information in the shape of statistical data or on the implementation of Community decisions - e.g. when they reach the Common Position stage. They are not as such available for sale.

5. The 'C' document

   The legislative documents that the Commission has to issue in its everyday role of supervisor and administrator of European Community policy such as the Common Agricultural Policy are first drafted in the form of 'C' documents. The final text of Commission decisions and regulations will eventually be published in the Official Journal of the European Communities.

   A useful guide is: The European Commission and the Administration of theCommunity, European Documentation Series No. 3/1989 (see Section B). The booklet describes the way the Commission administers the European Community and the development of the European public service. Free from Commission Offices.

Addresses:

Commission of the European Communities
200 Rue de la Loi
B1049 Brussels

Commission of the European Communities
Jean Monnet House
8 Storey's Gate
London
SW1P 3AT
Tel: (071) 973 1992
Fax: (071) 973 1900

4 Cathedral Road
Cardiff CF1 9SG
Tel: 0222 371631
Telex: 497727 EUROPA G
Fax: 0222 395489

7 Alva Street
Edinburgh EH2 4PH
Tel: 031 225 2058
Telex: 727420 EUEDIN G
Fax: 031 226 4105

Windsor House
9/15 Bedford Street
Belfast
Tel: 0232 240708
Telex: 74117 CECBEL G
Fax: 0232 248241

IV. The Court of Justice

1. The Court of Justice of the European Communities
   European Documentation No. 5/1986
   free from the Offices of the Commission

   Guide to the powers, composition and working methods of the court.

2. Synopsis of the Work of the Court of Justice of the European Communities in 1986 and 1987
   Court of Justice Information Office, 1988
   free
   ISBN 92-829-0141-6

   Information on the administration of the Court together with a summary of the most important judgements of the year.

3. Digest of case-law relating to the European Communities Court of Justice of the European Communities
   'A' Series: Judgements of the Court relating to the EC, ECSC, and EAEC Treaties and secondary law.
   Loose-leaf form with periodical updatings

Issue 1 - 1983 (1069pp)	£40.80
Issue 2 (1st updating) - 1985	£20.40
Issue 3 (2nd updating) - 1986	£20.80

4. Digest of case-law relating to the European Communities
   Court of Justice of the European Communities
   'D' Series: Case-law on the Convention of 27 September 1968 on jurisdiction and the enforcement of judgements in civil and commercial matters.
   Issue 1 - 1979 (basic edition) £20.80
   Issue 2 (1st updating) - 1984 £20.40
   Issue 3 / December 1985 (base edition: 1981) £20.80

5. Reports of cases Before the Court
   Irregular
   Volume XXXIV covering 1988
   Price: Ecu105

   Contains the judgements of the cases of the Court of Justice and is published with an annual index.

6. Proceedings of the Court of Justice of the European Communities
   Weekly
   Available only from the Court of Justice in Luxembourg

   Gives a summary of the judgements, opinions, oral proceedings and new cases. Indispensable for professional advisers.

Address

Court of Justice of the European Communities
Service Interieur
L 2925 Luxembourg
Tel: (010 35 2) 430 31

V. The Court of Auditors

The Court of Auditors is the Community body in charge of external auditing of the Community's general budget and the ECSC's operating budget.

1. The Court of Auditors of the European Communities 1988
   free from the Court of Auditors, Luxembourg

   Small booklet giving basic information on the work of the Court.

2. Annual Report of the Court of Auditors concerning the financial year 1988 accompanied by the replies of the institutions
   published in the 'C' series of the Official Journal

   Report on how the Community institutions have spent the Community budget and the institutions' own budget - the latest report published is C 312 of 12.12.89 and covers the year 1988

3. Special Reports of the Court of Auditors on specific aspects e.g.:

   Special report No. 5/88 on management and control of public storage together with the Commission's replies: O.J. C 274 of 24.10.88

   Special report No. 1/89 on the agri-monetary system accompanied by the replies of the Commission: O.J. C 128 of 24.5.89

Address

Court of Auditors of the European Communities
12 Rue Alcide de Gasperi
L 1615 Luxembourg
Tel: (010 35 2) 4 39 81

VI. The Economic and Social Committee

1. The Other European Assembly
   Economic and Social Committee, 1989
   free from the Economic and Social Committee, Brussels

2. Annual Report of the Economic and Social Committee - 1989
   published 1990
   ISBN 92-830-0171-0
   Price: Ecu12

3. Bulletin of the Economic and Social Committee
   monthly
   annual subscription
   ISBN 0256-5846
   Price: £19.00

4. Opinions and Reports of the Economic and Social Committee
   approximately daily
   annual subscription
   Price: £184

   The opinions and reports are also published later in the 'C' series of the Official Journal

Address

Economic and Social Committee
Press, Information and Publications Division
2 Rue Ravenstein
B 1000 Bruxelles
Tel: (010 32 2) 519 90 11

In order to enable users to obtain information relating to their fields of interest it is possible to subscribe to Commission, European Parliament and Economic and Social Committee documents via a joint subscription scheme which enables selection by topic. Contact the sales offices.

VII. The European Foundation for the Improvement of Living and Working Conditions

The Foundation aims at planning and establishing better living and working conditions through a concrete dissemination of knowledge.

1. European Foundation for the Improvement of Living and Working Conditions - Catalogue of Publications 1988
   free from the Foundation
   ISBN 92-825-8729-0

   Cumulative list of all Foundation publications since its beginning

2. European Foundation for the Improvement of Living and Working Conditions - Annual Report 1989
   ISBN 92-826-0198-6
   Price: Ecu8.75

3. EF-News
   Newsletter, published five times a year
   free of charge from the Foundation

   In addition to highlighting the activities of the Foundation, selectively covers other work being done in Europe on themes relevant to the Foundation's aims

Address

European Foundation for the Improvement of Living and Working Conditions
Loughlinstown House
Shankill
Co. Dublin
Ireland
Tel: Dublin 82 68 88

VIII. CEDEFOP (European Centre for the Development of Vocational Training)

Its aim is to promote cooperation among the Member States of the Community in the field of vocational training by exchanging information relating to the national vocational training systems.

1. CEDEFOP - Annual Report 1990
   free from the Centre

2. CEDEFOP News
   free from CEDFOP

   Multilingual journal in German, French and English

3. Vocational Training
   published three times yearly
   ISBN 0378-5068
   Price: single copy - Ecu5
   annual subscription - Ecu12

   Example:
   No. 1/1988 Wanted - new media for vocational training!
   No. 2/1988 The Social dialogue - bridging the divide
   No. 3/1988 Selective funding - a regulative instrument for initial and continuing training
   No. 1/1989 Education and training - the keys to the future
   No. 2/1989 Our European neighbours - UDSSR, Poland, GDR, CSSR, Hungary and Bulgaria
   No. 3/1989 Europe: A labour market without frontiers?

Address

CEDEFOP
Bundesallee 22
D - 1000 Berlin 15

B. BREAKDOWN OF EUROPEAN PUBLICATIONS BY CATEGORY

I. General Publications

The following publications are available free of charge from the Commission offices

1. Europe at a Glance
   Basic 4-sided leaflet giving general information on the European Community and its policies.

2. Working Together
   By Emile Noel
   Detailed booklet on the European Community institutions and how they work together

3. Political Map of the European Community
   Small map (42 x 30 cm) which includes some basic statistics

4. Development
   20-page illustrated booklet on official development assistance from the European Community and its Member States

5. The European Community and the Third World
   Colour map of the world highlighting the Community and developing countries. Also includes graphics on aid and trade.
   Available in two sizes: 100 x 70 cm or 40 x 28 cm

6. The European Community as a publisher
   Catalogue of EC publications, mainly sales items

7. Film list
   List of films and videos available for free hire

II. Mailing List Publications

The European Commission's London Office provides information on the European Community to an extensive mailing list which is open to everyone. Key publications are:

1. The Week in Europe
   Summary of Community events, issued each Thursday. A useful one-sheet reference and update.

2. Background Reports
   Surveys of particular Community policies, written in popular style with reference to source documents.

3. Press Releases
   Immediate news as issued to the media.

It is possible to obtain a list of previous reports from which you can select appropriate back copies.

III. Periodicals

1. Europe in Northern Ireland
   published by the European Commission Office in Northern Ireland: Windsor House, 9/15 Bedford Street, Belfast BT2 7EG
   Free

2. EUROPE - Magazine of the European Community
   published by the Delegation of the Commission of the European Communities in Washington
   10 issues per year
   available by subscription from the European Community Information Service, 2100 M Street, N.W., Suite 707, Washington, D.C. 20037
   Price: $14.95 per year

3. Target 1992
   Monthly newlsetter on the Single Internal Market published by the Directorate-General Information,

Communication and Culture and Directorate-General XXIII, Commission of the European Communities, 200 Rue de la Loi, B-1049 Brussels
It is possible to obtain back copies from the Offices of the Commission
Free

There are other periodicals relating to specific areas which will be referred to in the appropriate section dealing with these policy areas (see Part C).

IV. European Documentation Series

Booklets describing in detail the origin and the working of various EC policies. They are available free of charge from Commission offices subject to availability. Free in limited quantities.

V. The European File

Shorter versions of the European Documentation topics, presented in the form of small essays. Free.

VI. The Treaties of the European Communities

Constitute the primary legislation of the European Communities whether they are the Founding Treaties, the Treaties amending these treaties (Volume I) or the later Treaties of Accession (Volume II). The treaties are published in all official languages of the Community.

Price:
Volume 1 - £33.00
Volume II - £58.00
Volume I & II - £75.00

Available from HMSO and agents

VII. The Official Journal of the European Communities

This is the daily legal gazette of the European Communities. It is obtainable on a subscription basis from H.M.S.O. or may be purchased in single copies. The Official Journal is available in the 9 languages of the Community, though it is currently available in the United Kingdom in English only. It is sub-divided in 3 series: L, C and S. Additionally, the Debates of the European Parliament are published as an Annex to the O.J.

1. The 'L' Series or legislative series covers secondary legislation.

a. Regulations:	binding in their entirety and directly applicable to all Member States;
b. Directives:	binding on Member States as to the result to be achieved, but leave the Member States the choice as to how to implement them in their national legislation;
c. Decisions:	are similar to regulations, are directly applicable, but are addressed to specific parties (one or more Member States or to individuals);
d. Recommendations and Opinions:	have no binding force.

2. The 'C' Series or communications series is sub-divided into three sections:

a. Information:	daily rate of the Ecu, opinions of the European Parliament, written questions, notices of

	actions brought before the Court of Justice etc.
b. Preparatory Acts:	proposals for legislation, opinions of the ESC and of the Court of Auditors
c. Notices:	invitations to tender relating to agricultural products or notices of competitions for recruitment in the Community institutions, etc.

Neither of these series is independently available; subscription is to both series whether on paper or on microfiches. Retrospective annual collections of the two series are available on microfiche only.

Together with the subscription to the Official Journal 'L' and 'C' Series, comes the bi-annual Directory of Community Legislation in Force. This can also be obtained independently for Ecu75. The latest edition, the 14th, covers the situation as at June 1 1990.

Indices to the 'L' and 'C' series are published monthly, with a cumulative index annually.

3. The 'S' Series or supplement to the Official Journal series is published daily and contains notices of public works and supply contracts, whether they are contracts where the projects concerned are financed by the European Development Fund, supply or works contracts compulsorily published under Community rules, or contracts not required to be published under Community rules.

   The 'S' Series may be subscribed to independently from the 'L' and 'C' series, but is not available on microfiche. The contents of the Supplement are published electronically on TED (Tenders Electronic Daily) which is updated daily.

4. The Annex or Debates of the European Parliament can be obtained by annual subscription or independently. They are available on paper or microfiche, while retrospective collections may be obtained only on microfiche.

VIII. The General Reports on the Activities of the European Communities

Yearly. These give a review of all Community activities over the past year.

Twenty-fourth General Report on the Activities of the European Communities 1989
1990
ISBN 92-825-9348-7
Price: £8.40

In conjunction with the General Reports, the Community publishes three separate reports covering specific areas of its policy.

1. The Agricultural Situation in the Community - 1989 Report
   1990
   ISBN 92-826-0913-8
   Price: Ecu25.50

2. Report on Social Developments - Year 1988
   1990
   ISBN 92-826-0226-5
   Price: Ecu16.50

3. Eighteenth Report on Competition Policy
   1989
   ISBN 92-826-0623-6
   Price: Ecu17.50

   (Nineteenth report now available from DG IV.)

IX. The Bulletin of the European Communities

Published eleven times a year, the Bulletin covers the activities of the Community institutions on a monthly basis.

Jointly published with the Bulletin is the Supplement to the Bulletin of the European Communities. The Supplement will reprint the text of specific and most important documents, e.g. the text of the Single European Act.

Annual subscription
Eleven issues per year + index + supplements
Price: £66.00

It is also possible to buy specific supplements to the Bulletin independently. Available from HMSO and agents.

X. The Eurostat Publications

The European Communities have their own Statistical Office which publishes their own series of statistics under the general heading of EUROSTATS.

It is impossible to cover all available titles in this section. A good 'EUROSTAT Catalogue - Publications and Electronic Services' is available free of charge from the UK Offices of the Commission and it is also possible to obtain a free quarterly publication entitled 'Eurostat News' from the Statistical Office in Luxembourg.

The main themes are:

1. General Statistics (dark blue cover)

   a. Basic Statistics: annual, pocket-size book, covering a large selection of general statistics comparing the EC countries with other industrialized countries.

   b. Eurostat Review: previously annual, covers a broad economic overview of the Community over a ten-year period compared with Japan and the U.S.A. (No longer published, but useful as background review.)

c. Regional statistics: annual, the only one of its kind which covers all statistical groupings on a regional basis.

2. Economy and Finance (violet cover)

a. National Accounts ESA: Aggregates 1970-86: gives the main national accounts aggregates of the EC countries, the U.S.A. and Japan;

b. National Accounts ESA: Detailed tables by branch

c. National Accounts ESA: Detailed tables by sector

d. General Government Accounts and Statistics: Yearbook

e. Consumer Price Indices: Monthly

and various others

3. Population and Social Conditions (yellow cover)

a. Demographic Statistics: yearly
including population projections. All statistics given in considerable detail for each country;

b. Employment and Unemployment Statistics: yearly

c. Unemployment Statistics: monthly
detailed breakdown of unemployment statistics on a monthly basis and a comparison with previous years;

d. Labour Force Sample Survey: yearly
provides considerable data on the structure of economic activity, employment and unemployment, and working time;

and various others

4. Energy and Industry (pale blue cover)

a. Industry Statistical Yearbook: yearly
analysis of the industrial structure of the Community, its analysis of the industrial structure of the Community, its member states, Japan and the U.S.A.;

b. Industrial Trends: monthly
covers industrial activity in the European Community;

c. Structure and Activity of Industry
coordinated annual inquiry into industrial activity, carried out by the Member States of the Community;

d. Energy Statistical Yearbook
extensive volume of statistical data relating to the energy economy of the Community and the Member States;

e. Iron and Steel Statistical Yearbook
detailed data on the structure and the economic situation of the Community's iron and steel industry;

and various other titles

5. Agriculture, Forestry and Fisheries

a. Agriculture Statistical Yearbook
vital statistical vade-mecum containing the most important data published by Eurostat in the specialised booklets dealing with agriculture, forestry and fisheries;

b. Economic Accounts - Agriculture, Forestry 1980-85
the data include tables showing time series for final output, intermediate consumption, value-added and fixed capital formation for each of the member states and the Community;

and various other titles

6. Foreign Trade

a. External Trade Statistical Yearbook
contains the main series from 1958 to 1986 of the external trade statistics of the European Communities.
The data is broken down by country and by commodity;

b. Analytical Tables of External Trade - Nimexe
Exports 1987 (13 volumes)
Imports 1987 (13 volumes)
breakdown by external trade statistics of the European Community and of the Member States according to the nimexe nomenclature;

and various other titles.

Address

EUROSTAT
Information Office
L - 2920 Luxembourg
Tel: (010 35 2) 4301 4567

XI. European Economy

This series of publications contains important reports and communications from the Commission to the Council and to the European Parliament on the economic situation and developments and on the lending and borrowing activities of the Community.

Four issues per year
Subscription, specific issues may be bought separately
Price: Ecu58.00

Two Supplements accompany the main periodical:

1. Series A - Economic Trends
   11 issues per year

Describes with tables and graphs the most recent trends of industrial production, consumer prices, unemployment, balance of trade, exchange rates etc. together with the Commission's microeconomic forecasts and communications to the Council on economic policy;
annual subscription: Ecu23.50

2. Series B - Business and Consumer Survey Results
11 issues per year
Gives the results of opinion surveys of industrial chief executives and of consumers in the Community together with other business cycle indicators;
Annual subscription: Ecu23.50

both supplements: annual subscription: Ecu37.00
combined subscription (European Economy + Supplements): Ecu87.50

XII. Series 'Documents'

This series covers all sectors of EC policy or re-print documents no longer available in their original format.

e.g.:
Completing the Internal Market
White paper from the Commission to the European Council
Series Document
ISBN 92-825-5436-8
Price: £3.90

Disharmonies in EC and US Agricultural Policy Measures
1988
Series Document
ISBN 92-825-7949-2
Price: £43.00
Experts' report on the differences between the agricultural policy of the European Community and of

the United States of America

Disharmonies in EC and US Agricultural Policies: A Summary of Results and Major Conclusions
1988
Series Document
ISBN 92-825-8599-9
Price: £5.20

XIII. European Perspectives

This series is presented in a glossy book format and gives an insight into the main factors involved in making an EC policy work.

e.g.:
Transport and European Integration
European Perspectives
ISBN 92-825-6199-2
Price: £9.60

The European Communities in the International Order
European Perspectives
ISBN 92-825-5137-7
Price: £3.00

Thirty Years of Community Law
European Perspectives
ISBN 92-825-2652-6
Price: £8.50

XIV. 'A Frontier-Free Europe'

New publications, presenting varied formats but with a common 'A Frontier-Free Europe' logo, reporting on different aspects of the Community plan to create a large frontier-free market by 1992.

e.g:
A Guide to Working in a Europe without Frontiers
by Jean-Claude Seche
1988
ISBN 92-825-8067-9
Price: £13.00

Common Standards for Enterprises
by Florence Nicolas
1988
ISBN 92-825-8554-9
Price: £6.20

XV. Series 'Study on Concentration, Competition and Competitiveness'

This series looks specifically at the concentration of industry in some areas and its effect on the European market.

e.g:
The Textile Machinery Industry in the EC
1985
Study on concentration, competition and competitiveness
ISBN 92-825-4780-9
Price: £5.40

The European Consumer Electronics Industry
1985
Study on concentration, competition and competitiveness
ISBN 92-825-5110-5
Price: £11.10

A list of the various studies on concentration of industry is given as an annex to the Annual Report on Competition Policy.

XVI. 'EUR' Reports

These are reports published on completion of research programmes and scientific and technical studies funded by the Commission. These documents are usually difficult to trace as they are, for the most part, extremely technical, but are easy to order on the basis of the 'EUR' numerification.

DG XIII (Telecommunications, Information Industries and Innovation) produces a monthly publication entitled 'Euro-abstracts' which lists and gives details of all EUR publications:

Euro Abstracts

Section I: Euratom and EC R&D and demonstration projects;
scientific and technical publications and patents
Monthly
Annual subscription - Price £52.00

Section II: Coal, steel and related social research
monthly + annual index
Annual subscription - Price £69.00

Combined subscription (Section I & II) - Price £101.00

B. BREAKDOWN OF EUROPEAN PUBLICATIONS BY POLICY SECTOR

I. Agriculture, Forestry and Fisheries

Periodicals, annual reports

Green Europe
An amalgamation of the former 'Green Europe Newsletter' (analysis and overview of a range of agricultural topics) and 'Green Europe: Newsflash' (analysis of a single, current agricultural topic).

Free from the European Commission, Directorate-General for Information, Communication and Culture, DGX. Separate isues can also be obtained free of charge from European Commission Offices.

Situation on the Agricultural Markets: Report 1988
Annual report giving an analysis of the agricultural market organizations and agricultural markets of the European Communities.
COM(88)796 final 18.01.89

The European Agricultural Guidance and Guarantee Fund (EAGGF): Annual Reports
17th financial report
Guidance Section COM(88)437 final; 18th Report: SEC(89)1984 final
Guarantee and Food Aid COM(88)563 final
18th Report SEC(89)1343 final
19th Report COM(90)397 final

Other agriculture titles

Directory of European Agricultural Organisations
Handbook describing the structure of European and national agricultural organizations, their decision-making procedures, priority policies and activities.
Economic and Social Committee
1984
ISBN 92-830-0032-3
Price: £45.00

The Agricultural Situation in the Community 1989 Report
Comprehensive report with analyses and statistics on agriculture; factors of production, structures and situation of markets for agricultural products, obstacles to the common agricultural market, the position of consumers and producers, financial aspects, together with an analysis of the general prospects and market outlook for agricultural products.

1990
ISBN 92-826-0913-8
Price: Ecu25.50

Economic Situation of Agricultural Holdings in the EEC: Report 1987
Financial results of Farmers throughout the European Community in 1984/85 and 1985/86.
The Farm Accountancy Data Network
1988
ISBN 92-825-8718-5
Price: £9.20

Green Paper on Perspectives for the CAP
Available free of charge from the European Commission London Office.
COM(85) 333 final, later re-printed in Green Europe: Newsflash series, 33/1985

A Future for Community Agriculture
Commission guidelines following the consultations in connection with the Green Paper.
Available for reference only at the library of the European Commission London Office.
COM(85)750 final
Later re-printed in Green Europe: Newsflash series, 34/1985

Report from the Commission on the Economic Effects of the Agri-Monetary System
Updated 1987
COM(87)168 14.08.87

Environment and Agriculture
COM(88)338 final

Completing the Internal Market: Current Status December 1989
Veterinary and Plant Health Controls
Issues and problems in creating an Internal Market in veterinary and plant health controls, approach adopted or proposed to achieve the Internal Market in the sector.
European Commission

One of a set of five brochures
ISBN 92-826-0887-5
Price: Ecu15.00

The Common Agricultural Policy and its Reform
Analysis of the CAP, simply explained
European Document series, 1/1987

The Common Fisheries Policy
European File series, 10/1986

The Community's Agricultural Policy on the Threshold of the 1990s
European File series, 1/1990

II Competition

Reports, series, studies

Eighteenth Report on Competition Policy
Latest in yearly series
1989
ISBN 92-826-0623-6
Price: Ecu17.50
(Nineteenth report available from DGIV.)

First Survey on State Aids in the European Community
Document series, 1989
ISBN 92-825-9535-8
Price: Ecu7.00

Second Survey on State Aids in the European Community
1990
Available from DGIV

Studies on Concentration, Competition and Competitiveness
Series looking at the concentration of industries from the point of view of competition and competitiveness.

The most recent titles in this series are listed in the annual competition report (see above). Examples:

The EC Telecommunications Industry: The Adhesion of Spain and Portugal
1987
ISBN 92-825-7551-9
Price: £15.10

The Likely Impact of Deregulation on Industrial Structures and Competition in the Community
1987
ISBN 92-825-7591-2
Price: £12.90

Other competition titles

Competition Rules in the EC and the ECSC Applicable to State Aids
A collection of the basic texts on State aid of different kinds and differing legal status.
1987
ISBN 92-825-6735-4
Price £13.40

Competition Law in the EC and the ECSC
1986
ISBN 92–825-5832-0
Price: £4.00

Recent Trends of Concentration in Selected Industries of the European Community, Japan and the US
Document series, 1988
ISBN 92-825-8617-0
Price Ecu12.00

Innovation in the EC Automative Industry: An Analysis from the Perspective of State-aid Policy
Document series, 1988
ISBN 92-825-8776-2
Price £10.50

Community Framework on State-aid to the Motor Vehicle Industry
Official Journal of the European Communities C123 of 18.5.89

The Aid Element in State Participation to Company Capital
Document series, 1989
ISBN 92-825-9510-2
Price: Ecu19.50

Barriers to Entry and Intensity of Competition in European Markets
Document series, 1989
ISBN 92-825-9625-7
Price: Ecu9.00

Horizontal Mergers and Competition Policy in the European Community
European Economy 40, May 1989

EC Competition Policy in the Single Market
European Documentation series, 1/1989
Explains the objectives and rules of European competition policy applying not only to big companies but also to SMEs, showing how they may benefit from cooperation with other firms and thus take full advantage of a unified market.

III Consumer Affairs

Selected titles

A New Impetus for Consumer Protection Policy
Supplement 6/86 to the Bulletin of the European Communities
ISBN 92-825-6649-8
Price: £1.70

Individual Choice and Higher Growth: The Task of European Consumer Policy
E. Lawlor
A Frontier-Free Europe publication
1989
ISBN 92-826-0087-4
Price: Ecu8.00

Reports of the Scientific Committee for Food (22nd series)
EUR 12535
1989
ISBN 92-826-1070-5
Price: Ecu6.25

The European Community and Consumers
European File series, 12/1987

Three Year Action Plan of Consumer Policy in the EC (1990-1992)
COM(90)98 final

IV Customs and Fiscal Controls

Selected titles

The Customs Union of the European Economic Community
The mechanism of the customs union, its role in European integration, the external Commons Customs Tariff as a commercial instrument with regard to non-member countries, the application of the customs regulation and trade with the Community.
European Perspectives, 1985
ISBN 92-825-1911-2
Price £2.60

Explanatory Notes to the Combined Nomenclature of the European Communities
1987
ISBN 92-825-7813-5
Price: Ecu17.50
Addendum 1988 to the 1987 explanatory notes
ISBN 92-825-8723-1
Price: Ecu13.25

Customs Valuation
Compendium of European Community legislation relating to customs valuation
Document series, 1989
ISBN 92-825-8835-1
Price: Ecu38.25

European Customs Inventory of Chemicals: A Guide to the Tariff Classification of Chemicals in the Combined Nomenclature
Document series, 1988
ISBN 92-825-7919-0
Price: £23.50

List of Authorized Customs Offices for Community Transit Operations
1986
ISBN 92-825-6575-0
Price £8.00

Practical Guide to the Use of the European Communities' Scheme of Generalized Tariff Preferences
1986
ISBN 92-825-6139-9
Price: £8.10

Completing the Internal Market: Current Status December 1989
Elimination of frontier barriers and fiscal controls
Control of goods
Control of individuals
Value-added tax
Excise duties
European Commission

One of a set of five brochures
ISBN 92-826-0860-3
Price: Ecu15.00

The Cost of Non-Europe
Volume 4
Border-related Controls and Adminstrative Formalities: An illustration in the road-haulage sector
ISBN 92-825-8618-9
Price: Ecu15.00

Generalized Preferences for the Third World
European File series, 16/1987

The Removal of Technical Barriers to Trade
European File series, 18/1988

Europe Without Frontiers: Completing the Internal Market
European Documentation series, 2/1989

V Economic, Monetary and Financial Affairs

Annual reports, series, business surveys, economic papers, EC budget, European Investment Bank, monetary union, the Ecu

European Economy
Series containing important reports and communications from the Commission to the Council and to the European Parliament on the economic situation and developments, and on the lending and borrowing activities of the Community.
Quarterly
Subscription, or separate issues
Price: Ecu58.00

Two supplements accompany the main periodical:

Series A: Economic Trends
Eleven issues per year. Describes with tables and graphs recent trends of industrial production,

consumer prices, unemployment, balance of trade, exchange rates etc. together with Commission staff's microeconomic forecasts and communications to the Council on economic policy.
Annual subscription: Ecu23.50

Series B: Busines and Consumer Survey Results
Eleven issues per year. Gives the results of opinion surveys of industrial chief executives and of consumers in the Community together with other business cycle indicators.
Annual subscription: Ecu23.50

Both supplements: annual subscription: Ecu37.00
Combined subscription (European, Economy and supplements): Ecu87.50

Annual Economic Reports

Annual Economic Report 1988-1989: Preparing for 1992
First published as COM (88) 591 Vol. I & II
Later published as European Economy 38, November 1988
ISSN 0379-0991

Facing the Challenges of the Early 1990s: Annual Economic Report 1989-1990
COM (89) 497 final
Later published as EUR Economy 42, November 1989

Twenty-ninth Activity Report of the Monetary Committee
1988
ISBN 92-825-8995-1
Price: £3.25

The Community Budget: Facts in Figures
The full budget is published yearly in the L series of the Official Journal of the European Communities. This publication aims at explaining the budget in a more digestible format.

Annual publication
1989 edition
ISBN 92-825-9716-4
Price: Ecu10.00

Financial Report 1987
Information on the implementation of the budget in an accessible format.
1988 report is in French.

Financial Report 1988: European Coal and Steel Community
Financial activity of the European Commission in the field covered by the ECSC Treaty
1989
ISBN 92-826-0693-7

Results of the Business Survey Carried out Among Managements in the Community
Monthly
ISSN 0378-4479
Annual subscription Ecu58.50

EURECOM

Monthly bulletin of European Community economic and financial news. Published by the European Commission, 3 Dag Hammarskjold Plaza, 305 East 47th Street, New York, NY 10017.

DGII: Economic Papers

Papers written by officials in European Commission Directorates-General for Economic and Financial Affairs (DGH). Reports on a macro-economic scale. The full collection of the reports is available for reference in the library of the European Commission London Office. Examples:

65 The Completion of the Internal Market: results of macro-economic model simulations
M. Catinat, E. Donni, A. Italianer
1988

66 Europe After the Crash: economic policy in an era of adjustment
C. Bean
1988

67 A Survey of the Economies of Scale
C. Pratten
1988

74 The Exchange Rate Question in Europe
F. Giavazzi
1989

76 Europe's Prospects for the 1990s
H. Giersch
March 1989

77 1992, Hype or Hope: A Review
Alexander Italianer
February 1990

78 European Labour Markets: A Long Run View (CEPS Macroeconomic Policy Group 1989 Annual Report)
J. -P. Danthine, Ch. Bean, P. Berhnholz and E. Malinvaud
February 1990

79 Country Studies - The United Kingdom
Tassos Belessiotis and Ralph Wilkinson
July 1990

80 Country Studies - The Federal Republic of Germany
Françoise Moreau, Werner Schüle, Manfred Teutemann and Luc Veron
July 1990

81 Country Studies - The Netherlands
Filip Keereman, Françoise Moreau and Cyriel Vanbelle
July 1990

The European Investment Bank in 1988 and Subsequent Years
Overview of the Bank's activity

European Investment Bank
ISBN 92-861-0181-3
Free from the European Investment Bank, 68 Pall Mall, London SW1Y 5ES, tel: (071) 839 3351.

The European Investment Bank: Annual Report 1988
EIB activities in 1988 with statistics, in particular loans within and outside the Community.
European Investment Bank,
1989
Free from the European Investment Bank (address above).

The European Monetary System: Origins, Operation and Outlook
European Perspectives series
1985
ISBN 92-825-3468-5
Price £3.00

Report on Economic and Monetary Union in the European Community
Known as the Delors Report, this document details the stages by which the complete economic and monetary union will be achieved. A summary of the report can be obtained free of charge from the European Commission London Office.
1989
ISBN 92-825-0655-4
Price: Ecu10

The Ecu
European Documentation series, 5/1987

The European Financial Area
European Documentation series, 4/1989

Other economic and monetary titles

Community Public Finance: The European Budget After

the 1988 Reform

The publication is an informative guide on the working of the budgetary and financial policy after the reform of the budgetary procedure.
ISBN 92-825-9830-6
Price: Ecu10.50

Efficiency, Stability and Equity: A Strategy for the Evolution of the Economic System of the European Community

Report of a study group appointed by the Commission of the European Communities. In-depth analysis of the problems encountered between now and 1992 in order to achieve a single Internal Market.
T. Padoa-Schioppa
1987
ISBN 0-19-828629-5
Oxford University Press

The Economics of 1992

European Economy series, 35, March 1988
CB-AR-88-035-EN-C
Price: £11.50

Compendium of Community Monetary Texts

Legal texts of importance to the Monetary Committee
Monetary Committee 1989
ISBN 92-825-9489-0
Price: Ecu10.00

Inventory of Taxes Levied to Member States of the European Communities 13th Edition

Analysis of tax law in the member states
ISBN 92-825-8829-7
Price: Ecu47.50

The Single Financial Market

D. Servais
1988
ISBN 92-825-8572-7
Price: £4.10

Completion of the Internal Market: Approximation of Indirect Tax Rates and Harmonization of Indirect Tax Structures
COM(87)320 final
COM(89)260 final

The Approximation of European Tax Systems
European File series, 9/1986

A European Financial Area: The Liberalization of Capital Movements
European File series, 12/1988

The Big European Market: A Trump Card for the Economy and Employment
European File series, 14/88

Towards a Big Internal Market in Financial Services
European File series 17/1988

VI Education and Cultural Policy

Education Training Youth
Guide of the European Community Programmes in those fields.
Free from the European Commission London Office.

COMETT, ERASMUS, EURYDICE, PETRA, SPES

ERASMUS (Community programme for the mobility of university students)
Directory of programmes 1987-88
Published for the Commission by the Erasmus Bureau, Rue d'Arlon 15, B-1040 Brussels
Free

ERASMUS Annual Report 1989
COM(90) 128 final

ERASMUS Newsletter
Commission newsletter on the joint study programe
Three issues per year
Annual subscription £6.00

COMETT (Community programme for co-operation between universities and enterprises in the field of training for technology and its applications: Annual report 1988
COM(89)171 final

COMETT: The training needs of staff in the Community's higher education sector engaged in co-operation with industry
Document series 1988
ISBN 92-825-8763-0
Price: Ecu47.75

SPES (stimulation plan for economic science) 1989-92
Commission document explaining the plan to encourage academic links in the fields of economics throughout the countries of the community. A free information pack is available from the European Commission London Office.
COM(88)98 final

PETRA: The European Community action programme for the vocational training of young people and their preparation for adult and working life
Free information note available from the European Commission London Office

EURYDICE Info
Published for the European Commission, Directorate-General for Employment, Social Affairs and Education, DGV by the European Unit of EURYDICE, Education Information network in the European Community, Rue Archimede 17, Bte 17, B-1040 Brussels.

Other education and culture titles

European Educational Policy Statements

Third edition
Council of the European Communities
1988
ISBN 92-825-0471-4
Price: £8.00

The Education Structures in the Member States of the European Communities
1987
ISBN 92-825-7543-8
Price: £11.00

Transition Education for the 1990s
Supplement 1/88 to Social Europe
1988
Price: £3.60

Education in the European Community: Medium-term Perspectives 1989-92
Communication from the Commission
COM(88)280 final

Higher Education in the European Community: Student Handbook
Fifth edition
Directory of courses and institutions in 12 countries. Basic information needed by those seeking higher education in another member state.
1988
ISBN 1-85091-501-6
Price: £11.95

Young Europeans in 1987
Survey of attitudes of young Europeans towards Europe, including languages.
Document series
1989
ISBN 92-825-9511-0
Price: Ecu14.70

Employees' Organisations and their Contribution to the Development of Vocational Training Policy in the European Communities
CEDEFOP document

1988
ISBN 92-825-7734-1
Price: £3.50

The European Community and Culture
European File series, 10/1988

The European Community and Recognition of Diplomas for Professional Purposes
European File series 13/1989

A Fresh Boost for Culture in the European Community
Supplement 4/87 to the Bulletin of the European Communities
ISBN 92-825-8241-8
Price: Ecu3.50

The Public Administration and the Funding of Culture in the European Community
Document series
1989
ISBN 92-825-6737-0
Price: Ecu16.20

Books and Reading: A Cultural Challenge for Europe
Communication from the Commission
COM(89)258 final

VII Energy

Periodicals

Energy in Europe
Energy policies and trends in the European Communities
Three issues per year
Annual subscription: £24.00

The Internal Energy Market
Energy in Europe special issue. Reprint of COM(88)238 final, together with the inventory of obstacles to an internal energy market and a number of conclusions.
ISBN 92-825-8507-7
Price: Ecu12.70

Major Themes in Energy
Energy in Europe special issue.
1989
ISBN 92-826-0724-0
Price: Ecu12.70

Nuclear energy

EURATOM Supply Agency: Annual Report 1988
ISBN 92-826-0023-8
Price: Ecu5

Nuclear Safety in the European Community
European Documentation series, 5/1985

Nuclear Energy in the European Community
European File series, 18/1987

Other energy titles

Recueil des Textes Legislatifs et des Actes Relatifs au Domaine de l'Energie
Compendium of EC legislation relating to the energy field, available in French only.
Document series
1988
ISBN 92-825-8725-8
Price: Ecu58.75

Collection of Legislation and Acts Relating to Energy: Situation at 1.1.89
EC legislation relating to the energy field with Official Journal references.

Document series
1989
ISBN 92-825-9549-8
Price: Ecu5.00

The Internal Energy Market
Commission report outlining the expected results of an internal energy market and priorities which should be addressed in order to remove the obstacles to its creation.
COM(88)238 final

Towards a Continuing Policy for Energy Efficiency in the European Community
Commission communication
COM(87)223 final

Accelerating Discrete Energy Efficiency Investments Through Third Party Financing
Commission Communication
COM(88)175 final

Commission Communication on Transparency of Consumer Energy Prices
COM(89)123/2 final

The Market for Solid Fuels in the Community in 1988 and Outlook for 1989
SEC(89)280
Official Journal of the European Communities C148 15.6.89

Investment in the European Coal and Steel Community 1988
Yearly
ISBN 92-825-9369-X
Price: Ecu19

National Laws and Regulations Relating to the Natural Gas Industry
EUR document 11433
1988
ISBN 92-825-8543-3
Price: Ecu8.75

Energy and the Environment
Commission Communication
COM(89)369 final

VIII Environment

Selected titles

The State of the Environment in the European Community 1986
EUR 10633
ISBN 92-825-6973-X
Price: £11.60

European Environment Policy: Air, Water & Waste Management
Economic and Social Committee
1987
ISBN 92-830-0108-7
Price: £2.60

European Community Environmental Legislation 1967-1987
Vol I General policy and nature protection
Vol II Air and noise
Vol III Waste
Vol IV Water
Published by the European Commission, Directorate-General for Environment, Consumer Protection and Nuclear Safety (DGXI).

Living Conditions in Urban Europe
European Foundation for the Improvement of Living and Working Conditions
1988
ISBN 92-825-7054-1
Price: £3.60

The Impact of Biotechnology on the Environment
European Foundation for the Improvement of Living and Working Conditions

1987
ISBN 92-825-7529-2: Price: £4.10
ISBN 92-825-7532-2: Price: £5.80
ISBN 92-825-6767-2: Price: £6.60

EINECS (European Inventory of Existing Commercial Chemical Substances)
Official journal - Annex C146A
Volumes I and II
Also available on magnetic tape
Price £250.00

Working for a Better Environment: The Role of the Social Partners
European Foundation for the Improvement of Living and Working Conditions
1989
ISBN 92-825-8781-9
Price: £3.30

Fourth Environmental Action Programme 1987-1992
Official Journal of the European Communities C328 7.12.87

The Greenhouse Effect and the Community
Commission working programme concerning the evaluation of policy options to deal with the greenhouse effect.
COM(88)656 final

1992: The Environmental Dimension
Report by a task force chaired by a Commission official and including independent experts.
Available for reference in the library of the European Commission London Office.

Energy and the Environment
Commission communication
COM(89)369 final

The European Community and Environmental Protection
European Documentation series 4/1990

IX External Relations, Foreign Trade, Overseas Development

Periodicals, series

The Courier
Magazine published every two months, covering ACP/EC relations including contract tender information.
Free subscription available from the European Commission, Directorate-General for Development (DGVIII).

Europe Information: Development
Publications covering development topics:

Lome III: Mid-term Review 1986-88
European Information series: Development DE61
ISSN 1012-2184

Lome IV: 1900-2000 Background, Innovations, Improvements
European Information series: DE64
March 1990

STABEX
The STABEX system, EC system of export earnings from agricultural commodities for Third World countries.
Europe Information series, Development DE59
1988

Europe Information: External relations
Publications dealing with a country or group of countries' relations with the EC:
The European Community and China 90/88
The European Community and the Yemen Arab Republic 91/88
The European Community and ASEAN 92/88
The European Community and Bangaldesh 93/88
The European Community and Yugoslavia 94/88
The European Community's relations with COMECON and its East European members 1/89

Other foreign trade and external relations titles

Corps Diplomatique Accredite Aupres des Communautes Europeennes
Annual directory, updated at intervals, of the diplomatic corps accredited to the European Community.
1990 edition
ISBN 92-826-1399-2
Price: Ecu7.50

International Trade of the European Community
A review of certain aspects of the external trade of the Community
European Economy series, 39, March 1989

Thirteen Years of Development Co-operation with the Developing Countries of Latin America and Asia
Data and results
SEC(89)713 final

European Community Report on US Trade Barriers and Unfair Trade Practices 1990
Published by the European Commission, Directorate-General for External Relations, DGI. Available for reference at the library of the European Commission London Office.

Report of the European Parliament on Protectionism in Trade Relations Between the European Community and the United States of America
Rapporteur: Dame Shelagh Roberts
Report by the European Parliament committee on external economic relations.
PE doc A2-89/88

The Internal Market of North America: Fragmentation and Integration in the USA and Canada
The Cost of Non-Europe Volume 16
ISBN 92-825-8630-8
Price: Ecu13.50

Relations Between the Community and Japan
Commission communication
COM(88)136 I & II final

Seventh Annual Report of the Commission on the Community's Anti-Dumping and Anti-Subsidy Activities
COM(90)229 final

Relations Between the European Community and International Organisations
A Frontier-Free Europe publication
1989
ISBN 92-826-0085-8
Price: Ecu30.75

Europe in the World
European File series, 16/1988
Free from the European Commission London Office

The Europe-South Dialogue in Practice
EC development policy: Rural development, industry and trade, education, training and health, regional co-operation.
1988
ISBN 92-825-8436-4

Economic Transformation in Hungary and Poland
European Economy, 43, March 1990

PHARE - Assistance for Economic Restructuring in Poland and Hungary
Free from the Commission Offices

The Effects on Intra-Community Competition of Export Subsidies to Third Countries
The case of export credits, export insurance and official development assistance
Document series
1990
ISBN 92-826-0352-0
Price: Ecu16.00

X Industry

Selected titles

Completing the Internal Market for Industrial Products
Document series
ISBN 92-825-6481-9
Price: £8.30

Panorama of EC Industry
Overview of more than 125 sectors of manufacturing and services industries with some comparisons with the US and Japan.
1990
ISBN 92-825-9924-8
Price: Ecu38.00

Completion of the Internal Market: A Survey of European Industry's Perception of the Likely Effects
The cost of non-Europe Volume 3
ISBN 92-825-8610-3
Price: Ecu25.50

Technical Barriers in the EC: An Illustration by Six Industries
The cost of non-Europe Volume 6
ISBN 92-825-8649-9
Price: Ecu21.00

The EC 1992 Automobile Sector
The cost of Non-Europe Volume 11
ISBN 92-825-8619-7
Price: Ecu27.75

The Cost of Non-Europe in the Foodstuffs Industry
The cost of non-Europe Volume 12
Part A: ISBN 92-825-8642-1
Part B: ISBN 92-825-8643-X
Price: A + B Ecu120

Le Cout de la Non-Europe des Produits de la Construction
The cost of non-Europe Volume 13
In French. NEDO has its own translation.

ISBN 92-825-8631-6
Price: Ecu14.25

The Cost of Non-Europe in the Textile/Clothing Industry
The cost of non-Europe Volume 14
ISBN 92-825-8641-3
Price: Ecu21.75

Rules Governing Medicinal Products in the European Community
Volume 1
The Rules Governing Medicinal Products for Human Use in the European Community
ISBN 92-825-9563-3
Price: Ecu13.50
Volume II
Notice to Applicants for Marketing Authorizations for Medicinal Products for Human Use in the Member States of the European Community
ISBN 92-825-9503-X
Price: Ecu16.50
Volume III
Guidelines on the Quality, Safety and Efficacy of Medicinal Products for Human Use
ISBN 92-825-9619-2
Price: Ecu23.25
Volume IV
Guide to Good Manufacturing Practice for the Manufacture of Medicinal Products
ISBN 92-825-9572-2
Price: Ecu9.75

The Community's Pharmaceutical Industry
Document series, 1985
ISBN 92-825-5224-1
Price: £8.30

The Cost of Non-Europe in the Pharmaceutical Industry
The cost of non-Europe Volume 15
ISBN 92-825-8632-4
Price: Ecu13.50

The Tourism Sector in the Community
A study of concentration, competition and competitiveness.
1985
ISBN 92-825-5276-4
Price: £9.00

Business Plan - European Year of Tourism 1990: Book One
Summary available free from the Commission Office

ECSC Investments 1989
Overview of investments in the coal and steel sector.
European Commission
ISBN 92-826-1470-0
Price: Ecu20.00

The European Aerospace Industry: Trading Position and Figures 1989
III/4100/89-EN final
Available from the European Commission,

Directorate-General for the Internal Market and Industrial Affairs (DGIII).

XI Law

Annual reports

Fifth Annual Report to the European Parliament on Commission Monitoring of the Application of Community Law
1987
COM(88)425 final, or Official Journal C310, 5.12.88

Sixth Annual Report to the European Parliament on Commission Monitoring of the Application of Community Law
1989
COM(89)411 final, or Official Journal C330, 30.12.89

Seventh Annual Report
COM(90) 288, or Official Journal C232, 17.09.90

Community Law: Offprint from the 22nd General Report
Offprint from the Annual General Report on the activities of the European Communities, pertaining to legal matters, including summaries of important judgements.
ISBN 92-825-9693-1
Price: Ecu4.00

Other law titles

The ABC of Community Law
Guide with basic information on Community law, specifically orientated to use by the layman.
European Documentation series, 2/1986

Lawyers in the European Community
Comparison of the legal profession in 10 of the member states of the European Community (not Spain and Portugal - to be covered in a future edition).
S.P. Laguette and P. Latham
European Perspectives series, 1987
ISBN 92-825-6978-0
Price: £9.60

Harmonization of Company Law in the European Communities: Measures Adopted and Proposed - Situation as at 1.1.89
Document series, 1989
ISBN 92-825-9578-1
Price: Ecu29.25

Completing the Internal Market: Current Status December 1989
Conditions for industrial cooperation
Company law
Intellectual property
Taxation
European Commission
One of a set of five brochures

ISBN 92-826-0869-7
Price: Ecu15.00

Commission Green Paper on Copyright and the Challenge of Technology
Copyright issues requiring immediate action.
COM(88)172 final

The European Economic Interest Grouping (EEIG)
European File series, 6/1989

Complaint to the European Commission for Failure to Comply with Community Law
Standard complaint form issued by the commission
Official Journal of the European Communities C26, 1.2.89.

Company Law in the European Community
European File series, 14/1989

Patents, Trade Marks and Copyright in the European Community
European File series, 14/1989

XII Public Procurement

Selected titles

Public Procurement and Construction: Towards an Integrated Market
European Documentation series, 1988
ISBN 92-825-8891-2
Free from the European Commission London Office

The Cost of Non-Europe in Public Procurement
The Cost of Non-Europe Volume 5
Part A: ISBN 92-825-8646-4
Part B: ISBN 92-825-8647-2
Price: A + B Ecu120

A Single Public Procurement Market
Completing the Internal Market: Current status
December 1989, part 2
European Commission
One of a set of five brochures
ISBN 92-826-0869-7
Price: Ecu15.00

XIII Regional Policy, European Regional Development Fund (ERDF), STRIDE

Annual reports

European Regional Development Fund: Fourteenth Annual Report (1988) from the Commission to the Council, the European Parliament and the Economic and Social Committee
1990
ISBN 92-826-0357-1
Price: Ecu14.00

Other regional policy titles

Main Texts Governing the Regional Policy of the European Communities
Document series, 1985
ISBN 92-825-5283-7
Price: £5.60

The Regions of the Enlarged Community: Third Periodic Report on the Social and Economic Situation and Development of the Regions of the Community - Summary and Conclusions
Document series, 1987
ISBN 92-825-7526-6
Price: £16.50

Long-term Regional Demographic Developments up to the Beginning of the Next Century and Regional Policy

Document series, 1988
ISBN 92-825-8620-0
Price: £11.50

Peripheral Regions in a Community of 12 Member States
Document sries, 1988
ISBN 92-825-8640-5
Price: £8.30

Research and Technological Development in the Less-favoured Regions of the Community (STRIDE)
1988
ISBN 92-825-7852-6
Price: £19.50

STRIDE: Science and Technology for Regional Innovation and Development in Europe
1988
ISBN 92-825-7858-5
Price: £26.50

Urban Problems and Regional Policy in the European Community
Document series, 1988
ISBN 92-825-7871-2
Price: £18.50

Living Conditions in Urban Europe
European Foundation for the Improvement of Living and Working Conditions
1988
ISBN 92-825-7054-1
Price: £3.60

ERDF in Figures 1988 (1975-88)
1989
ISBN 92-826-0055-6
Available for reference in the library of the European Commission London Office

European Regional Policy
European File series, 14/1987

The Integrated Mediterranean Programme
European File series, 7/1989

XIV Services

Selected titles

The Cost of Non-Europe: Obstacles to Trans-border Business Activity
The Cost of Non-Europe Volume 7
ISBN 92-825-8638-3
Price £8.50

The Cost of Non-Europe for Business Services
The Cost of Non-Europe Volume 8
ISBN 92-825-8637-5
Price: £9.00

The Cost of Non-Europe in Financial Services
The Cost of Non-Europe Volume 9
ISBN 92-825-8636-7
Price: £78.00

The Benefits of Completing the Internal Market for Telecommunications Services and Equipment in the Community
The Cost of Non-Europe Volume 10
ISBN 92-825-8650-2
Price: £11.50

The Single Financial Market: Liberalization of Capital Movements and Financial Integration
D. Servais
A Frontier-free Europe publication
1988
ISBN 92-825-8572-7
Price: Ecu6.00

Creation of a European Financial Market
European Economy series, 36, May 1988

Towards a Big Internal Market in Financial Services
European File series, 17/1988

The European Financial Area
European Documentation series, 4/1989

The Insurance Industry in the Countries of the EEC: Structure, Conduct and Performance
Document series, 1985
ISBN 92-825-4919-4
Price: £10.80

Insurance - Community Measures Adopted or Proposed
Situation at March 1990
Document series, 1990
ISBN 92-826-0346-6
Price: Ecu39.00

The Creation of the Internal Market in Insurance
B. Pool
Document series, 1990
ISBN 92-826-0246-X
Price: £7.60

Completing the Internal Market: Current Status December 1989
A Common Market for Services
Banking, insurance, securities, transport, new technologies and services, capital movements, free movement of labour and the professions.
European Commission
One of a set of five brochures
ISBN 92-826-0851-4
Price: Ecu15.00

Credit Institutions: Community Measures Adopted or Proposed - Situation at January 1989
Compendium of texts of EC proposed and exisitng legislation relating to the banking sector.
Document series, 1989

ISBN 92-825-9508-0
Price: Ecu24.75

Securities Markets - Community Measures Adopted or Proposed
Document series, 1989
ISBN 92-826-0017-3
Price: Ecu15.00

XV Small and Medium-sized Enterprises (SMEs)

Periodicals/annuals

Euro/Info
SME craft industry newsletter for small business and craft trades. Available from the European Commision, Directorate-General for Business Policy, Commerce, Tourism and Social Economy (DG XXIII), 200 Rue de la Loi, B-1049 Brussels.

Operations of the European Community Concerning Small and Medium-sized Enterprises: Practical Handbook
Document series
ISBN 92-825-8741-X
Price: £14.70

Other SME titles

Evaluation of Policy Measures for the Creation and Development of Small and Medium-sized Enterprises: Synthesis Report
Part A: Analysis of measures taken by the member states and the Community to create and develop SMEs.
Part B: In-depth analysis of the situation in Portugal
ISBN 92-826-0104-9
Price: Ecu15.75

Practical Guide to Legal Aspects of Industry Sub-contracting within the European Community
Volume I: The Sub-contract
A Frontier-free Europe publication, 1989
ISBN 92-825-9593-5
Price: Ecu11.25

Methods of Promoting the Supply of Risk Capital: Utilizing Innovative Banking to Improve the Equity Capital Resources of SMEs
Pilot study designed to look at the existing role of the banks and the role banks could play in the market for risk capital assets.
Enterprise Policy Document series, 1989
ISBN 92-826-0105-6
Price: Ecu8.25

Strengthening Co-operation Between European Firms: A Response to the 1992 Internal Market Deadline
The BC-net Euro-partnership promoting transnational sub-contracting.
Commission communication
COM(88)162 final

SME Task Force: Data Banks of Interest to SMEs
Directory of databases of special interest to SMEs
Produced by the SME Task Force, Rue de la Loi 200, ARLN, B-1049 Brussels.

Report from the Commission to the Council: Improvement of the Business Environment, in Particular for SMEs, in the Community
COM(90) 200 final

The Action Programme for Small and Medium-sized Enterprises
European File series, 3/1988

The European Community and Co-operation Among Small and Medium-sized Enterprises
European file series, 11/1988

XVI Research and Development, Science and Technology, Communications

Periodicals

Innovation and Technology Transfer
Newsletter (5-6 issues per year) replacing the New Technologies and Innovation Policy newsletter covering the activities and fields of interest of Directorate-General Telecommunications, Information Industries and Innovation (DGXIII).
Free from DGXIII, C-3 (Exploitation of Research, Technological Development, Technology Transfer and Innovation), European Commission, JMO B4-091, L-2920 Luxembourg.

Eurotec
Research and Development news periodical, published by the European Commission, Directorate-General for Information, Communication and Culture (DGX).
Free from DGX.

Eurotec: Technology in Europe
Special issue of Eurotec, drawing attention to the existence of Community information and providing details of access to its databanks.
Issue No. S 4/1986
1986
Available for reference at the library of the European Commission London Office.

Information Market
Newsletter published by the European Commission, Directorate-General Telecommunications, Information Industries and Innovation (DGXIII).
Research and development activities relating to the information market, covering notices of conferences, etc.
Free from the European Commission, Directorate-General for Exploitation of Research, Technological Development, Technology Transfer and Innovation (DGXIII), Jean Monnet Building B4-091, L2920 Luxembourg.

ESRA (European Safety and Reliability Association) Newsletter

Three times a year

Published by the Joint Research Centre of the European Commission, Ispra Establishment, I-21020 Ispra, Italy.

Other R & D technology titles

European Community Research Programmes: Status at 1.9.89

New published catalogue of research programmes within the Framework Programme of the European Community 1987-1991.

Published by the European Commission, Directorate-General for Science, Research and Development (DGXII).

EC Research Funding - A Guide for Applicants

European Commission, January 1990

Free from the European Commission London Office

First Report on the State of Science and Technology in Europe

First published as COM(88)647 final

Reprinted and available free of charge from the European Commission London Office

Vade-mecum of Community Research Promotion 1987

1980-90: A New Development on the European Scientific Policy

EUR 7121, 1982

ISBN 92-825-3111-2

Price: £21.00

Scientific Research and Technological Development in the Community: The Facts in Figures 1988

Short analysis of European Communities R & D presented in statistics.

EUR 11975

ISBN 92-825-9286-3

Publications on Science and Technology
Booklet issued by the European Commission, Directorate-General for Telecommunications, Information Industries and Innovation (DGXIII). Free from DGXIII/C-3, European Commission, Jean Monnet Building, L-2920 Luxembourg.

Publicly Funded Research and Development in the European Community: Improving the Utilisation of Results
EUR 11528, 1988
ISBN 92-825-8269-8
Price: Ecu8.75

Utilisation of the Results of Public Research and Development in the UK
EUR 11539, 1989
ISBN 92-825-9054-2
Price: Ecu10.00

Directory of Contract Research Organisations in the EEC
Directory aiming at furthering the integration of technological progress into the Community industrial structure.
EUR 12112, 1989
ISBN 92-825-9766-0

The Impact of Biotechnology on Working Conditions
European Foundation for the Improvement of Living and Working Conditions, 1988.
ISBN 92-825-6767-2
Price: £6.60

Copyright and the Challenge of Technology: Copyright Issues Requiring Immediate Action
Background discussion paper on various issues such as piracy, copyright, home copying, distribution rights, computer programmes, databases, etc.
COM(88)172 final

Progress Report on the Implementation of a Community Telecommunications Policy
COM(88)240-1

Working Towards Telecom 2000 (Launching of the Programme RACE)
COM(88)240-II

The Benefits of Completing the Internal Market for Telecommunications Services and Equipment in the Community 1988
The Cost of Non-Europe - Volume 10
ISBN 92-825-8650-2
Price: £11.50

Completing the Internal Market: Current Status December 1989
Banking, insurance, securities, transport, new technologies and services, capital movements, free movement of labour and the professions.
European Commission
One of a set of five brochures
ISBN 92-826-0851-4
Price: Ecu15.00

Telecommunications in Europe
H. Ungerer with N.P. Costello
Basic objectives ensuring a free choice for the user in Europe's 1992 market. The challenge for the European Community.
European Perspectives series, 1988
ISBN 92-825-8209-4
Price: £7.50

The European Consumer Electronics Industry
Study on concentration, competition and competitiveness, 1985
ISBN 92-825-5110-5
Price: £11.10

The MEDIA Programme
Measures to encourage the development of the industry of audiovisual production.
1988

Media Vade-mecum 1990
Free from the European Commission London Office
ISBN 92-826-1326-7

Action Programme to Promote the Development of the European Audiovisual Industry 'Media' 1991-1995
Commission Communication
COM(90)132 final

TV Broadcasting in Europe and the New Technologies
Prof. G. Locksley
Document series, 1988
ISBN 92-825-8759-2
Price: Ecu31.50

Telecommunications: The New Highways for the Single European Market
European File series, 15/88

The Audio-visual Market in the Single European Market
European Documentation series, 4/1988

XVII Technical Barriers

Selected titles

Technical Barriers
The Cost of Non-Europe - Volume 6
An illustration by six industries: Some case studies on technical barriers.
ISBN 92-825-8649-9
Price: Ecu21.00

Catalogue of Community's Legal Acts and Other Texts Relating to the Elimination of Technical Barriers to Trade for Industrial Products
Document series
ISBN 92-825-7908-5
Price: £9.00

Common Standards for Enterprises
F. Nicolas and J. Repussard
A Frontier-Free Europe publication

ISBN 92-825-8554-9
Price: £6.20

Completing the Internal Market: A New Community Standards Policy, Current Status December 1989
The new approach in harmonization
Motor vehicles
Tractors and agricultural machinery
Food
Pharmaceuticals
Chemicals
Construction products
European Commission
One of a set of 5 brochures
ISBN 92-826-0878-6
Price: Ecu15.00

The Removal of Technical Barriers to Trade
European File series, 18/1988

Guide to the Reform of the Structural Funds
ISBN 92-826-0029-7
Price: Ecu11.25

XVIII Social Affairs

Annual reports, special reviews, series

1992: The Single European Market - The Social Dimension
Series of European Commission pamphlets, 1988
First four titles:
Questions and Answers: Workers' Rights in the Single European Market
Women's Rights and Equal Opportunities
Social Security Will Apply to Workers in All Member States in the Single European Market
Workers' Rights
Free from the European Commission London Office

Employment in Europe

First annual report of the series. In-depth analysis of employment developments in the Community, sectoral analysis and other trends in the member states.

European Commission 1989

First published as COM(89)399 final

Later produced in book form

ISBN 92-825-9769-5

Price: Ecu11.25

Employment in Europe

Second report

ISBN 92-826-1517-0

Price: Ecu11.25

Seventeenth Report on the Activities of the European Social Fund - Financial Year 1988

Report from the Commission to the Council and the European Parliament.

SEC(89) 2200 final

Social Europe

Three part review of social affairs in Europe:

1 Overview of current developments in social affairs

2 Conferences, studies and other information destined to stimulate the debate on social affairs

3 Developments in national policies and introduction of new technologies.

Plus annual statistics on social trends in the member states.

Published 3 times a year

Annual subscription £21.00

Social Europe Supplements

In-depth analysis of specific subjects: technologies of the future, equal treatment for men and women, etc.

Up to ten per year

Combined annual subscription (Social Europe plus Supplements: £51.00)

Comparative Tables of the Social Security Schemes in the Member States of the European Communities: General Scheme (Employees in industry and

Commerce)
15th edition: Situation as at 1 July 1988
ISBN 92-825-9523-4
Price: Ecu12.00

Vocational Training Systems in the Member States of the European Community
Published by CEDEFOP - European Centre for the Development of Vocational Training
Vocational Training in Belgium
HX-48-85-252-EN-C 1987
Price: £2.50
Vocational Training in Denmark
HX-47-86-195-EN-C 1988
Price: £7.00
Vocational Training in France
HX-49-87-971-EN-C 1988
Price: £3.50
Vocational Training in the Federal Republic of Germany
HX-48-86-044-EN-C 1987
Price: £5.00
Vocational Training in Greece
HX-45-86-846-EN-C 1987
Price: £2.50
Vocational Training in Ireland
HX-46-86-880-EN-C 1987
Price: £3.50
Vocational Training in Italy
HX-47-86-745-EN-C 1988
Price: £2.50
Vocational Training in Luxembourg
New edition being prepared
Vocational Training in the Netherlands
New edition being prepared
Vocational Training in Portugal
HX-45-85-276-EN-C 1987
Price: £2.50
Vocational Training in Spain
HX-45-85-280-EN-C 1987
Price: £2.50
Vocational Training in the United Kingdom
HX-46-86-864-EN-C 1987
Price: £2.60

Women of Europe

Twice-monthly information bulletin plus supplements
The effect of Community policies on the daily life of women
Published by the European Commission, Directorate-General for Information, Communication and Culture (DGX), Women's Information Service.
Free from DGX

HELIOS Journal

Quarterly
Formerly published as Interact News. The work of HELIOS (Handicapped People in the European Community Living Independently in an Open Society) programme.
Available from HELIOS, Information Service, 79 Avenue de Cortenberg, B-1040 Brussels.

Trade Union Information Bulletin

Quarterly
Published by the European Commission, Directorate-General for Information, Communication and Culture (DGX).

InforMISEP

Quarterly bulletin covering activities of MISEP (Mutual Information System on Employment Policies). Changing policies and actions at national level aimed at promoting and improving employment within the European Community.
Published by and available from the European Commission, Directorate-General for Employment, Industrial Relations and Social Affairs.

Other social affairs titles

Report on Social Developments: Year 1988

Review on the development of EC policy together with a review of the current social situation in the member states
ISBN 92-826-0226-5
Price: Ecu16.50

Compendium of Community Provisions on Social Security
3rd edition
1988
ISBN 92-825-7317-6

Commission Report on the Medium-term Projections of Social Protection Expenditure and its Financing
1990 projections summary report
COM(88)655 final

A Guide to Working in a Europe Without Frontiers
Community policy and legislation about freedom of movement and establishment of professional people within the large Internal Market.
J.C. Seche
A Frontier-Free Europe publication, 1988
ISBN 92-825-8067-9
Price: Ecu18.50

Freedom of Movement in the Community: Entry and Residence
Collection of EC legislative texts relating to the freedom of movement of workers.
A Frontier-Free Europe publication, 1988
ISBN 92-825-8660-X
Price: Ecu7.50

Employment in Europe: Trends and Priorities
Report posing a set of questions on specific issues analysed in COM(89)399 final
SEC(89)1880

The Social Dimension of the Internal Market
Interim Report of the Interdepartmental Working Party
Special edition of Social Europe 1988
ISBN 92-825-8256-6
Price: Ecu4.20

The Social Aspects of the Internal Market
Volume I
Synthesis of 3 seminars held in Brussels in November/December 1987 and January 1988.

Further seminars to be reported in later volumes.
Social Europe Supplement 7/1988
ISBN 92-825-9316-9
Price: Ecu5.10

1992: The European Social Dimension
P. Venturini
A Frontier-Free Europe publication, 1989
ISBN 92-825-8703-7
Price: Ecu9.75

Social Europe 1/90
Essential document with regards to the social dimension of 1992 containing:
The Community Charter of Basic Social Rights, the action programme relating to the implementation of the Charter, and the Social Policy Progress Review for 1989.
ISSN 0255-0776
Price: Ecu13.50

Europe 1992: The Social Dimension
Address by Jacques Delors to the TUC 8.9.88
Free from the European Commission London Office

1992 and Beyond: New Opportunities for Action to Improve Living and Working Conditions in Europe
European Foundation for the Improvement of Living and Working Conditions
1989
Free from the Foundation

People's Europe: Information Handbook
Loose-leaf publication covering all aspects of the People's Europe concept.
Published by the European Commission, Directorate-General for Information, Communication and Culture (DGX).
Free from DGX
Available for reference only at the European Commission London Office

1992 - The Social Dimension
European Documentation 2/1990

A Human Face for Europe
European Documentation 4/1990

The Social Policy of the European Community
European File series, 13/1988

The Big European Market: A Trump Card for the Economy and Employment
European File series, 14/1988

Health and Safety at Work in the European Communities
European File series, 3/1990

The Re-insertion of Women in Working Life: Initiatives and Problems
1987
ISBN 92-825-7165-3
Price £10.70

The Rights of Working Women in the European Community
E. Landau
European Perspectives series, 1986
ISBN 92-825-5341-8
Price: £3.00

First Report Concerning the First Three Years of Operation of the First Joint Programme for Exchange of Young Workers, 1985-1987
COM(88)382 final

Childcare and Equality of Opportunity
Consolidated report to the European Commission
1988
Peter Moss (co-ordinator)

Caring for Children: Services and Policies for Childcare and Equal Opportunities in the United Kingdom
B. Cohen
Published by the European Commission's Childcare Network
1988
Available from Family Policy Studies Centre, 231

Baker Street, London NW1 6XE
Price: £8.00

Who Cares for Europe's Children?
Short report of the European Childcare Network
Angela Phillips and Peter Moss
1989
ISBN 92-825-9607-9
Price: Ecu10.50

XIX Transport

Annual reports series

Europa Transport: Observations of the Transport Market
Annual subscription: Four issues, annual report and annual analysis and forecasts: £24.00

Europa Transport: Observations of the Transport Market
Annual Report 1987
Review of the recent developments in the carriage of goods between member states.
1988
ISBN 92-825-9092-5
Price: Ecu7.50

Europa Transport: Observations of the Transport Market
Analysis and forecasts
1989
ISBN 92-825-9611-7
Price: Ecu6.25

Other transport titles

Transport and European Integration
Carlo Degli Abbati

European transport policy of the European Community and other international institutions.
European Perspectives series, 1987
ISBN 92-825-6199-2
Price £9.60

The Cost of Non-Europe: Border-related Controls and Administrative Formalities - An Illustration in the Road Haulage Sector
The Cost of Non-Europe - Volume 4
ISBN 92-825-8618-9
Price: £15.00

Electronics and Traffic on Major Roads: Technical, Regulatory and Ergonomic Aspects
EUR 9793 EN 1986
Price: £24.00

EEC Maritime Transport Policy
Economic and Social Committee
1986
ESC-86-008-EN
Available from the ESC

Air Transport: ESC Opinion and Report on Civil Aviation
Memorandum No. 2: Progress Towards the Development of a Community Air Transport
Economic and Social Committee
1985
ESC-85-010-EN
Available from the ESC

Community Rail Policy: Stocktaking and Prospects
Economic and Social Committee
1987
ESC-87-007-EN
Available from the ESC

Proceedings of the Air Safety Symposium
Report on a symposium held in Brussels on 26-27 November 1987
Document series, 1988
ISBN 92-825-8788-6

Price: Ecu15.00

Communication on a Community Railway Policy

Commission Communication

COM (89) 564 final

Air Transport and Aeronautics: Towards a Europe of the Skies

European File series, 1/1989

26. Select Bibliography

1. Research on the Cost of Non-Europe
   P. Cecchini - Series of Publications Vol 1-16
   Vol 1 ISBN 92-825-8605-7
   Vol 2 ISBN 92-825-8616-2
   Vol 3 ISBN 92-825-8610-3
   Vol 4 ISBN 92-825-8618-9
   Vol 5
   Pt. A ISBN 92-825-8646-4
   Pt. B ISBN 92-825-8647-2
   Vol 6 ISBN 92-825-8649-9
   Vol 7 ISBN 92-825-8638-3
   Vol 8 ISBN 92-825-8637-5
   Vol 9 ISBN 92-825-8636-7
   Vol 10 ISBN 92-825-8650-2
   Vol 11 ISBN 92-825-8619-7
   Vol 12
   Pt. A ISBN 92-825-8642-1
   Pt. B ISBN 92-825-8643-X
   Vol 13 ISBN 92-825-8631-6
   Vol 14 ISBN 92-825-8641-3
   Vol 15 ISBN 92-825-8632-4
   Vol 16 ISBN 92-825-8630-8

2. The Big European Market: A trump card for the economy and employment
   Commission of the European Communities
   Euro File No. 14/88
   ISSN: 0379-3133

3. Europe without Frontiers - Completing the Internal Market
   Commission of the European Communities
   Euro Doc 1989
   ISBN 95-825-9895-0

4. The European Challenge 1992 - The Benefits of a Single Market
   Paolo Cecchini & others
   Wildwood House 1988
   ISBN 0-7045-0613-0

5. Pocket Guide to the European Community
   D. Leonard
   B. Blackwell and Economist Publications 1988

6. The EEC : A Guide to the Maze (3rd Edition)
   Stanley A. Budd
   Kogan Page1989
   ISBN 0-7494-0023

7. The EEC: A Guide to the Maze (4th Edition)
   A. Jones
   Kogan Page 1991

8. The Economics of the Common Market
   D. Swann
   Penguin 1984
   ISBN 0-14-022781-4

9. Europe - More than a Continent
   M. Butler
   Heinemann 1986
   ISBN 0-434-09925-2

10. Making Sense of Europe
    C. Tugendhat
    Viking 1986
    ISBN 0-670-80604-8

11. Europe's Domestic Market
    J. Pelkmans & Alan Winters
    Chatham House Papers No 43. 1988
    ISBN 0-415-00213-3

12. The European Community - Past, Present and Future
    Loukas Tsoukalis
    Blackwell 1983
    ISSN 0021-9886

13. The European Community: Progress or Decline?
M. Kaiser
Royal Institute of International Affairs 1983
ISBN 0-905031-26-1

14. 1992 - Implications and Potential
J. Elles
The Bow Group, 1988

15. Vachers European Companion (quarterly)
Vachers's Publications
ISSN 0958-0336

16. Whose Europe? Competing Visions for 1992
R. Dahrendorf, J. Hoskyns, V. Curzon Price,
B. Roberts, G. Wood, E. Davis, L. Sealy
Institute of Economic Affairs 1989
ISBN 0-255-36222-6

17. Eurojargon: A Dictionary of European Community
Acronyms, Abbreviations and Sobriquets
A. Ramsay
Capital Planning Information, Stamford, 1989

18. The Challenge of Europe - Can Europe Win?
Michael Heseltine
Weidenfeld & Nicholson 1989
ISBN 0-297-79608-9

19. CBI Initiatives:
Mercury Books published by W H Allen & Co Plc

(i) Company Law and Competition
S J Berwin & Co
ISBN 1-85-251-0277

(ii) Employment and Training
Blue Arrow Plc
ISBN 1-85-251-057-9

(iii) Finance for Growth
National Westminster Bank Plc
ISBN 1-85-251-022-6

(iv) Information Technology: The Catalyst for Change
PA Consulting Group
ISBN 1-85-251-042-0

(v) Marketing: Communicating with the Consumer
D'Arcy Masius Benton & Bowles
ISBN 1-85-251-032-3

(vi) Marketing to the Public Sector and Industry
Rank Xerox Limited
ISBN 1-85-251-037-4

(vii) Mergers, Acquisitions and Alternative Corporate Strategies
Hill Samuel Bank Limited
ISBN 1-85-251-012-9

(viii) Property
Erdman Surveyors
ISBN 1-85-251-052-8

(ix) Tax: Strategic Corporate Tax Planning
Price Waterhouse
ISBN 1-85-251-017-X

(x) Transport and Distribution
TNT Express
ISBN 1-85-251-047-1

20. Copyright Law in the United Kingdom and the European Community
Peter Stone
The Athlone Press
ISBN 0-485-70004-2

21. DTI - Europe Open for Business. The Single Market
Prepared for the Department of Trade and Industry and the Central Office of Information
Published 1989
DTI 1992 Hotline: 081 200 1992

(i) The Facts

(ii) Standards - Action Plan for Business

(iii) A Guide to Public Purchasing

(iv) An Action Checklist for Business

(v) 1992 - for You

(vi) 'Brussels Can You Hear Me?'
Influencing Decisions in the European Community

(vii) Company Law Harmonisation

(viii) Financial Services

(ix) Removing Technical Barriers
Directives Under Discussion

(x) Toy Safety

22. DOD's European Companion
DOD's Publishing & Research Ltd 1990
ISBN 1-872-110-35-5

23. EEC Environmental Policy & Britain
(2nd Revised Edition)
Nigel Haigh
Longman, 1989
ISBN 0-582-05959-3

24. The Environmental Policy of the European Communities
Stanley P. Johnson and Guy Corcelle
International Environmental Law Policy Series 1989
ISBN 1-85333-225-9

25. Croner's Europe
Croner Publications Ltd
Updated periodically

26. The European Community 1991 - The Professional Guide for Business, Media and Government

Editors: Brian Morris, Klaus Boehm and Maurice Geller
Macmillan Press Ltd 1990
ISBN 0-333-39838-6

27. Europe Relaunched - Truths and Illusions on the Way to 1992
Nicholas Colchester and David Buchan
Hutchinson/Economist Books 1990
ISBN 0-09-174382-6

28. Financing the European Community
Michael Shackleton
Pinter Publishers Ltd 1990
ISBN 0-86187-875-2

29. IBI - International Business Intelligence
Eurofi Publications, Butterworths 1990

(i) 1992 - Planning for Chemicals, Pharmaceuticals and Biotechnology
ISBN 0-408-04095-5

(ii) 1992 - Planning for the Engineering Industries
ISBN 0-408-04097-1

(iii) 1992 - Planning for Financial Services and the Insurance Sector
ISBN 0-408-04089-0

(iv) Planning for the Food Industry
ISBN 0-408-04091-2

(v) Planning for the Information Technology Industries
ISBN 0-408-04093-9

30. 1992: Eurospeak Explained
Stephen Crampton
Rosters 1990
ISBN 1-85631-001-9

31. 1992: Strategies for the Single Market
James W. Dudley

Kogan Page 1989
ISBN 1-85091-240-8

32. Setting Up a Company in the European Community
A Country by Country Guide
Brebner & Co., London Chamber of Commerce
Kogan Page 1989
ISBN 1-85091-860-0

33. The Times Guide to 1992 - Britain in a Europe without Frontiers (2nd Edition)
Richard Owens and Michael Dynes
Times Books 1990
ISBN 0-7230-0316-5

34. Your Business 1992
James Dewhurst
Rosters 1989
ISBN 0-948032-18-9

35. 1992: A Zero Sum Game
Amin Rajan
Industrial Society 1990
ISBN 0-852-90594-7

36. A Common Man's Guide to the Common Market (2nd Edition)
Hugh Arbuthnot & Geoffrey Edwards
Macmillan 1989
ISBN 0-333-40913-2

37. Butterworths Guide to the European Communities
Butterworth & Co.
Butterworths 1989
ISBN 0-406-16999-3

38. Planning for Europe
William M. Clarke (Editor)
Waterlow 1989
ISBN 0-08-036903-0

39. Europe sans Frontiers (1992 - how it affects you)
Confederation of British Industry 1988
Briefing pack with quarterly updates

40. European Communities Information
Michael Hopkins (Editor)
Mansell 1985
ISBN 0-7201-1701-1

41. Understanding the European Communities
William Nicoll & Trevor C Salmon
Philip Allan 1990

42. The Documentation of the European Communities: A Guide
Ian Thomson
Mansell 1989
ISBN 0-7201-2022-5

43. After 1992: The United States of Europe
E. Wistrich
Routledge 1989
ISBN 0-415-04451-0

44. Panorama of European Industry 1990
Office for Official Publications of the Euoropean Communities
ISBN 92-825-9927-8

45. European Business Strategies
Richard Lynch
Kogan Page
ISBN 074-940-2172

46. The Marketing Challenge of 1992
Quelch, Buzzell and Salama
Addison Wesley
ISBN 020-156-4009

27. Short List of European Abbreviations and Glossary

ACE Action by the Community relating to the Environment. A Programme aimed at protecting the environment.

ACP The African, Caribbean and Pacific states which make up the more than 70 members of the Lomé Convention.

ASEAN Association of South East Asian Nations. An association of SE Asian countries who work together to accelerate economic and social progress.

BCC Business Cooperation Centre. Set up in 1972 to help small and medium-sized companies cooperate across Community boundaries.

BRITE Basic Research in Industrial Technologies in Europe. A Community framework programme covering cost-shared research projects.

CAP Common Agricultural Policy of the Community.

CBI Confederation of British Industry

CCC Consumer Consultative Committee. Represents consmers' opinions.

CEDEFOP European Centre for the Development of Vocational Training

CEN/CENELEC European standards body including both EC and EFTA countries.

COM Commission of the EC proposals for legislation. The abbreviation marking Commission documents.

COMETT Community Action Programme for Education and Training for Technology.

Commission The seventeen Commissioners who collectively propose legislation to the Council. Also refers to the officials who work for the Commission.

COREPER The Committee of Permanent Representatives. The Member States' ambassadors to the European Community.

COST Committee on European Cooperation in the field of Scientific and Technical Research. An inter-governmental body providing scientific and technical collaboration to member countries.

CREST Committee on Scientific and Technical Research. Coordinates national science and technological research policies and jointly implements projects of interest to the Community.

Council of Ministers Ministers of the Twelve meeting to agree Community legislation proposed by the Commission.

Decisions Community decrees addressed to a state, a company or an individual and binding on them.

Directives Community legislation binding on Member States but leaving them free to decide how to carry it out.

EAGGF The European Agricultural Guidance and Guarantee Fund which finances the CAP within the Community budget.

EBRD The European Bank for Reconstruction and Development, established in 1991 to assist Central and East European Countries.

EC The European Community (previously called EEC)

ECSC The European Coal and Steel Community. Established in 1951. Its responsibilities were taken over by the Commission of the European Communities on signature of the Treaty of Rome in 1957.

Ecu European Currency Unit

EDF European Development Fund

EEC European Economic Community. Established by the Treaty of Rome in 1957. Now called **EC** - European Community.

EFTA The European Free Trade Association. Its members are Austria, Switzerland, Norway, Sweden, Iceland, Finland and Liechtenstein.

EIB European Investment Bank. It makes loans and provides guarantees to facilitate the financing of Community projects.

EMS European Monetary System. A system aimed at stabilising exchange rates between European currencies.

EPU European Political Union

ERASMUS European Community Action Scheme for the Mobility of University Students

ERDF European Regional Development Fund

ERM Exchange Rate Mechanism. Instrument for linking EMS currencies by means of a central rate accompanied by margins of fluctuation.

ESC or **ECOSOC** The Economic and Social Committee which gives opinions on Council proposals.

ESF European Social Fund

ETUC European Trade Union Confederation

EUREKA European Research Coordination Agency. A technological research body from government, industrial and commercial initiatives of 18 countries.

Euronet-Diane Direct Information access network for Europe.

European Council Summit meeting at least twice a year of the EC heads of government. The most powerful body influencing the future developments of the Community.

Eurydice The Education Information Network in the European Community

EVCA European Venture Capital Association

FAST Forecasting and Assessment in Science and Technology

GATT General Agreement on Tariffs and Trade. An international body set up to promote free trade, reduce tariffs and establish an international code of practice for fair trading.

GSP Generalized System of Preferences under which developed countries grant preferential tariff treatment to most goods originating from developing countries.

INSIS Community Inter-Institutional Information System

JET Joint European Torus. A doughnut-shaped vacuum vessel designed to study the creation of cheap, clean energy by the fusion of hydrogen atoms. It is based at Culham near Oxford.

NTB Non-tariff barrier

OECD Organization for Economic Cooperation and Development. The economic organization of twenty-three of the worlds industrialized nations, most of which are in Europe.

OJ Official Journal. A daily Community publication available in all the Community languages.

PHARE Assistance for economic restructuring in Poland and Hungary. A Community action fund started in 1990 and extended to Czecoslovakia, Bulgaria and Yugoslavia.

SME Small and Medium-sized Enterprises

TED Tenders Electronic Daily. A databank of information on national governments' public works contracts which is available on line via EC Office for Official Publications.

TEMPUS University exchange programme with Eastern Europe.

Regulations A form of Community law binding and directly applicable in all Member States.

SEA Single European Act

UCITS Undertakings for Collective Investment in Transferable Securities

UNCTAD United Nations Conference on Trade and Development

UNICE Union of Industrial and Employers Confederation of Europe

Index